AF485950

RETRIBUTIVE
TO
RESTORATIVE JUSTICE

250 Questions answered

Dr. Maxwell Shimba

Copyright © 2023 – Dr. Maxwell Shimba

All rights reserved. No portion of this book may be reproduced, stored in a retrieval system, or transmitted in any form or by any means – electronics, mechanical, photocopy, recording, scanning, or other – except for brief quotations in critical revies or articles, without the prior written permission of the publisher.

Published in Manhattan, New York by Shimba Publishing, LLC.

Scripture quotations are from THE NEW KING JAMES VERSION. Copyright © 1982 Used by permission. All rights reserved.

The Scripture quotation noted KJV is from KING JAMES VERSION of the Bible.

Printed in the United States of America

Shimba Publishing LLC
Printed in the United States of America

First Printing Edition, 2023

Table of Contents

INTRODUCTION iv

Why there has been growing dissatisfaction with this justice system?

Chapter I 1
The Traditional View of Justice 1
Chapter II 11
Why Restructure the Criminal Justice System?
.... 11
Chapter III 31
A Different View of Justice 31
Chapter IV 58
Conceptual Frameworks Of Restorative Justice 58
Chapter V 79
Promising Practices of Restorative 79
Justice 79
Chapter VI 132
Should the Church Get Involved in Restorative Justice? 132
Chapter VII 161
The Restorative Justice Ministry 161
Paradigm 161
Chapter VII 188
How the Church Can Impact Corrections
.... 188
Chapter IX 206
Organizational Change 206
Chapter X 220
Conclusion 220

INTRODUCTION

Justice is a fundamental principle in all societies. When wrongdoing occurs, there is a need to address it and restore justice. However, different societies have different approaches to justice. Retributive justice and restorative justice are two approaches that aim to address wrongdoing and restore justice. In this book, we will discuss the differences between retributive justice and restorative justice, and the advantages and disadvantages of each approach.

Retributive Justice:

Retributive justice is a system of justice that seeks to repair justice through the imposition of punishment. It is based on the principle of "an eye for an eye, a tooth for a tooth." This means that when a person commits a crime, they must be punished in proportion to the harm they have caused. Retributive justice focuses on punishing the offender, rather than repairing the harm caused by the offense.

Advantages of Retributive Justice:

One of the advantages of retributive justice is that it sends a clear message to society that crime will not be tolerated. When offenders are punished, it acts as a deterrent to others who may be considering committing a crime. It also provides closure to victims and their families, who may feel that justice has been served. Retributive justice is also based on the principle of equality before the law, meaning that everyone is subject to the same punishment for the same offense.

Disadvantages of Retributive Justice:

One of the main disadvantages of retributive justice is that it does not address the root cause of the problem. It focuses on punishing the offender, rather than addressing the underlying issues that led to the offense. It also does not provide an opportunity for the offender to make amends or take responsibility for their actions. Retributive justice can also be costly, both in terms of the financial resources required for the criminal justice system and the human cost of incarcerating offenders.

Restorative Justice:

Restorative justice is a system of justice that seeks to repair justice through a bilateral process that involves the offender, victim, and community. It focuses on repairing the harm caused by the offense, rather than punishing the offender. Restorative justice is based on the principle of reconciliation and aims to restore relationships and rebuild communities.

Introduction

Advantages of Restorative Justice:

One of the advantages of restorative justice is that it addresses the root cause of the problem by focusing on repairing the harm caused by the offense. It provides an opportunity for the offender to take responsibility for their actions and make amends. It also provides closure to the victim and their families by giving them a voice in the process and the opportunity to be heard. Restorative justice is also cost-effective, as it can often be resolved without the need for a lengthy court process.

Disadvantages of Restorative Justice:

One of the main disadvantages of restorative justice is that it can be difficult to implement in practice. It requires a high level of cooperation and participation from all parties involved, and not all offenders may be willing to take responsibility for their actions. It can also be challenging to ensure that the process is fair and equitable for all parties involved. Restorative justice may also be perceived as being too lenient, as it does not focus on punishing the offender.

What is the deference between Retributive and Restorative Justice?

Retributive justice and restorative justice are two different approaches to addressing wrongdoing and restoring justice. Retributive justice focuses on punishing the offender, whereas restorative justice focuses on repairing the harm caused by the offense. Both approaches have their advantages and disadvantages, and the choice between them depends on the nature of the offense and the goals of the justice system. In conclusion, it is important to recognize the strengths and weaknesses of each approach and to develop a justice system that is effective, fair, and equitable for all.

Restorative justice is a form of justice that focuses on repairing the harm caused by a crime or conflict, rather than solely punishing the offender. This approach is often used in many African and Asian communities as a way to resolve conflicts and restore relationships within the community.

In these communities, restorative justice typically involves bringing together the victim, offender, and community members in a facilitated dialogue to discuss the harm that has been caused and to find ways to repair the harm and restore relationships. The process is often guided by cultural and traditional values, such as the importance of community, forgiveness, and reconciliation.

Restorative justice in these communities is often seen as a way to address crime and conflict that is more effective and meaningful than the traditional criminal justice system. It allows for a more participatory approach, where all members of the community are involved in finding solutions and repairing harm.

Hence, restorative justice in African and Asian communities is a culturally specific approach that prioritizes healing and relationship-building over punishment, and it has been found to be effective in promoting social cohesion and reducing recidivism.

Restorative justice is indeed a conflict resolution paradigm that emphasizes the importance of bringing together all parties affected by a crime or dispute in order to find ways to repair harm and restore relationships.

Community participation is also a key component of restorative justice in many African and Asian communities. This involves engaging community members in the process of resolving conflicts and addressing crime, in order to promote a sense of ownership and responsibility for the well-being of the community.

Furthermore, restoration takes many forms, such as compensation, reparation or apology, and helps mend broken relationships. This makes perfect sense because African peoples tend to live communally and abhorred anything that could strain relationships, disconnect an individual or family with the community, and paralyze their social relationships (Ladan, 2013). A Comparative Analysis of Restorative Justice Practices in Africa - GlobaLex (nyulawglobal.org)

Indeed, in Tanzania, for example, restorative justice has been practiced for millennia. The Nyamwezi of Tabora, formerly Kazeh, town, *West-Central Tanzania through* Mtyela Kasanda (1840–1884), better known as King Mirambo, was a Nyamwezi king, from 1860 to 1884. He created the largest state by area in 19th-century "East Africa" in present day Urambo district in Tabora Region of Tanzania. Urambo district is named after him, he resolved conflict amongst its members through restorative justice processes. Thus, whenever a conflict occurred either between family members or between families of a clan, the community concerned called for a meeting to reconcile the parties.

Community members would sit in circles around the fire place, a kind of court setting controlled by Chiefs, and then a complainant would narrate the incident or present their account of what happened and the defendant or defendants allowed responding to the accusations and defending him/herself or themselves. The reconciliation of the parties is sealed or solemnized with a sharing, from the same pot, of some alcohol, and eating roasted meat.

Restorative justice has a long history in Tanzania and has been practiced by various communities for many centuries. The Nyamwezi of Tabora, in particular, have a rich tradition of restorative justice that has been passed down through generations.

As I construed previously, Mtyela Kasanda, better known as King Mirambo, was a prominent Nyamwezi king who ruled from 1860 to 1884. During his reign, he was known for his efforts to promote justice and resolve disputes in his kingdom through a restorative justice approach. He encouraged the use of mediation and negotiation to resolve conflicts, and he placed a strong emphasis on repairing harm and restoring relationships within the community.

King Mirambo's approach to restorative justice was based on traditional Nyamwezi values and beliefs, such as the importance of community, forgiveness, and reconciliation. His legacy continues to inspire restorative justice practitioners in Tanzania and beyond, and his example serves as a reminder of the power of restorative justice to promote healing and reconciliation in communities.

The practice of resolving conflict and reconciling parties to it differed and depended on the gravity of the wrong committed and the number of people involved. For a minor conflict, for example, one member insulting another, only the parties to the conflict could attempt to resolve it. But grave offences or serious disputes required the involvement of clan members and the community. This usually happened when members of the community, sitting around the fireplace, and listening attentively to the parties, interrogated them and helped them get to the bottom of the problem and bring out the truth. Getting to the truth, including understanding the root causes of the dispute, and not how one convinced the members of the community of his or her innocence, as practiced in the conventional justice system is one of the main distinguishing features of the restorative justice system. The search for truth had more to do with lessons learnt, understanding the causes and advising the parties and community how to avoid in future similar problems (Ilomo, 2013).

The practice of restorative justice in Tanzania, as in many African and Asian communities, varies depending on the nature and severity of the conflict or wrong committed. For minor conflicts or offenses, such as insults or minor theft, the parties involved may attempt to resolve the conflict among themselves, without the need for community intervention.

However, for more serious offenses or disputes, such as assault, theft, or land disputes, the involvement of the community and clan members is often required. This is because these types of conflicts can have a broader impact on the community and can threaten social cohesion.

In these cases, the community may come together to hold a traditional community court, where elders or other respected community members act as mediators to help resolve the conflict. This may involve bringing together the victim, offender, and their families to discuss the harm that has been caused and to find ways to repair the harm and restore relationships.

Hence, restorative justice in Tanzania and many other African and Asian communities is a flexible and adaptable approach that can be tailored to meet the needs of each unique situation. It emphasizes the importance of community involvement and the restoration of relationships, and it has been found to be effective in promoting social cohesion and reducing recidivism.

The offender, having told the truth, had to voluntarily confess or acknowledge responsibility for their words, actions, or failure to act that caused harm or injury to the victim and his or her family; he or she also had to show remorse for his or her acts. When the truth is known and acknowledged, and responsibility owned, reconciliation follows due course and the broken relationship is repaired and restored. Thus, reconciliation is at the centre of the restorative justice model and cannot happen before the offender, victim and members of the community hear them out and establish the truth. Indeed, if it happened that a victim of a crime or a conflict or dispute suffered further harm or suffering before mending the broken relationship through the restorative justice system because of the recalcitrant behaviour of the community member suspected to be in the wrong or is the offender, the community members cast the blame on the suspect; hence communities had to resolve conflicts quickly (Ilomo, 2013).

1. Crime has become the World's most serious problem.
2. Crime is certainly a serious problem that affects many people around the world. Crime can take many different forms, from petty theft and fraud to violent crimes such as murder and assault. It can have a profound impact on individuals, families, and communities, causing physical, emotional, and financial harm.
3. However, it's important to note that crime rates vary widely depending on the country and region in question. While some countries have relatively low levels of crime, others may struggle with high rates of crime and violence.
4. It's also worth noting that the causes of crime are complex and multifaceted. Factors such as poverty, inequality, social exclusion, and lack of access to education and employment opportunities can all contribute to the prevalence of crime in a given society.
5. Addressing crime requires a comprehensive approach that addresses the underlying causes of criminal behavior, as well as implementing effective policies and programs to prevent crime, provide support for victims, and hold offenders accountable for their actions. This may involve a range of strategies, including community-based policing, restorative justice, education and training programs, and social welfare policies.

2. a) The current criminal justice system is impotent in crime prevention and, for some time now.

Crime control involves going after criminal offenders through arrest, prosecution, criminal conviction, and incarceration. But this process has not had a significant impact on the problem. Approximately thirteen million people (approximately 5% of the U.S. population) are victims of crime every year. Approximately one and a half million are victims of violent crime.

The effectiveness of the criminal justice system in preventing crime is a complex and multifaceted issue that involves a range of factors, including law enforcement strategies, social and economic conditions, and the legal and political systems that shape the administration of justice.

Some argue that the current criminal justice system is indeed ineffective in preventing crime and reducing recidivism rates, citing high rates of incarceration, disparities in the treatment of marginalized communities, and limited resources for crime prevention programs.

Others contend that the criminal justice system plays a critical role in protecting public safety and deterring criminal behavior, but acknowledge that there is room for improvement in areas such as rehabilitation and reentry programs for offenders.

Ultimately, the effectiveness of the criminal justice system in preventing crime depends on a wide range of factors, and it is up to policymakers, law enforcement officials, and communities to work together to find solutions that address the root causes of crime and promote public safety.

Why there has been growing dissatisfaction with this justice system?

There are a number of reasons why there has been growing dissatisfaction with the criminal justice system in recent years. Here are a few:

1. *Racial and socioeconomic disparities:* Many people believe that the criminal justice system unfairly targets and punishes individuals from certain racial and socioeconomic groups. There is evidence to support this claim, as studies have shown that Black and Hispanic individuals are more likely to be stopped, searched, and arrested than their white counterparts, even when controlling for factors such as criminal history and offense severity.

2. *Mass incarceration:* The United States has one of the highest incarceration rates in the world, and many people believe that the criminal justice system has become overly punitive, resulting in high rates of incarceration and longer prison sentences. This has led to concerns about the impact of incarceration on families and communities, as well as the financial cost of maintaining large prison populations.

3. *Lack of rehabilitation:* Many people believe that the criminal justice system does not do enough to rehabilitate offenders and reduce recidivism rates. This is particularly true for individuals with mental health or substance abuse issues, who may need specialized treatment and support to address the underlying causes of their criminal behavior.

4. *Police misconduct:* High-profile cases of police brutality and misconduct have eroded public trust in law enforcement and the criminal justice system more broadly. Many people believe that the police are not held accountable for their actions, which can lead to a sense of impunity and further undermine public confidence in the system.

Accordingly, the growing dissatisfaction with the criminal justice system is rooted in concerns about fairness, effectiveness, and accountability. These issues are complex and multifaceted, and addressing them will require a concerted effort from policymakers, law enforcement officials, and communities.

3. Below are some of the dissatisfaction created by the current criminal system.:

a) Citizens feel disconnected

b) Victims are dissatisfied,

c) Offenders are embittered

d) and those working in the system are frustrated.

The dissatisfaction with the current criminal justice system is widespread and affects various groups of people in different ways. Here is a breakdown of some of the key areas of dissatisfaction:

a) Citizens feel disconnected: Many citizens feel that the criminal justice system is out of touch with their needs and concerns. They may believe that the system is too focused on punishment and not enough on prevention or rehabilitation. This can lead to a sense of disconnection and mistrust between the public and the criminal justice system.

b) Victims are dissatisfied: Victims of crime may feel dissatisfied with the criminal justice system if they feel that their needs are not being met or if they feel that the system is not providing them with the support and resources they need to recover from their experience. This can lead to a sense of frustration and disillusionment with the system.

c) Offenders are embittered: Offenders who come into contact with the criminal justice system may feel embittered if they believe that the system is treating them unfairly or if they feel that they are not being given a second chance to turn their lives around. This can lead to a sense of resentment and a lack of trust in the system.

d) Those working in the system are frustrated: People who work in the criminal justice system, such as police officers, lawyers, and judges, may also feel frustrated with the system if they believe that it is not working as effectively as it could be. This can lead to a sense of disillusionment and burnout among those who are responsible for enforcing the law and administering justice.

Therefore, the dissatisfaction with the current criminal justice system is complex and multifaceted, affecting various groups of people in different ways. Addressing these issues will require a comprehensive and collaborative effort from policymakers, law enforcement officials, and communities.

In addition to the financial cost, Americans are feeling the psychological cost of devastated lives and the loss of a feeling of security.

4. Why don't tall fences, razor-wire, and iron bars deter crime?

Because these devices only respond to symptoms and never address the root causes of criminal behavior.

Tall fences, razor wire, and iron bars are physical measures that can be used to prevent or deter crime by making it more difficult for potential offenders to access a particular location or target. However, these measures are only a part of a larger strategy to prevent and address criminal behavior.

Crime prevention is not just about physical barriers or punishment, but also about addressing the root causes of criminal behavior. Many offenders are driven to commit crimes by factors such as poverty, lack of education, social isolation, mental illness, and substance abuse. Addressing these underlying issues is critical to reducing crime rates and preventing recidivism.

In addition, focusing solely on punishment and incarceration can actually perpetuate cycles of criminal behavior. Incarceration often separates individuals from their families and communities, limits their opportunities for education and employment, and exposes them to violence and trauma. Without addressing these factors, individuals may be more likely to reoffend after their release from prison.

Therefore, while physical measures such as tall fences, razor wire, and iron bars can be useful tools in preventing and deterring crime, they must be used in conjunction with efforts to address the root causes of criminal behavior and promote rehabilitation and reintegration into society.

Consider the flu virus and how it will manifest itself through symptoms such as a sore throat, fever, or coughing. I can take a Halls drop for the sore throat, a couple of Tylenols for the fever and cough syrup for the coughing. Two weeks later I wonder why I'm still ill with the flu. We should realize that all we've done is medicate the symptoms. This same approach is being taken today by our criminal justice system when dealing with the offender and his or her problems

5. a) There has been growing interest in new approaches to justice which involve the community.
    b) and focus on the victim.

6. There has been a growing interest in new approaches to justice that involve the community and focus on the needs of the victim. These approaches are often referred to as "restorative justice" or "community justice" and are based on the principles of repairing harm, involving stakeholders, and addressing the underlying causes of criminal behavior.

Restorative justice emphasizes the importance of repairing the harm caused by crime and restoring the relationships between the victim, offender, and community. This can be done through a variety of means, such as victim-offender mediation, community conferencing, and circle sentencing. These processes allow the victim to have a voice in the justice process and can lead to greater accountability and understanding on the part of the offender.

Community justice is an approach that involves the active participation of the community in addressing crime and its underlying causes. This can include community policing, neighborhood watch programs, and community-based diversion programs. These programs aim to prevent crime by building stronger relationships between law enforcement and the community, addressing the root causes of criminal behavior, and providing support and resources to those in need.

7. Overall, the focus on restorative and community justice reflects a growing recognition that traditional approaches to justice may not be effective in reducing crime or addressing the needs of victims and communities. These new approaches are grounded

in a more holistic and collaborative understanding of justice, which seeks to address the underlying causes of criminal behavior and promote healing and restoration for all stakeholders.

6. The current criminal justice system considers crime an act against the State.

The current criminal justice system often considers crime as an act against the state or society as a whole. This is because the state has a responsibility to ensure public safety and maintain social order, and crime is seen as a threat to these goals.

Under the current system, criminal offenses are prosecuted by the state through the court system, with the state representing the interests of society as a whole. This approach can be effective in ensuring that offenders are held accountable for their actions and that justice is served for victims of crime.

However, some critics argue that this approach to justice can be overly punitive and fails to consider the needs and perspectives of individual victims and communities. Restorative and community justice approaches, on the other hand, emphasize the importance of involving all stakeholders in the justice process and prioritizing the needs of victims and communities.

Thus, while the current criminal justice system is designed to protect the interests of the state and society, there is a growing recognition that it must also prioritize the needs of victims and communities and take a more holistic and collaborative approach to justice.

7. Our current criminal justice system works on a premise that largely ignores the rehabilitation of the offender, the victim, and the community that is hurt most by the crime.

Yes, there is a growing recognition that the current criminal justice system often fails to prioritize rehabilitation and restoration for the offender, victim, and community. Instead, the focus has traditionally been on punishment and retribution.

This approach to justice can be seen as problematic because it fails to address the underlying causes of criminal behavior and does little to prevent recidivism. Punishment alone is often not enough to deter offenders from committing further crimes, and it may actually contribute to a cycle of criminal behavior by exacerbating the social, economic, and psychological factors that can lead to criminal activity.

Moreover, the current criminal justice system often neglects the needs and perspectives of victims and communities affected by crime. Victims may feel isolated and powerless in the face of the justice system, and communities may experience a loss of trust in law enforcement and the broader justice system.

In contrast, restorative and community justice approaches prioritize rehabilitation and restoration for all stakeholders. These approaches recognize the importance of addressing the underlying causes of criminal behavior and promoting healing and restoration for victims and communities. They also emphasize the importance of involving all stakeholders in the justice process and building stronger relationships between law enforcement and the community.

Consequently, while the current criminal justice system serves an important role in holding offenders accountable for their actions, there is a growing recognition that it must also prioritize rehabilitation, restoration, and community engagement to promote long-term public safety and prevent recidivism.

8. What is the primary focus of today's criminal justice system?

The primary focus of today's criminal justice system is often seen as punishing offenders for their crimes. While this is an important aspect of the justice system, critics argue that the system often fails to address the underlying causes of criminal behavior and does little to help offenders face the impact of their crimes.

Under the current system, offenders are typically punished through incarceration, fines, or other forms of legal penalties. While these penalties can serve as a deterrent for future criminal behavior, they may not address the underlying issues that led to the crime in the first place. Additionally, the current system may not offer enough support for offenders to reintegrate into society once their sentence is completed, which can lead to recidivism and further criminal behavior.

Moreover, the current criminal justice system may not adequately address the impact of the crime on victims and communities. Victims may feel ignored or disrespected by the justice system, and communities may feel a lack of trust in law enforcement and the broader justice system.

In contrast, restorative and community justice approaches prioritize rehabilitation and restoration for all stakeholders. These approaches recognize the importance of addressing the underlying causes of criminal behavior and promoting healing and restoration for victims and communities. They also emphasize the importance of involving all stakeholders in the justice process and building stronger relationships between law enforcement and the community.

Accordingly, while the current criminal justice system serves an important role in holding offenders accountable for their actions, there is a growing recognition that it must also prioritize rehabilitation, restoration, and community engagement to promote long-term public safety and prevent recidivism.

Note: This is very true. Many years ago, Texas prisons were called the Texas Department of Corrections. They were supposed to rehabilitate the offender. However, this was not the case and an offender successfully sued the State over the matter. As a result, the prison system is now called the Texas Department of Criminal Justice. This system punishes the offender without helping them face the impact of their crimes.

9. The restorative justice principles offer more inclusive processes and reorient the goals of justice.

Yes, the principles of restorative justice offer a more inclusive and community-oriented approach to justice. Restorative justice focuses on repairing harm caused by crime by involving all stakeholders in the process of addressing the harm and preventing future harm. The goals of restorative justice include not only holding offenders accountable for their actions but also promoting healing and restoration for victims and communities, and addressing the underlying causes of criminal behavior.

Restorative justice principles include:

1. Focus on harm: Restorative justice prioritizes repairing the harm caused by crime, rather than punishing offenders.
2. Inclusivity: Restorative justice involves all stakeholders in the justice process, including victims, offenders, and communities.
3. Empowerment: Restorative justice seeks to empower victims and communities by giving them a voice in the justice process and by allowing them to play an active role in the resolution of the harm caused by the crime.
4. Collaboration: Restorative justice emphasizes collaboration and problem-solving, with the goal of finding solutions that are satisfactory to all stakeholders.

5.   Accountability: Restorative justice holds offenders accountable for their actions while providing them with opportunities for rehabilitation and reintegration into society.

Thence, the principles of restorative justice offer a more inclusive, collaborative, and community-oriented approach to justice that seeks to promote healing and restoration for victims and communities, while also addressing the underlying causes of criminal behavior.

Note: The primary stakeholders in the restorative justice process are the person who caused the harm (the offender), the person harmed (the victim), and the affected community. It is the goal of restorative justice to create healing by identifying and addressing harms, needs, and obligations that resulted from wrongdoing.

10. Why has restorative justice been finding a receptive audience?

"Because it creates common ground which accommodates the goals of many constituencies and provides a collective focus."

Restorative justice has been finding a receptive audience because it offers a more inclusive and collaborative approach to justice that accommodates the goals of many constituencies and provides a collective focus.

Restorative justice seeks to involve all stakeholders in the justice process, including victims, offenders, and communities. By involving these stakeholders in the process of repairing harm caused by crime, restorative justice promotes healing and restoration for victims and communities, while also holding offenders accountable for their actions. This collaborative approach to justice creates common ground among stakeholders and can build stronger relationships between law enforcement and the community.

Additionally, restorative justice prioritizes addressing the underlying causes of criminal behavior, which can help to prevent future crime and promote long-term public safety. By focusing on rehabilitation and reintegration, restorative justice can help to reduce recidivism rates and improve outcomes for offenders and communities.

Accordingly, restorative justice's emphasis on collaboration, inclusivity, and addressing the root causes of criminal behavior has resonated with many communities and stakeholders who are looking for a more effective and humane approach to justice. By providing a collective focus on repairing harm and promoting healing, restorative justice offers a promising alternative to traditional punitive approaches to justice.

11. Has restorative justice been recognized by the United States Department of Justice?

This nation-wide trend has been recognized by the United States Department of Justice.

Restorative justice has been recognized by the United States Department of Justice. The Department of Justice has acknowledged the potential benefits of restorative justice and has provided funding and support for restorative justice programs throughout the country.

In 2014, the Department of Justice's Office of Justice Programs launched the National Center for Restorative Justice, which provides training and technical assistance to jurisdictions and organizations seeking to implement restorative justice programs. The Department of Justice has also funded a variety of restorative justice initiatives, including victim-offender mediation programs and community conferencing programs.

Additionally, several states and local jurisdictions have implemented restorative justice programs with the support and encouragement of the Department of Justice. These programs have shown promising results in reducing recidivism rates and improving outcomes for victims and communities.

Therefore, the recognition and support of the Department of Justice have helped to legitimize and promote restorative justice as a viable alternative to traditional punitive approaches to justice in the United States.

12. Briefly describe community justice.:

A concept that builds on the problem-solving approach of community policing and creates strong linkages between the police, courts, prosecutors, correction systems and the communities they serve.

Community justice is a concept that builds on the problem-solving approach of community policing and creates strong linkages between the police, courts, prosecutors, correction systems, and the communities they serve. It emphasizes collaboration between justice system stakeholders and community members to identify and address the underlying causes of crime and disorder.

Community justice recognizes that crime is often the result of complex social problems, such as poverty, substance abuse, and mental health issues, that cannot be addressed through traditional punitive approaches alone. Instead, it seeks to involve community members in the justice process, encourage community-based problem-solving, and promote the use of alternative approaches to justice, such as diversion programs and restorative justice.

Community justice also emphasizes the importance of cultural competence and responsiveness, recognizing that different communities may have different needs and perspectives regarding justice. By working closely with communities to understand their unique concerns and needs, justice system stakeholders can develop more effective and responsive strategies for addressing crime and promoting public safety.

Wherefore, community justice represents a collaborative, community-based approach to justice that seeks to build trust, promote accountability, and address the underlying causes of crime and disorder in a more holistic and effective manner.

Community Justice is a concept that builds on the problem-solving approach of community policing and creates strong linkages between the police and courts, prosecutors, correction systems and the community they serve.

DR. MAXWELL SHIMBA

CHAPTER I
THE TRADITIONAL VIEW OF JUSTICE

1. Describe the traditional view of justice.

The traditional view of justice is based on the idea that offenders should be punished for their wrongdoing, and that the punishment should fit the crime. This view is often referred to as retributive justice, as it is focused on giving offenders what they deserve for their actions.

Under the traditional view of justice, the primary goal of punishment is to provide retribution or payback for the harm caused by the offender. This may involve imposing fines, community service, or imprisonment, depending on the severity of the offense.

In this model, the victim's role is often limited to providing testimony and assisting with the prosecution of the offender, rather than being actively involved in the justice process. Similarly, community involvement is often limited to serving on juries or providing input on sentencing decisions.

Wherefore, the traditional view of justice is focused on punishing offenders for their wrongdoing, rather than rehabilitating them or addressing the root causes of crime. While this approach may provide a sense of justice for victims and society, it may not be effective in reducing recidivism or promoting long-term public safety.

Note: This type of justice is driven by a need for revenge. In this concept, incarceration has a twofold purpose: to punish the offender and to protect society from them.

2. The term "lex talionis" means "Law of Retaliation," and is used to describe the view of an eye for an eye and a tooth for a tooth. Discuss:

"Lex talionis" is a Latin term that translates to "law of retaliation" or "law of retribution." It refers to the principle of punishment that advocates for the infliction of punishment on the offender that is equivalent or proportionate to the harm they have caused.

The concept of "an eye for an eye and a tooth for a tooth" is often associated with the principle of lex talionis, and is frequently used to describe the idea of retributive justice. The idea behind this principle is that punishment should be proportional to the harm inflicted, and that offenders should receive what they deserve based on their actions.

It was developed in early Babylonian law and was present in both biblical and early Roman law.

While the principle of lex talionis has been influential in shaping traditional views of justice, modern justice systems often prioritize rehabilitation, restoration, and community involvement over strict retribution. As a result, the use of the principle of lex talionis in contemporary justice systems is limited.

3. What is the natural response to violent crimes?

The natural response to violent crimes often involves a desire for revenge or retribution against the offender. When a person or a community has been harmed by a violent crime, it is natural to want the offender to be punished and to suffer in a way that reflects the harm that was done.

However, it is important to recognize that revenge and retribution are not always effective in promoting healing, restoring justice, or preventing future crime. In some cases, revenge can lead to a cycle of violence and perpetuate harm, rather than promoting healing or reconciliation.

Instead of simply seeking revenge, modern justice systems often prioritize rehabilitation, restoration, and community involvement in addressing the harm caused by violent crimes. This approach may involve providing support to victims, addressing the root causes of crime, and working with offenders to help them understand the impact of their actions and take responsibility for their behavior.

While it is understandable to feel anger and a desire for revenge in the aftermath of a violent crime, it is important to consider the potential consequences of this approach, and to explore more restorative and constructive alternatives to promote healing and prevent further harm.

4. Why our nation "USA" cries out for retribution and punishment of the offender?

It is true that there are instances when the public's demand for retribution and punishment of the offender can be strong, particularly in cases of violent crime. However, it is important to recognize that the pursuit of retribution and punishment alone is not always sufficient to address the complex social, psychological, and systemic issues that underlie criminal behavior.

Modern justice systems often seek to balance the need for accountability and punishment with a focus on rehabilitation, restoration, and community involvement. This approach recognizes that punishment alone may not be enough to deter future crime or promote healing for victims, and that addressing the root causes of criminal behavior is essential for creating safer and more just communities.

While retribution and punishment have a place in the justice system, it is important to consider the broader context of criminal behavior and to explore alternative approaches that prioritize rehabilitation, restoration, and community involvement. By doing so, we can create a more effective and just system that supports both victims and offenders in the process of healing and restoration.

5. Describe some of the effects of our outrages and demands for protection from the offender.

The effects of our outrages and demands for protection from offenders can have significant consequences for the justice system and society as a whole. Some of these effects include:

a) Harsher punishment and longer sentences: When politicians respond to public outrage by passing new laws mandating harsher punishment and longer sentences for offenders, it can lead to an increase in the number of people incarcerated and a strain on the criminal justice system. This approach may also fail to address the root causes of criminal behavior and may not effectively reduce crime rates.

b) "Three strikes" laws: Some states have enacted "three strikes and you're out" laws, which mandate lengthy prison sentences for repeat offenders. While these laws may deter some offenders from committing further crimes, they can also lead to disproportionate sentencing and may not effectively address the underlying issues that contribute to criminal behavior.

c) Abolishing parole and truth in sentencing: Other states have abolished parole and implemented truth in sentencing reforms, which require offenders to serve a minimum amount of time in prison before being eligible for release. While these reforms may help ensure that offenders serve their full sentences, they may also fail to address the underlying issues that contribute to criminal behavior and can lead to overcrowding in prisons.

Hence, it is important to consider the potential consequences of harsh punishment and sentencing policies, and to explore alternative approaches that prioritize rehabilitation, restoration, and community involvement. By doing so, we can create a more effective and just system that supports both victims and offenders in the process of healing and restoration.

In addition to these effects, our outrages and demands for protection have resulted in laws that operate on a premise that says, "Three strikes and you're out!" Some states have even abolished parole.

6. Why in the State of Texas, the conservative push for "justice" has caused politicians to place more emphasis on building prisons than on rehabilitation and prevention efforts?

In the state of Texas, there has been a conservative push for "tough on crime" policies that emphasize punishment over rehabilitation and prevention. As a result, politicians have prioritized building more prisons and expanding the state's criminal justice system, rather than investing in programs and services that could help address the root causes of crime and reduce recidivism rates.

For example, Texas has one of the largest prison systems in the country, with a high rate of incarceration and a focus on punishment and retribution. The state has also faced challenges with prison overcrowding and understaffing, which can have negative consequences for both inmates and correctional staff.

Some advocates and experts have argued that Texas could benefit from a more balanced approach to criminal justice that incorporates restorative justice principles, community involvement, and rehabilitation services. By prioritizing prevention and rehabilitation, Texas could potentially reduce crime rates, save money on prison costs, and create a more just and equitable system for all Texans.

The philosophy behind this movement is: "If you can't stand the time don't do the crime."

7. Briefly explain why the prison population in Texas has grown over 500% in less than a quarter century. Of the 238,000 individuals incarcerated in the Texas Department of Criminal Justice, less than 2,000 will receive the help they need. The rest will simply serve their sentence and, if paroled, will take with them the same needs they had before incarceration?

The prison population in Texas has grown significantly in the past few decades, with the number of incarcerated individuals increasing by over 500% since the 1970s. As of 2021, there are approximately 130,000 individuals incarcerated in Texas state prisons and another 100,000 in local jails, for a total of around 238,000 people.

Despite this large prison population, relatively few individuals receive the help they need to successfully reintegrate into society after their release. According to some estimates, less than 2,000 individuals in the Texas Department of Criminal Justice receive treatment for mental health or substance abuse issues, which are common among incarcerated individuals and can contribute to recidivism if left untreated.

This lack of support and resources for rehabilitation and reentry can make it difficult for individuals to successfully reintegrate into society after their release, leading to a cycle of incarceration and recidivism. Some advocates and experts have called for a greater focus on prevention, rehabilitation, and community-based alternatives to incarceration in Texas and elsewhere, in order to reduce the harm caused by mass incarceration and create a more just and equitable criminal justice system.

8. Why the only other nations close to our world's highest incarceration rates are Russia and South Africa.

There are a number of factors that contribute to high incarceration rates in certain countries, including Russia, South Africa, and others. Here are a few possible explanations:

1. Crime rates: High levels of crime can lead to higher rates of incarceration, as law enforcement agencies seek to bring perpetrators to justice. In some countries, such as South Africa, high levels of violent crime have been linked to historical factors such as segregation and economic inequality.

2. Criminal justice policies: The policies and practices of a country's criminal justice system can also contribute to high incarceration rates. For example, mandatory minimum sentencing laws, three-strikes laws, and other tough-on-crime policies can result in longer sentences and more people behind bars.

3. Drug policies: Drug policies can also play a role in high incarceration rates, as many drug offenses are punishable by imprisonment. Countries that have adopted strict drug laws and have aggressive law enforcement strategies for drug offenses may see higher incarceration rates.

4. Socioeconomic factors: Socioeconomic factors such as poverty, unemployment, and lack of access to education or healthcare can contribute to higher levels of criminal activity and ultimately lead to higher incarceration rates. In some cases, individuals may turn to crime as a means of survival or to escape poverty, leading to a cycle of incarceration.

5. Cultural attitudes towards crime and punishment: Cultural attitudes towards crime and punishment can also play a role in high incarceration rates. Some countries may prioritize punishment over rehabilitation or may view incarceration as the only effective response to criminal behavior.

It's worth noting that the specific reasons for high incarceration rates can vary from country to country, and there is likely no one single factor that can explain it all. However, these are some of the common factors that have been identified as contributing to high incarceration rates around the world.

The United States has one of the highest incarceration rates in the world, with over 2 million people currently incarcerated in prisons and jails. According to data from the World Prison Brief, the United States has an incarceration rate of around 639 per 100,000 population, which is the highest in the world. The only other countries with incarceration rates even close to this level are Russia and South Africa, which have rates of around 418 and 341 per 100,000 population, respectively.

9. Criminologist Nils Christie has stated that it is incomprehensible that a nation so religious could misuse incarceration to this extent.

Nils Christie, a prominent criminologist, has argued that the United States' high rates of incarceration are difficult to reconcile with the country's religious and moral values. Christie has advocated for a more rehabilitative approach to criminal justice, in which prisons function more like hospitals, focusing on addressing the emotional and spiritual needs of offenders, rather than just punishing them. This approach would recognize that offenders are often in need of help and support to overcome the issues that led them to commit crimes in the first place, rather than simply being bad people who need to be locked away.

Christie believes that a prison's function should be similar in nature to that of a hospital. In other words, a prison should care for the emotional and spiritual needs of the offender just as a hospital care for the physical needs of a patient. Both the offender and the patient are sick and desperately need help!

10. Why after centuries of dealing with crime, America is incarcerating over two Million people each year?

The reasons why America is incarcerating over two million people each year are complex and multifaceted. Some of the main factors include:

1. Tough-on-crime policies: In the 1980s and 1990s, there was a shift towards tough-on-crime policies, which emphasized longer sentences, mandatory minimums, and increased penalties for drug offenses. These policies were often implemented in response to rising crime rates and concerns about public safety.

2. War on drugs: The War on Drugs, which began in the 1970s and continued through the 1980s and 1990s, led to increased criminalization of drug offenses and mandatory minimum sentences for drug-related crimes. This resulted in a sharp increase in the number of people incarcerated for drug offenses.

3. Racial disparities: There are significant racial disparities in the American criminal justice system, with people of color disproportionately represented in prisons and jails. This is due in part to systemic racism and bias in law enforcement and the criminal justice system.

4. Privatization of prisons: The privatization of prisons in the United States has led to a profit-driven criminal justice system that prioritizes filling beds over rehabilitation and reducing recidivism. This has led to longer sentences, harsher conditions, and a lack of resources for rehabilitation programs.

5. Poverty and inequality: Poverty and inequality are also contributing factors to the high incarceration rates in America. People living in poverty are more likely to be incarcerated, and incarceration can also lead to increased poverty and economic instability.

Accordingly, the high incarceration rates in America are the result of a complex interplay of policies, systemic issues, and societal factors. Addressing these issues will require a multi-faceted approach that addresses the root causes of crime and promotes restorative justice and rehabilitation over punishment.

11. Why our thirst for revenge has not been satisfied and, as a result, our hatred, anger and intolerance for the offender has grown grotesquely out of proportion?

The human desire for revenge is a natural response to being wronged or harmed. However, revenge does not always lead to satisfaction and can often lead to further negative consequences. In the context of the criminal justice system, the desire for revenge can result in a focus on punishment and retribution, rather than on rehabilitation and healing.

When we seek revenge, our anger and hatred for the offender can grow to an extreme degree. This can result in a dehumanization of the offender and a lack of empathy for their situation. As a result, we may become more intolerant and less willing to consider alternative approaches to justice, such as restorative justice.

Furthermore, the desire for revenge can also perpetuate cycles of violence and harm. When we seek revenge, we are essentially perpetuating the harm that was done to us. This can lead to a cycle of retaliation and further harm, without addressing the underlying causes of the initial harm.

Restorative justice, on the other hand, seeks to address the harm caused by a crime in a more holistic way. It aims to bring together the victim, the offender, and the community to address the harm caused and to promote healing and reconciliation. This approach can lead to greater empathy and understanding, and can help break cycles of harm and violence.

In conclusion, while the desire for revenge is a natural response to being wronged or harmed, it can lead to extreme anger, hatred, and intolerance. Restorative justice offers a more empathetic and holistic approach to addressing harm and promoting healing, and can help break cycles of harm and violence.

12. How do we justify our demands for retribution?

Retribution is often justified on the basis of several different arguments. Some of the main justifications for retribution include:

1. Deterrence: The idea that punishing offenders serves as a deterrent to others who might consider committing similar crimes.

2. Just desserts: The belief that offenders deserve to be punished for their crimes, based on the principle of "an eye for an eye" or the idea that they have violated a social contract and should be held accountable.

3. Restitution: The idea that punishment should include some form of restitution to the victim or the community, such as monetary compensation or community service.

4. Protection: The belief that punishing offenders protects society from future harm, either by removing them from society or by discouraging them from committing future crimes.

However, it is important to note that there are also arguments against retribution as a primary goal of the criminal justice system. Some of the main criticisms of retribution include:

1. Lack of effectiveness: Research has shown that punishment alone may not be effective in reducing crime rates, and that other approaches such as rehabilitation and restorative justice may be more effective in promoting positive outcomes.

2. Human dignity: Punishing offenders can be seen as a violation of their human dignity, especially if the punishment is excessive or inhumane.

3. Racial disparities: The criminal justice system has been shown to have significant racial disparities, with people of color disproportionately represented in prisons and jails. This raises questions about the fairness of retribution as a primary goal of the criminal justice system.

4. Moral objections: Some people argue that retribution is morally objectionable, as it involves intentionally causing harm to another person, even if they have committed a crime.

In conclusion, while retribution can be justified on the basis of several different arguments, there are also valid criticisms of retribution as a primary goal of the criminal justice system. Ultimately, the most effective and just approach to addressing crime may involve a combination of different approaches, including punishment, rehabilitation, and restorative justice.

Do we punish individuals for being sick with cancer? Do they heal without any treatment? Of course not. We send them to a doctor or to a hospital to receive treatment. Does every cancer patient recover from their illness? No! Shouldn't our approach to carrying out justice be similar in nature to how we care for the physically ill?

13. Why Americans love the feeling associated with revenge and retribution?

"because it partially satisfies our emotional needs"

It is true that revenge and retribution can provide a sense of emotional satisfaction for some people. The desire for revenge is a natural human response to being wronged or harmed, and seeking retribution can provide a sense of justice or closure for the victim and their loved ones.

However, it is important to recognize that the desire for revenge and retribution can also be problematic. Seeking revenge can lead to a cycle of harm and violence, perpetuating the harm that was initially done. It can also lead to extreme anger and hatred towards the offender, which can cause further harm and prevent healing and reconciliation.

Additionally, the desire for revenge and retribution can be driven by social and cultural factors, such as a belief in punitive justice or a desire for retribution against certain groups or individuals. This can lead to bias and injustice in the criminal justice system, with certain groups or individuals being disproportionately punished or targeted.

Therefore, while the desire for revenge and retribution is understandable, it is important to also consider alternative approaches to justice that prioritize healing and restoration, such as restorative justice. These approaches can provide a more holistic and effective response to crime, addressing the harm caused to the victim and the community, while also promoting accountability and preventing further harm.

CHAPTER II
WHY RESTRUCTURE THE CRIMINAL JUSTICE SYSTEM?

---

1. One of the most hotly debated subjects of the 21st century has been the burgeoning cost of justice and its impotence in crime prevention.

The cost of justice has been a major concern in the United States and many other countries in recent years. The traditional approach of punishing offenders with incarceration has proven to be incredibly expensive, with costs ranging from $31,286 to $69,355 per inmate per year, depending on the state. Moreover, the high rate of recidivism (re-offending) among released inmates shows that this approach does little to prevent crime in the long term.

As a result, there has been increasing interest in alternative approaches to justice, such as restorative justice and community justice, which focus on prevention, rehabilitation, and addressing the root causes of criminal behavior. These approaches are generally more cost-effective than incarceration and have the potential to reduce crime rates over time.

Expenditures for corrections have increased from 44 billion in 1997 to over 100 billion in 2006. As the prison population grows so does the price of carrying out justice.

2. Why have most evaluations of the criminal justice system not been favorable?

Evaluations of the criminal justice system have not been favorable because the system tends to focus on punishing offenders rather than addressing the underlying causes of crime. In addition, the system has been criticized for its high cost, ineffectiveness in reducing recidivism, and disproportionate impact on marginalized communities. Many argue that a more comprehensive and restorative approach to justice is needed, one that addresses the root causes of crime and includes meaningful support for victims and rehabilitation for offenders.

3. The sweeping judgment, often applied toward both the offenders and criminal justice personnel, tend to globalize the public's fear and anxiety.

The fear and anxiety caused by crime are often generalized to all offenders, as well as to those working in the criminal justice system, leading to negative attitudes and perceptions towards them. This can create a cycle of fear and mistrust, which can further harm the effectiveness of the justice system.

4. How do we solve the public's response to the lack of familiarity with the justice process?

The public's response to the lack of familiarity with the justice process can indeed be one of frustration and anger. This is because the justice system can often seem opaque, bureaucratic, and impersonal, making it difficult for people to understand how it works and how they can participate in it.

One of the main sources of frustration is the perceived lack of transparency in the justice process. Many people feel that the legal system is shrouded in mystery, with decisions made behind closed doors and little information provided to the public. This can lead to a sense of mistrust and suspicion towards the justice system, especially in cases where the outcome seems unfair or unjust.

Another source of frustration is the perceived lack of accountability in the justice system. Many people feel that judges, lawyers, and other legal professionals are too insulated from public opinion, making it difficult to hold them accountable for their actions. This can be exacerbated by cases where judges or lawyers seem to be more concerned with protecting their own interests than with promoting justice.

Finally, there is a sense of anger that the justice system often seems to prioritize the interests of the wealthy and powerful over those of ordinary people. Many people feel that the justice system is rigged against them, and that they have little chance of obtaining justice in cases where they are pitted against more powerful opponents.

To address these frustrations and concerns, it is important for the justice system to become more transparent, accountable, and responsive to the needs of the public. This can be achieved through greater access to information, greater public participation in the legal process, and greater emphasis on fairness and impartiality in the administration of justice. By building trust and confidence in the justice system, we can create a society that is more just and equitable for all.

5. Why earlier in history, the courts were closely connected to the community in comparison to today's courts?

In earlier times, the courts were closely connected to the community in which they operated. This was largely due to the fact that the justice system was less formalized and centralized, and communities were responsible for maintaining order and resolving disputes within their own boundaries.

In many traditional societies, the community played a central role in resolving conflicts and ensuring justice. Disputes were often settled through mediation or arbitration, with community leaders or elders serving as neutral mediators. This approach was rooted in a sense of communal responsibility, with the understanding that all members of the community had a stake in maintaining peace and resolving conflicts.

As legal systems became more formalized and centralized, the role of the community in justice became more limited. Courts became more distant from the people they served, and the legal process became more bureaucratic and impersonal. This was particularly true in urban areas, where the sheer scale of the justice system made it difficult for individual communities to have a meaningful impact on the process.

However, in recent years, there has been a growing movement towards restorative justice, which emphasizes the importance of community involvement in the justice process. Restorative justice programs often involve mediation or dialogue between the victim and the offender, with the goal of repairing harm and addressing underlying issues that may have contributed to the crime.

Through restorative justice, communities can play a more active role in promoting justice and healing, by supporting victims, holding offenders accountable, and working to prevent future harm. This approach recognizes the importance of community connections and relationships in promoting a more just and peaceful society.

Note: Community affairs, including the problems of crime, were a concern for the entire community. They assumed responsibility for all matters and thus maintained a close connection to the courts.

6. Societal change and the passing of antidotal laws (laws passed by a legislature in reaction to some high-profile crime) prompted the modern justice service delivery process. Discuss:

The modern justice service delivery process in many countries has been shaped by societal change and the passing of antidotal laws. Societal change refers to changes in the attitudes, values, and beliefs of people in a society, while antidotal laws are laws passed in response to a high-profile crime or a perceived problem in society.

Societal change can impact the justice system in several ways. For example, changes in societal attitudes towards certain crimes or offenders may lead to changes in the way those crimes are punished or how offenders are treated. Changes in public opinion can also influence the development of new laws or policies that aim to address emerging social issues, such as the legalization of marijuana or the recognition of same-sex marriage.

Antidotal laws, on the other hand, are often passed in response to a high-profile crime or a perceived problem in society. These laws are often passed quickly and with little debate, in an effort to show that the government is taking action to address the problem. Examples of antidotal laws include mandatory minimum sentencing laws, three-strikes laws, and sex offender registration laws.

However, while these laws may be well-intentioned, they can also have unintended consequences. For example, mandatory minimum sentencing laws can result in disproportionately harsh sentences for minor offenses, while three-strikes laws can result in life sentences for relatively minor crimes. Similarly, sex offender registration laws can make it difficult for individuals to reintegrate into society, even after they have served their sentences.

In conclusion, societal change and the passing of antidotal laws have both played a role in shaping the modern justice service delivery process. While both can have positive effects, it is important to carefully consider the potential consequences of new laws or policies, in order to ensure that they are fair, just, and effective.

7. List four factors that have affected the court's judicial system.:

While I can certainly provide a list of four factors that have affected the court's judicial system, I must clarify that this will be a broad overview and not specific to any particular country or jurisdiction. With that said, here are four factors that have historically affected the court's judicial system:

1. The shift of control from the community: In many traditional societies, the community played a significant role in the administration of justice. Disputes were resolved through mediation, arbitration, or other means of conflict resolution that involved the community. However, with the rise of centralized states, the administration of justice shifted from the community to the state. This led to the creation of formal legal systems that are independent of the community.

2. Specialization: As legal systems became more complex, the need for specialized courts and judges arose. This led to the creation of separate courts for civil, criminal, and administrative matters. This specialization has allowed for greater expertise and efficiency in the administration of justice.

3. Court unification: In some countries, courts were historically organized into separate jurisdictions based on geographic or subject matter. Over time, however, many jurisdictions have been unified into a single court system. This has led to greater consistency in the interpretation and application of the law.

4. Severance of the link between the courts and community politics: In some societies, the courts were closely linked to community politics, and judges were appointed or elected based on political considerations. However, this practice has led to the perception of judicial bias and has undermined the independence of the judiciary. As a result, many countries have taken steps to separate the judiciary from politics, such as establishing judicial selection commissions or independent judicial councils.

8. Why the current criminal justice system's process isolates the public and creates a fear and anxiety-based cycle?

The current criminal justice system's process and its impact on society is a complex and multifaceted topic. I will provide a general overview of the ways in which the criminal justice system can affect the public:

a) Isolates: The criminal justice system can isolate individuals who are accused or convicted of a crime from society. This can include pre-trial detention, imprisonment, and other forms of punishment that physically separate individuals from their families, communities, and other support networks.

b) Fear: The criminal justice system can create fear among the public, particularly among those who are vulnerable or marginalized. This fear can arise from concerns about crime rates, police brutality, racial profiling, and other issues related to the administration of justice.

c) Anxiety-based: The criminal justice system can also create anxiety among individuals who are involved in the system, such as victims, witnesses, and defendants. The process of going to court, testifying, and waiting for a verdict can be stressful and traumatic, and can have long-lasting psychological effects.

It's worth noting that the criminal justice system can also have positive impacts on society, such as deterring crime, protecting victims' rights, and promoting justice and accountability. However, the system is not perfect, and there is ongoing debate about how it can be reformed to better serve the needs of all members of society.

9. What are some features in our current criminal justice system that tend to create an isolation effect?

There are several features of the current criminal justice system that tend to create an isolation effect, including:

1. Pre-trial detention: Individuals who are accused of a crime and are unable to post bail may be held in jail for an extended period before their trial. This can lead to isolation from family, friends, and community support networks, as well as from their employment and other responsibilities.

2. Prison sentences: Individuals who are convicted of a crime may be sentenced to a term in prison, which can result in long-term isolation from their family, friends, and community. This can have a detrimental effect on mental health and well-being, as well as on the individual's ability to reintegrate into society upon release.

3. Solitary confinement: Some prisons use solitary confinement as a form of punishment or to manage difficult or dangerous inmates. However, prolonged periods of solitary confinement can cause psychological harm and exacerbate feelings of isolation and despair.

4. Geographic isolation: Prisons are often located in remote areas, far from the inmate's home community. This can make it difficult for family members to visit and provide support, and can exacerbate feelings of isolation and disconnection.

Hence, these features of the criminal justice system can contribute to an isolation effect that can have long-lasting negative effects on individuals and their communities. It's important to consider alternatives to incarceration that prioritize rehabilitation, community support, and reintegration into society.

Addendum:

a): Data Privacy Access to Information: Every State has data privacy laws prohibiting the release of private information on the offender. Such laws isolate the public and create a fear of the unknown. The sensibility of these laws cannot be argued. For example:

b): Sterilization of Information: All public agencies are given access to private data which is vital to the development of public policy. When this information is shared with the public, it is often sterilized and usually takes persistent inquiries and thorough analysis to deter mine what major policy implications might be drawn from the data.

c): Imposing Courthouse Structures: The architectural design of most courthouses is imposing and intimidating to the public. Each has a majestic air, complete with marble tile and mahogany paneling. Judges, wearing robes, sit higher than others. Occupants of the courtroom must stand as the judge is introduced. The judge in some instances maintains order through the surroundings, bulletproof glass, metal detectors, use of the gavel, the presence of a bailiff and the power inherent in the position. Even the courthouse jargon and legal process is foreign to most participants, especially offenders and victims. In this setting, there is no formal or informal welcome by any participants, neither is one's input solicited or valued.

d): Emotions forbidden in the Justice Process: The orderly environment of the justice process is intolerant of the expression of emotions. When individuals succumb to their raw emotions, attempts are made to control or even remove these expressions from the proceedings. Since crime is a form of interpersonal conflict, it is precisely these emotions that are needed while evaluating witnesses in the justice process. Crime is an emotionally charged conflict and the expression of raw emotions should not be restricted. In addition, the system's goal of "speedy processing" eliminates the opportunity of restoration of the victim, offender and the community. Our justice system should have as its objective, determining responsible parties seeking a dispositional process and outcome which addresses and corrects the harm to the degree possible. Otherwise, our justice system's priority becomes efficiency rather than effectiveness.

e): Professionalism: The entire justice system and its' process is confusing and intimidating. Understanding its carefully scripted procedures, court rules, laws, policies and practices requires extensive education and experience background. As justice system personnel gain more education and expertise in their field, there is a tendency to use the specialized jargon and procedures like a foreign language. A type of dress and conduct is quickly established in each courtroom and you cannot know or understand the unwritten rules as to appropriate protocol, unless you are an approved and accepted member of the "justice club." As friendships and social cliques develop, a type of closed system emerges that shuns public influence. In fact, public input tends to interfere with the tidy set of procedures for those working within the justice system. Therefore, one quickly discovers that one should not "speak unless spoken to."

f): Convenience of Public Service: The American society does not know how to handle its interpersonal conflicts (crime) and in a very real sense is handicapped by a 911 mentality. Whenever problems arise between the members of the community, the natural reaction is to dial 911 without trying to resolve the conflict. In each instance, the conflict is seldom resolved directly by the parties involved, but is referred to those in authority. These conflicts are then resolved by "professional experts", whether that be the police, the Child Protective Services, the housing authorities, the animal control officer, the Environmental Protection Agency, or the probation and parole officer.

10. Discuss why Criminologist Nils Christie describes interpersonal conflict as personal property?

Nils Christie, a prominent criminologist and sociologist, argued that interpersonal conflict can be seen as personal property. He believed that in modern societies, conflict is often seen as a matter to be dealt with by the State, with the State taking on the role of a neutral third party in resolving disputes. However, Christie argued that this approach overlooks the fact that conflicts are often deeply personal and emotional, and that individuals have a strong sense of ownership over their conflicts.

According to Christie, conflicts can be seen as personal property in several ways. First, conflicts are often based on personal values, beliefs, and experiences, and are therefore deeply connected to an individual's sense of identity. Second, conflicts can be seen as a form of social currency, as individuals may use conflicts to gain status, power, or resources within their social networks. Finally, conflicts can be seen as a form of social exchange, as individuals may use conflicts to negotiate and establish relationships with others.

By seeing conflicts as personal property, Christie argued that individuals should be given greater control over the resolution of their conflicts. He advocated for alternative forms of conflict resolution, such as mediation and restorative justice, that prioritize the needs and perspectives of those involved in the conflict. Overall, Christie's work has contributed to a broader shift in criminology towards a more humanistic and restorative approach to justice, which prioritizes the needs and experiences of individuals over the needs of the state.

11. According to Christie, our justice representatives are "professional thieves," who are trained at stealing our conflicts. Discuss.

Nils Christie did use the phrase "professional thieves" to describe justice representatives, but it's important to understand the context and nuance of his argument. Christie's work focused on the ways in which the state and criminal justice system often takes control of conflicts that are deeply personal and emotional, and which individuals may feel a strong sense of ownership over. He argued that the criminal justice system can sometimes be seen as a form of theft, in that it takes away individuals' control over their own conflicts and imposes a solution that may not be in their best interests.

However, it's worth noting that Christie did not view justice representatives as inherently corrupt or malicious. Rather, he saw them as operating within a system that was often structured in a way that prioritized the needs of the state over the needs of individuals. He believed that by recognizing the personal and emotional nature of conflicts, and by involving individuals more directly in the resolution process, it was possible to create a more just and humanistic approach to conflict resolution.

Therefore, Christie's work was influential in promoting alternative forms of conflict resolution, such as restorative justice and mediation, that prioritize the needs and perspectives of those involved in the conflict. While he was critical of certain aspects of the criminal justice system, his work was ultimately aimed at creating a more equitable and humanistic approach to justice.

12. Describe what happens when justice representatives take over our conflicts.

When justice representatives take over conflicts, it can have a paralyzing effect on victims and communities by disempowering them and depriving them of agency and control over their own conflicts. This can happen in several ways:

1. Loss of control: When the state takes over the resolution of a conflict, victims and communities may lose control over the process and outcome. The criminal justice system often operates according to a set of legal procedures and rules, which may not take into account the specific needs and perspectives of those involved in the conflict. This can lead to a sense of disempowerment and frustration, as victims and communities may feel that their voices and experiences are not being heard or valued.

2. Lack of participation: Victims and communities may also be excluded from the resolution process altogether. For example, in a criminal trial, victims may be required to testify as witnesses, but they may not have a say in the ultimate outcome of the trial. This can be particularly disempowering for victims who have experienced trauma or other forms of harm.

3. Impersonal nature: The criminal justice system can be impersonal and bureaucratic, which can further disempower victims and communities. Justice representatives may be seen as distant and unapproachable, and the legal language and procedures may be confusing and intimidating.

Consequently, when justice representatives take over conflicts, it can have a paralyzing effect by disempowering victims and communities. This can create a sense of frustration, disillusionment, and mistrust towards the criminal justice system, and may discourage victims and communities from seeking justice or participating in the resolution process. It's important to recognize the human and emotional dimensions of conflicts and to involve victims and communities more directly in the resolution process, in order to create a more empowering and just approach to conflict resolution.

13. Why after years of avoiding and relinquishing our conflicts to experts, we've lost all autonomy and our ability to influence the outcome of conflicts?

There is some truth to the idea that, over time, individuals and communities may come to rely too heavily on experts and professionals to resolve their conflicts, and in doing so, may lose their sense of autonomy and ability to influence the outcome of those conflicts.

One reason for this is that the criminal justice system can be complex and difficult to navigate, particularly for individuals who may be unfamiliar with the legal system or who lack resources and support. As a result, people may turn to lawyers, police, and other experts to help them resolve conflicts, and in doing so, may relinquish some of their own agency and autonomy in the process.

Another factor is that the criminal justice system is often designed to prioritize the needs of the state over the needs of individuals and communities. This can result in outcomes that may not align with the desires or interests of those involved in the conflict, and can lead to a sense of powerlessness and frustration.

Thus, it's important to recognize that conflicts are complex and multi-dimensional, and that there is no one-size-fits-all solution to resolving them. While experts and professionals can provide valuable guidance and support, it's important to also prioritize the needs and perspectives of individuals and communities, and to involve them more directly in the resolution process. This can help to foster a greater sense of autonomy and agency, and can lead to outcomes that are more just and equitable for everyone involved.

14. Why our willingness to seek solutions from professionals has ultimately diminished our sense of community responsibility?

There is some truth to the idea that relying too heavily on professionals to resolve conflicts can diminish our sense of community responsibility. When individuals and communities turn to experts and professionals to solve their problems, they may feel less of a personal stake in the outcome of the conflict, and may be less likely to take responsibility for resolving it themselves.

This can be particularly true in the criminal justice system, where individuals may feel that it is not their responsibility to address issues of crime and justice, but rather the responsibility of police, prosecutors, and other professionals. This can lead to a sense of detachment and disengagement from the issues that affect their communities, and may prevent individuals from taking an active role in addressing those issues.

At the same time, it's important to recognize that seeking solutions from professionals can also be an important and necessary step in resolving conflicts. Professionals can bring a wealth of knowledge and expertise to bear on complex issues, and can help to facilitate communication and understanding between conflicting parties.

The key is to strike a balance between seeking professional help and taking responsibility for our own conflicts and communities. This may involve finding ways to involve more people in the resolution process, and to encourage greater community engagement and responsibility. By doing so, we can create more just, equitable, and sustainable solutions to the conflicts that affect us all.

Note: We also breed a generation of people who do not know how to resolve conflict.

15. Do you know why crime has a paralyzing effect on victims and communities, causing them to respond with anger and fear?

Crime can have a paralyzing effect on both victims and communities, causing them to respond with anger and fear. Victims may feel helpless, violated, and afraid, while communities may feel threatened, anxious, and mistrustful of one another. These emotions can have a powerful impact on individuals and communities, and can make it difficult to move forward and address the underlying issues that contribute to crime. It's important to recognize and acknowledge these emotions, while also working to find ways to address the root causes of crime and to promote healing and justice for all those affected.

Furthermore, crime can also cause people to develop and respond with prejudice. For instance, if a member of a particular race committed the crime, others of the same race may be treated with contempt.

16. What do most people do when they experience anger and fear as a result of crime?

Many people may feel the need to take measures to protect themselves after experiencing anger and fear as a result of crime, but isolation may not always be the best or most effective response.

While it's natural to want to protect ourselves and our loved ones from harm, isolation can also contribute to a sense of disconnection and mistrust within communities, and can make it more difficult to address the root causes of crime.

Instead of isolating ourselves, it may be more effective to find ways to build stronger, more connected communities that can work together to address the underlying issues that contribute to crime. This may involve building relationships with neighbors and community members, getting involved in community groups and organizations, and supporting policies and programs that promote safety, justice, and equity for all.

It's also important to seek support and help if you or someone you know has been affected by crime. This may involve reaching out to friends, family members, or community organizations for support, or seeking professional help from a therapist or counselor.

By working together and seeking support, we can create stronger, more resilient communities that are better equipped to address the challenges and complexities of crime and justice.

Note: Some people move, build taller fences, install additional locks, alarms, floodlights, or even burglar bars. Yet others may purchase a firearm or some other device for protection.

17. In our pursuit of isolation, our collective responsibility for the safety and welfare of our neighbors has long been abandoned.

It's true that in some cases, our pursuit of isolation can lead to a diminished sense of collective responsibility for the safety and welfare of our neighbors and communities. When we focus solely on protecting ourselves and our immediate families, we may become less invested in the well-being of those around us, and may be less likely to take action to address broader social issues.

However, it's also important to recognize that isolation is not the only response to crime and fear. There are many ways to build stronger, more connected communities that can work together to address the root causes of crime and promote safety and well-being for all.

This may involve getting involved in community organizations, volunteering with local groups or charities, participating in neighborhood watch programs, or advocating for policies and programs that support safety, justice, and equity.

By taking these actions, we can demonstrate a commitment to the safety and well-being of our neighbors and communities, and can build stronger, more resilient communities that are better equipped to address the challenges of crime and justice.

Note: In many cases we don't even know the names of our neighbors, so we say to ourselves, "Why should we take responsibility for their safety and welfare?"

18. What happens when we look out for ourselves?

When we focus solely on looking out for ourselves and our own interests, it can lead to a breakdown of social bonding and a diminished sense of community connection and responsibility. This can have a number of negative consequences, including increased feelings of loneliness, disconnection, and mistrust.

By isolating ourselves and prioritizing our own needs over the needs of others, we may also miss out on the benefits of social connection, such as social support, shared resources, and a sense of belonging.

However, it's important to acknowledge that looking out for ourselves is also an important aspect of self-care and self-preservation. We all have the right to protect ourselves from harm and to prioritize our own well-being. The key is to strike a balance between taking care of ourselves and also recognizing our interconnectedness with others and our responsibility to our communities.

By finding ways to balance self-care with community connection and responsibility, we can build stronger, more resilient communities that are better equipped to address the challenges of crime and justice.

Note: This isolation is also producing a new generation of individuals who lack social bonding skills.

19. Is it true that interpersonal relationships are promoted through social bonding between neighbors?

Yes, interpersonal relationships can be promoted and strengthened through social bonding between neighbors. When we form social connections with those around us, we build a sense of community and shared responsibility for the well-being of our neighborhoods and communities.

Social bonding can take many forms, from casual interactions with neighbors to more formal community groups and organizations. By getting to know those around us and working together towards common goals, we can build trust, foster empathy and understanding, and create a sense of belonging and connectedness.

Strong social bonds can also have a number of positive impacts on crime and justice. By building strong relationships with our neighbors, we may be more likely to report suspicious activity or crimes, and may be more willing to work with law enforcement and other community organizations to address crime and promote safety.

Accordingly, social bonding is an important aspect of building stronger, more connected communities that are better equipped to address the challenges of crime and justice.

20. Activities that promote social bonding between neighbors.

There are many activities that can promote social bonding between neighbors. Here are some examples:

1. Block parties
2. Potluck dinners
3. Neighborhood picnics
4. Community clean-up events
5. Yard sales or flea markets
6. Walking groups or fitness classes
7. Book clubs or discussion groups
8. Movie nights or outdoor screenings
9. Volunteer projects or service activities
10. Sports leagues or recreational activities
11. Neighborhood gardens or community farming projects
12. Holiday celebrations or cultural events
13. Block or street-wide garage sales
14. Dog-walking groups or pet meet-ups
15. Outdoor games or competitions.

By participating in these types of activities, neighbors can get to know each other better, build relationships, and create a stronger sense of community and shared responsibility.

21. Social bonding activities produce familiarity and trust between individuals.

Yes, social bonding activities can help to produce familiarity and trust between individuals. By spending time together, sharing experiences, and engaging in common activities, neighbors can develop a greater sense of familiarity and understanding of one another. This can lead to increased levels of trust, empathy, and mutual support, which can in turn foster a stronger sense of community and shared responsibility.

Through social bonding activities, individuals may also be more likely to see each other as partners in promoting safety and preventing crime, rather than as strangers or potential threats. This can help to build a sense of collective efficacy, or the belief that together, community members can effectively address the challenges of crime and justice.

Thus, social bonding activities can be an important tool for promoting stronger, more connected communities that are better equipped to address the challenges of crime and justice. By fostering familiarity, trust, and mutual support, these activities can help to build a foundation for safer, more resilient neighborhoods and communities.

22. Name three things that isolation produces.:

Yes, isolation can produce several negative outcomes. Here are three examples:

1. Distrust: Isolation can lead to a lack of trust between individuals and communities, as people become less familiar with one another and less likely to rely on one another for support.
2. Unfamiliarity: Isolation can also lead to a lack of familiarity between individuals and communities, as people become less likely to interact and engage with those around them.
3. Cycle of Crime: Isolation can create a fertile environment for crime, as individuals and communities become more vulnerable and less equipped to prevent and address criminal activity. In isolated communities, there may be less social control, less willingness to report crime, and less access to resources and support that can help prevent crime.

Accordingly, isolation can have a number of negative impacts on individuals and communities, including decreased social cohesion, increased fear and anxiety, and increased vulnerability to crime and other forms of victimization. By promoting social bonding and connectedness, we can work to address these negative outcomes and build stronger, more resilient communities.

Note: These and many other things such as indifference, lack of empathy for others, and maybe even a hostile/negative attitude are produced by isolation.

23. Once a cycle of isolation is developed, it creates a fertile environment for crime.

If no one in the neighborhood is concerned about the safety and welfare of other neighbors then the drug dealer is free to deal drugs on the corner and the thief can easily kick in a back door without the worry of being seen or heard.

When isolation becomes the norm in a community, there may be fewer people looking out for each other's safety and welfare, which can create a more fertile environment for criminal activity. Criminals may be more likely to target isolated individuals or homes, knowing that there is less risk of being seen or caught.

In addition, when there is no sense of collective responsibility or shared concern for the safety and well-being of the community as a whole, there may be less willingness to report crime or work together to prevent it. This can create a cycle of isolation and vulnerability, in which individuals and communities become increasingly isolated and vulnerable to crime.

Addressing isolation and promoting social bonding and connectedness can be an important strategy for preventing crime and promoting community safety and well-being. By working together and supporting one another, individuals and communities can create a safer and more resilient environment for everyone.

24. Describe the condition created by isolation

Isolation can create a condition of anonymity for offenders, as they may be unknown to the community and free from informal constraints that would otherwise discourage criminal behavior. When individuals and communities are isolated from one another, there may be less opportunity for informal social control, such as gossip, peer pressure, or reputational damage, to discourage criminal activity.

For example, if a community is highly connected and individuals are familiar with one another, a criminal may be more reluctant to engage in illegal activity for fear of being caught or shunned by the community. However, if the community is isolated and individuals are unfamiliar with one another, there may be less informal social control, and the offender may feel freer to engage in criminal activity without fear of being identified or ostracized by the community.

Hence, the condition of anonymity created by isolation can make it more difficult to prevent and address crime, as offenders may be harder to identify and deter. By promoting social bonding and connectedness, individuals and communities can create a stronger sense of shared responsibility and encourage more informal social control, which can help to prevent crime and promote community safety and well-being.

25. Why the freedom resulting from the condition of anonymity is void of accountability and encourages the offender to participate in anti-social activities and criminal behavior?

The condition of anonymity resulting from isolation can create a sense of freedom for offenders, as they may feel that they can engage in criminal behavior without fear of being caught or held accountable. This lack of accountability can encourage the offender to continue engaging in anti-social activities and criminal behavior, as they may not face consequences for their actions.

When individuals and communities are isolated, there may be less opportunity for formal social control, such as law enforcement, to deter criminal activity. Additionally, the lack of informal social control, such as peer pressure and reputational damage, may further reinforce the sense of anonymity and freedom for offenders.

Therefore, the combination of anonymity and lack of accountability can create a dangerous environment in which criminal behavior is more likely to occur and persist. By promoting social bonding and connectedness, individuals and communities can help to prevent and address crime by increasing opportunities for formal and informal social control, and encouraging a sense of shared responsibility for community safety and well-being.

26. Why do the personnel in the justice system have a tendency to withdraw in isolation from those seeking to blame them for crime and recidivism in the community?

It is common for justice system personnel, such as police officers, prosecutors, judges, and correctional officers, to become isolated from the communities they serve, particularly when there is a perception of blame or criticism. This isolation can make it difficult for justice system personnel to understand and respond effectively to the needs and concerns of the community.

When justice system personnel feel isolated or defensive, they may be less likely to engage in community-oriented policing or other forms of community outreach and collaboration. This can contribute to a breakdown in communication and trust between the justice system and the community, and can make it harder to prevent and address crime and recidivism.

It is important for justice system personnel to recognize the importance of maintaining positive relationships with the communities they serve, and to take proactive steps to engage with community members and address their concerns. This can include participating in community events, listening to community feedback, and working collaboratively with community organizations and leaders to develop effective strategies for preventing and addressing crime. By building trust and rapport with the community, justice system personnel can help to create a safer and more cohesive society.

27. How does the justice system protect itself from the scrutiny and criticism of the public?

The justice system can protect itself from scrutiny and criticism by limiting access to information and controlling the nature of released information. This can include restricting public access to court records, sealing court proceedings, and limiting public statements or press releases about ongoing investigations or prosecutions.

In addition, the justice system may use its authority to shield its personnel from public scrutiny or criticism. For example, police departments may invoke qualified immunity to protect officers from civil lawsuits, and prosecutors may decline to prosecute cases where there is a risk of negative publicity or community backlash.

While there may be legitimate reasons for the justice system to restrict access to certain information or shield its personnel from undue criticism or scrutiny, it is important for the system to maintain transparency and accountability to the public. This can include providing regular updates on ongoing investigations or prosecutions, making court records and proceedings as accessible as possible, and engaging in meaningful dialogue with community members and leaders to address their concerns and feedback.

28. Describe the public's reaction to the obstacles encountered while seeking information.

When the public encounters obstacles while seeking information from the justice system, such as limited access to court records or restricted public statements, it can lead to frustration and anger. This can erode the trust between the public and the justice system personnel, creating a wall of separation and a spiraling effect of mistrust.

As the public perceives that the justice system is not being transparent or forthcoming with information, it can fuel suspicions and conspiracy theories, further damaging the relationship between the public and the system. This can also undermine the legitimacy of the justice system and make it harder for the system to effectively address issues of crime and public safety.

It is important for the justice system to recognize the value of transparency and accountability to the public, and to work towards making information as accessible as possible while still protecting the rights and privacy of those involved in legal proceedings. Building trust and maintaining open lines of communication with the public can help to bridge the gap and create a more collaborative and effective system for addressing issues of crime and justice.

29. One of the ways to understand the effects of isolation is to examine how the criminal justice system might answer four simple questions. List those questions.:

a): Is the current justice process easy for the public to understand or is it filled with expert and legal jargon that is largely incomprehensible?

b): Is the system accessible to the public or do they encounter roadblocks to participation?

c): Is the outcome entirely determined by system personnel or does the community truly have a voice and influence in the justice process?

d): Is the justice system respectful of gender, socio-economic and cultural differences by the way it operates or is it inflexible?

e): We could also ask, "Is the outcome entirely determined by system personnel or does the community truly have a voice and influence in the justice process?"

CHAPTER III
A DIFFERENT VIEW OF JUSTICE

---

1. Why the philosophy known as Restorative Justice has become one of the most widely debated subjects of the 21st century?

The statement that the philosophy of restorative justice has become one of the most widely debated subjects of the 21st century is largely true. Restorative justice has gained increasing attention and interest in recent years as an alternative approach to traditional punitive justice systems.

Restorative justice is based on the principle of repairing harm caused by a crime or wrongdoing, rather than solely punishing the offender. It aims to bring together the victim, the offender, and the community to address the harm caused and to promote healing and reconciliation. This approach has been seen as a way to create a more inclusive and collaborative justice system that focuses on restoring relationships and preventing future harm.

The growing interest in restorative justice can be seen in a variety of contexts. In criminal justice systems around the world, there has been increasing use of restorative justice processes in cases ranging from minor offenses to serious crimes. Restorative justice has also been used in schools, workplaces, and communities as a way to address conflicts and repair relationships.

At the same time, there has been significant debate and discussion about the effectiveness of restorative justice and its potential limitations. Some critics argue that restorative justice may not be appropriate in cases of serious or violent crimes, and that it may not always provide adequate protection for victims. Others question whether restorative justice is truly an alternative to punitive justice systems, or whether it simply serves as a supplement to them.

Thus, while restorative justice has become a widely debated subject in the 21st century, the effectiveness and appropriateness of this approach continue to be explored and debated by scholars, practitioners, and policymakers around the world.

2. What are some questions you should ask yourself while developing your own view of justice?

a) How do I view justice?

b) Do I believe in rehabilitation and restoration of the

offender?

c) Do I support retributive efforts to administer justice?

d) What should be the goal of our criminal justice system?

e) Is the current punitive justice system effective?

Here are some additional questions to consider:

- What role should the victim play in the justice process?
- How should the community be involved in the justice process?
- Should restorative justice be the primary approach to justice, or should it be combined with other approaches?
- How should we balance the needs of the victim, offender, and community in the justice process?
- How should we address systemic injustices and inequalities in the criminal justice system?
- Should punishment always be the primary goal of the justice system, or should rehabilitation and prevention also be prioritized?
- How should we address the root causes of crime, such as poverty, addiction, and mental illness?
- Should the justice system be focused on individual accountability, or should it also consider broader social and economic factors?
- How can we ensure that the justice system is fair, impartial, and equitable for all individuals, regardless of their background or circumstances?

If you feel that offenders and ex-offenders are a "lost cause," you won't be able to minister effectively to them.

3. Explain why restorative justice is the type of justice that brings resolution, healing, and reconciliation to the problem of crime?

Restorative justice aims to repair the harm caused by crime by involving the parties affected by the crime, including the victim, offender, and community, in a process of dialogue and reconciliation. It prioritizes the needs of the victim and seeks to address the underlying causes of the offender's behavior, with the goal of promoting healing and preventing future harm.

Restorative justice views crime as more than breaking the law – it also causes harm to people, relationships, and the community. So, a just response must address those harms as well as the wrongdoing.

Restorative justice recognizes that crime causes harm not only to the victim but also to the offender, the community, and the relationships between them. Therefore, a just response to crime should not only address the wrongdoing but also seek to repair the harm and restore relationships. Restorative justice involves the active participation of all parties affected by the crime in a process that allows them to communicate, understand each other's perspectives, and work together to find ways to repair the harm done.

4. To whom does restorative justice suggest that crime is an injury?

Restorative justice suggests that crime is an injury not only to the immediate victim but also to the wider community. It views crime as a violation of the relationships and trust that exist within a community, rather than simply a violation of laws and rules. The focus of restorative justice is on repairing the harm caused by the crime, rather than solely punishing the offender.

In the traditional criminal justice system, the focus is on punishing the offender for violating the law. However, restorative justice recognizes that punishment alone may not be sufficient to address the harm caused by the crime. Restorative justice aims to involve both the victim and the offender in a process of healing and repairing the harm caused by the crime. This process involves addressing the needs and interests of all parties involved, including the victim, offender, and community.

Restorative justice recognizes that crime has a ripple effect that can be felt beyond the immediate victim. By involving the community in the process of addressing the harm caused by the crime, restorative justice aims to strengthen relationships and build a stronger sense of community. This approach can lead to greater accountability and responsibility on the part of the offender, as well as greater healing and restoration for the victim and the community as a whole.

Restorative justice suggests that crime is an injury not only to the victim but also to the wider community. It seeks to address the harm caused by the crime by involving all parties in a process of healing and repair, rather than simply punishing the offender.

Effective restorative justice should have four components:

- Inclusion of all parties
- Encountering the other side
- Making amends for the harm

- Reintegration of the parties into their communities
- Restorative justice suggests that crime is an injury to the victim, the community, and the offender.

5. Explain why in a restorative justice paradigm, the offender at some point recognizes the hurt he has caused and experiences remorse for those actions, leading to repentance?

"Repentance is a very crucial aspect of the restorative justice paradigm. Someone has said that an offender can recognize the hurt they have caused and experience remorse without repenting but an offender that repents (changes) has certainly recognized the hurt they've inflicted and experienced true remorse."

In restorative justice, the focus is not just on punishing the offender, but on repairing the harm caused by the crime. This involves the offender taking responsibility for their actions, expressing remorse for the harm caused, and taking steps to make amends and repair the harm done. The goal is to restore relationships and heal the harm caused by the crime, rather than simply punishing the offender.

6. In order for the offender to move toward complete restoration, he or she must deal with both long- and short-term damages caused by their actions. Explain.

In a restorative justice paradigm, the offender is encouraged to take responsibility for the harm they have caused and make amends for the damage done, both in the short term and in the long term. This may involve repairing relationships with the victim and the community, making financial restitution, participating in community service or restorative justice programs, and taking steps to address any underlying issues or problems that may have contributed to their offending behavior. The goal is to not only hold the offender accountable for their actions, but also to help them become a responsible and productive member of society.

7. Explain why the victim cannot be the State or the system?

The victim in the context of restorative justice is typically the individual or community who has directly suffered harm as a result of a crime or wrongdoing. This can include physical, emotional, or financial harm, as well as a loss of trust or sense of safety. The victim may be an individual person or a community, but it is important to note that the victim cannot be the State or the system itself.

This is because the State or the system is not capable of experiencing harm in the same way that an individual or community can. While the State or the system may be affected by crime or wrongdoing, they are not the primary parties who have suffered harm as a result of the crime. Instead, the State or the system has a responsibility to uphold the law and to provide a fair and just process for addressing crime and wrongdoing.

In a restorative justice process, the State or the system may play a role in facilitating the process and ensuring that it is conducted fairly and justly. However, the primary focus is on repairing the harm caused to the victim and addressing the underlying causes of the crime or wrongdoing. By placing the victim at the center of the process, restorative justice seeks to create a more inclusive and collaborative approach to justice that prioritizes healing and restoration.

In summary, while the State or the system may be affected by crime or wrongdoing, they cannot be considered the victim in a restorative justice process. Instead, the victim is typically the individual or community who has directly suffered harm as a result of the crime or wrongdoing, and the focus is on repairing the harm and addressing the underlying causes of the crime.

Note: In the current justice system the State or system assumes the position of victim. They become an abstract entity in the entire criminal justice process.

8. Explain why the concept of restorative justice is a new paradigm for doing justice that starts at the grassroots with ordinary members of the community as well as victims and offenders?

Restorative justice is a concept that has gained significant attention in recent years as a new paradigm for doing justice. Unlike traditional criminal justice systems that focus on punishing offenders and upholding the law, restorative justice aims to repair the harm caused by crime and build stronger relationships between individuals and communities. One of the defining features of restorative justice is that it starts at the grassroots level, involving ordinary members of the community, victims, and offenders in the process of healing and restoration.

In traditional criminal justice systems, the process is often controlled by legal professionals, with little involvement from victims or the community. Restorative justice, on the other hand, recognizes the important role that victims and the community can play in the process of justice. Victims are given a voice and an opportunity to express their needs and desires, and offenders are held accountable for their actions in a way that involves them in the process of repair.

Restorative justice also recognizes that crime is not just an individual act, but has wider social and community impacts. It seeks to address the root causes of crime by involving the community in the process of healing and restoration. This approach can lead to greater understanding and empathy between individuals and communities, and can build stronger social bonds and relationships.

Overall, the concept of restorative justice is a new paradigm for doing justice that starts at the grassroots with ordinary members of the community, victims, and offenders. It is a more holistic and community-oriented approach to justice that seeks to repair the harm caused by crime and build stronger social connections. As restorative justice continues to gain recognition and support, it has the potential to transform our understanding of justice and create a more just and equitable society.

In addition, the offender becomes a taxpayer rather than a tax burden.

9. In restorative justice, what purpose does it serve to work offenders in closely monitored community projects?

In restorative justice, working with offenders in closely monitored community projects serves multiple purposes. Firstly, it provides an opportunity for offenders to take responsibility for their actions and make amends to the community that they have harmed. This can help to promote a sense of accountability and responsibility on the part of the offender, which can be an important step in the process of rehabilitation and reintegration.

Secondly, working on community projects can provide offenders with a sense of purpose and meaning, which can be particularly important for those who have experienced social exclusion and disconnection. By working on projects that benefit the community, offenders can develop a sense of belonging and connection, which can be an important factor in reducing the risk of reoffending.

Thirdly, closely monitored community projects can provide a supportive environment for offenders, where they can develop skills and competencies that can help them to reintegrate into society. This can include developing social and emotional skills, as well as vocational skills that can help them to find employment and make a positive contribution to the community.

Finally, working on community projects can also benefit the wider community, by promoting a sense of social cohesion and strengthening community bonds. It can provide an opportunity for members of the community to work together towards a common goal, which can help to build trust and understanding between individuals and groups.

Thus, working with offenders in closely monitored community projects serves multiple purposes in restorative justice. It provides an opportunity for offenders to take responsibility, develop a sense of purpose, develop skills and competencies, and benefit the wider community. By promoting a more holistic and community-oriented approach to justice, restorative justice can help to create a more just and equitable society for all.

Note: Restorative Justice sees crime as a breakdown of society and human relationships and attempts to mend these relationships through dialogue, community support, involvement, and inclusion.

10. Why with restorative justice, we hold offenders accountable and make the victim the center of the criminal justice process?

The statement that "with restorative justice, we hold offenders accountable and make the victim the center of the criminal justice process" is generally true. Restorative justice is a process that focuses on repairing the harm caused by a crime and bringing the offender, victim, and community together to find a solution that addresses the harm and promotes healing.

In a restorative justice process, the victim is often given a central role in the process. They are given an opportunity to share their experiences and feelings, and to express how the crime has affected them. This can be empowering for the victim, as they are given a voice in the process and are able to communicate directly with the offender.

At the same time, restorative justice also holds offenders accountable for their actions. Instead of simply punishing offenders, the process seeks to engage them in the process of repairing the harm they have caused. Offenders are given an opportunity to take responsibility for their actions, make amends, and take steps to ensure that they do not reoffend in the future.

Accordingly, restorative justice seeks to create a more inclusive and collaborative approach to justice, where the focus is on repairing harm and restoring relationships. By making the victim central to the process and holding offenders accountable for their actions, restorative justice can help to promote healing and prevent future harm.

11. Why is Restorative justice a noun referring (in the aggregate) to justice processes that create or restore equity, that make things right?

Restorative justice is a concept that refers to justice processes that aim to create or restore equity and make things right. It is based on the principle that justice should not only focus on punishing offenders but also on repairing the harm caused by their actions. The aim is to bring together the victim, offender, and community to collectively find solutions that address the harm caused by the crime and promote healing and restoration.

Restorative justice is a more holistic and community-oriented approach to justice that acknowledges the ripple effects of crime on individuals, families, and communities. It recognizes that crime is not just a violation of the law, but a breach of relationships and trust between individuals and communities. Therefore, it seeks to address the root causes of crime by promoting dialogue, understanding, and empathy.

In restorative justice, the focus is not just on punishing the offender but also on meeting the needs of the victim and repairing the harm caused by the crime. This involves bringing together all parties involved in the crime to find a resolution that is acceptable to everyone. This process can be facilitated by trained practitioners, who help to guide the conversation and ensure that everyone is heard and respected.

Restorative justice can take many different forms, from mediation between the victim and offender to community conferences involving the wider community. The aim is always to create a safe and supportive environment where all parties can share their experiences and find a way forward that promotes healing and restoration.

In conclusion, restorative justice is a noun referring to justice processes that prioritize repairing harm, restoring equity, and making things right. It is a more holistic and community-oriented approach to justice that aims to address the root causes of crime and promote healing and restoration for all parties involved.

In addition, Restorative Justice emphasizes the importance of working with prisoners and their victims in a way that promotes healing and encourages reconciliation.

12. Does restorative justice paradigm emphasizes the ways in which crime harms relationships in the context of community?

Yes, that's correct. The restorative justice paradigm recognizes that crime is not just a violation of the law, but also a harm to individuals, relationships, and the community. This approach emphasizes the importance of addressing the harm caused by the offense and restoring relationships and community well-being, rather than simply punishing the offender.

13. Authentic restorative justice is a continuum that includes:

1. Pre-conferencing: This involves preparing all parties for the conference, including explaining the process, answering questions, and setting goals for the conference.
2. The conference: This is a face-to-face meeting between the victim, offender, and other impacted parties, facilitated by a trained facilitator. The goal is to address the harm done and come up with a plan for repairing that harm.
3. Follow-up: This involves ensuring that the agreement reached during the conference is fulfilled, and that all parties are satisfied with the outcome. It may involve additional meetings or support services.
4. Community involvement: This involves engaging the community in the restorative justice process, including providing support to victims and offenders, and encouraging community members to take responsibility for preventing crime and repairing harm.

Included in authentic restorative justice is a sound, comprehensive understanding of the relationships affected by crime. It focuses on the full circle of injuries, needs and responsibilities of crime victims, offender, community and government.

14. Is it true that in Navajo Country, the practice of restorative justice promotes apology and forgiveness, including participation in culture-based cleansing ceremonies, traditional counseling and advisement?

That is correct. In Navajo Country, the practice of restorative justice is often based on traditional Navajo concepts of justice and includes elements such as apology and forgiveness, as well as participation in culture-based cleansing ceremonies and traditional counseling and advisement. The goal is to promote healing and restoration for both the victim and the offender, as well as the community as a whole.

15. In restorative justice, offender accountability is defined in terms of assuming responsibility and taking action to repair harm.

In restorative justice, offender accountability is not just about punishment but also about taking responsibility for their actions and making efforts to repair the harm they caused to the victim and the community. This approach focuses on the needs of the victim and the community, rather than just punishing the offender. By holding the offender accountable and encouraging them to make amends, restorative justice aims to promote healing, reconciliation, and a sense of closure for all parties involved.

16. Central to restorative justice is the recognition of the community, rather than the criminal justice agencies, as the prime site of crime control. Yes, that is correct. Restorative justice emphasizes the role of the community in addressing and preventing crime, rather than relying solely on the criminal justice system. The community is seen as having a central role in repairing harm and restoring relationships, and is involved in the process of holding offenders accountable and promoting healing for victims. This approach recognizes that crime is not just a violation of the law, but also a violation of the relationships and trust within the community, and therefore requires community-based solutions.

And to accomplish this, it takes not only the willingness of the offender and the victim to meet and plan amends, but also a cooperative effort by the community and law enforcement agencies.

17. Restorative justice emphasizes the importance of elevating the role of crime victim and community members through more active involvement in the justice process.

That's right and it does so by providing a wide range of opportunities for dialogue, negotiation, problem solving, which can lead to a greater sense of community safety, social harmony, and peace for all involved.

Restorative justice prioritizes the needs and concerns of the victim and the community, and involves them in the justice process in a more active and meaningful way. This approach recognizes that crime harms not only the victim, but also the community, and therefore, the community has a stake in the resolution and healing of the harm caused by the crime.

18. Why-Restorative justice is not retributive in nature, but redemptive?

Restorative justice is a philosophy and approach to justice that emphasizes repairing harm caused by crime or conflict, rather than punishing offenders. It is not retributive in nature, meaning that its focus is not on punishing offenders for their wrongdoing, but rather on repairing the harm caused and restoring relationships between victims, offenders, and communities.

In restorative justice, the offender is encouraged to take responsibility for their actions, make amends to the victim and the community, and work towards making positive changes in their lives. By doing so, they are able to move beyond their past mistakes and become productive members of society.

One of the key principles of restorative justice is that it is redemptive in nature. This means that it seeks to help offenders understand the impact of their actions on others, take steps to repair the harm caused, and make positive changes in their lives. By doing so, offenders are able to redeem themselves and make amends for their wrongdoing.

In contrast to retributive justice, which focuses on punishing offenders for their crimes, restorative justice emphasizes the importance of healing and reconciliation. It seeks to address the underlying causes of crime and conflict, rather than simply punishing offenders for their actions. By focusing on repairing the harm caused by crime, restorative justice is able to help victims and offenders move beyond their past experiences and work towards a brighter future.

In conclusion, restorative justice is a redemptive approach to justice that emphasizes repairing harm caused by crime or conflict, rather than punishing offenders. By focusing on healing and reconciliation, it is able to help offenders understand the impact of their actions, take responsibility for their wrongdoing, and make positive changes in their lives.

Note: Rather than seek revenge it focuses on helping bring about healing in relationships with God and the community of man.

19. Do you know why Restorative justice is not a set of programs, in contrast, it is a philosophy from which a response flows?

Restorative justice is not just a set of specific programs or practices, but rather a philosophy or approach to justice that emphasizes repairing harm, restoring relationships, and addressing the needs of all those impacted by a crime. From this philosophy, various programs and practices can be developed and implemented.

20. Explain why Restorative justice principles offer more inclusive processes which involve community justice?

Restorative justice is a philosophy and approach to justice that emphasizes repairing harm caused by crime or conflict, rather than punishing offenders. One of the key principles of restorative justice is that it offers more inclusive processes that involve community justice.

In traditional justice systems, the focus is often on punishing offenders for their crimes, with little involvement from the community. This can lead to a sense of alienation and disconnection between offenders and their communities, as well as a lack of understanding of the impact of crime on individuals and communities.

Restorative justice, on the other hand, emphasizes the importance of involving the community in the justice process. This includes not only the victim and the offender, but also family members, friends, and other members of the community who may have been affected by the crime or conflict.

By involving the community in the justice process, restorative justice is able to offer more inclusive and collaborative processes that promote healing and reconciliation. The community is able to play an active role in addressing the underlying causes of crime and conflict, and in supporting both the victim and the offender in making positive changes in their lives.

In addition, restorative justice is often seen as a more culturally responsive approach to justice, as it allows for greater input from diverse communities and promotes understanding and respect for different cultural perspectives.

Hence, restorative justice principles offer more inclusive processes that involve community justice, promoting healing and reconciliation, and offering a more culturally responsive approach to justice. By involving the community in the justice process, restorative justice is able to address the underlying causes of crime and conflict, promote positive change, and build stronger, more connected communities.

Note: Community justice includes all variants of crime prevention and justice, activities that explicitly include the community in their justice process.

21. Discuss why the primary goal of community justice is to mobilize communities to be active partners in crime-control and problem-solving efforts?

Community justice is a philosophy and approach to justice that emphasizes the importance of involving the community in crime-control and problem-solving efforts. The primary goal of community justice is to mobilize communities to be active partners in these efforts, working together with justice system professionals to create safer, healthier, and more vibrant communities.

One of the key principles of community justice is that crime is not just an individual problem, but a community problem. In order to effectively address crime and other community problems, it is necessary to involve the community in the process. This involves working with community members to identify the root causes of crime and develop strategies to address them, as well as creating opportunities for community members to be active partners in the justice system.

By involving the community in crime-control and problem-solving efforts, community justice is able to create a sense of ownership and investment in the justice system. This leads to increased trust and cooperation between community members and justice system professionals, as well as greater accountability and transparency.

Community justice also recognizes that traditional justice processes may not be effective in addressing all types of crime and community problems. Instead, it emphasizes the importance of utilizing a variety of approaches, including restorative justice, diversion programs, and community-based alternatives to incarceration.

Accordingly, the primary goal of community justice is to mobilize communities to be active partners in crime-control and problem-solving efforts, promoting greater trust and cooperation between community members and justice system professionals, and creating safer, healthier, and more vibrant communities.

22. Explain why the central focus of community justice is community-level outcomes, shifting the emphasis from individual incidents to systemic patterns, from individual conscience to social morals, from individual good to the common good?

Community justice is a unique approach to crime prevention. Community justice programs seek to integrate communities, government, and law enforcement agencies as an alternative response to, or for prevention of, criminal behavior. The primary focus of community justice programs is on outcomes that are directly related to the community.

Furthermore, community justice is a philosophy and approach to justice that emphasizes the importance of involving the community in crime-control and problem-solving efforts. The central focus of community justice is on achieving community-level outcomes, which involves shifting the emphasis from individual incidents to systemic patterns, from individual conscience to social morals, and from individual good to the common good.

One of the key principles of community justice is that crime is not just an individual problem, but a community problem. This means that addressing crime and creating a safer and more just society requires engaging community members in the process of problem-solving and decision-making. By involving the community in this way, community justice seeks to address the root causes of crime, such as poverty, inequality, and social disconnection, rather than simply punishing offenders after the fact.

Community justice also recognizes that traditional justice processes may not be effective in addressing all types of crime and community problems. Instead, it emphasizes the importance of utilizing a variety of approaches, including restorative justice, diversion programs, and community-based alternatives to incarceration. These approaches aim to provide meaningful opportunities for offenders to make amends for their actions and address the underlying issues that led to their criminal behavior.

Furthermore, community justice recognizes that achieving community-level outcomes requires a holistic and collaborative approach. This involves working with community members, law enforcement, courts, social service providers, and other stakeholders to develop comprehensive strategies that address the root causes of crime and promote community safety and well-being.

In summary, the central focus of community justice is on achieving community-level outcomes by engaging community members in the process of problem-solving and decision-making, addressing the root causes of crime, utilizing a variety of approaches, and taking a holistic and collaborative approach to justice. By doing so, community justice seeks to create a safer and more just society for everyone.

23. One of the goals of community justice is to facilitate the performance by private citizens of the functions that were once performed by the extended family, neighborhood and school.

Community justice is a philosophy and approach to justice that aims to involve private citizens and community members in crime control and problem-solving efforts. The concept of community justice recognizes that crime is not just an individual problem, but a community problem, and that the best way to address it is through a collaborative effort involving all members of the community.

One of the key goals of community justice is to empower community members to take on roles and responsibilities that were traditionally fulfilled by institutions like the extended family, neighborhood, and school. This includes promoting community involvement in restorative justice practices, which seek to repair harm caused by crime and restore relationships between offenders, victims, and the community.

Community justice also recognizes that crime is often rooted in social and economic conditions, such as poverty, unemployment, and inequality. To address these underlying issues, community justice initiatives often involve partnerships with social service providers and other community organizations to provide resources and support to individuals and families who are at risk of criminal behavior.

In addition, community justice involves promoting community policing practices, which aim to build trust and cooperation between law enforcement and community members. This can include initiatives like community patrols, citizen review boards, and police-community dialogues.

By involving private citizens and community members in crime control and problem-solving efforts, community justice seeks to create a more inclusive and responsive justice system that is better equipped to address the root causes of crime and promote community safety and well-being.

24. Community justice initiatives offer a new way of thinking about: Police, courts, and corrections that emphasize problem-solving. In other words, these three components operate differently from the past by emphasizing problem-solving and focusing on community concerns and the victim.

The traditional criminal justice system has been criticized for being too reactive and punitive, often resulting in high rates of recidivism and disproportionately affecting marginalized communities. In contrast, community justice initiatives aim to be more proactive and collaborative, involving community members in every stage of the justice process.

One of the key aspects of community justice is the promotion of restorative justice practices. Restorative justice seeks to repair harm caused by crime and address the needs of both the victim and the offender, with the ultimate goal of restoring relationships and promoting healing. This approach involves bringing together the victim, offender, and community members to discuss the harm caused and determine a way forward that addresses the needs of all parties involved.

Community justice initiatives also prioritize addressing the underlying social and economic conditions that contribute to crime. This involves working with community members to identify and address issues such as poverty, lack of access to education and healthcare, and systemic discrimination. By addressing these root causes, community justice initiatives aim to reduce the likelihood of future crime and create a safer and more just society.

In order for community justice initiatives to be successful, they must be grounded in strong relationships between community members, law enforcement, and other institutions. This requires building trust and engaging in open and transparent communication. Community justice initiatives also require adequate resources and support to ensure that they are sustainable over the long term.

Thus, community justice initiatives offer a promising alternative to traditional models of law enforcement and criminal justice. By involving community members in the process of problem-solving and decision-making, and addressing the underlying causes of crime, these initiatives have the potential to create more just and equitable societies.

25. Briefly explain the difference between community justice and restorative justice.

Both are more inclusive processes than the traditional criminal justice system, and both share the control with community to a greater extent. Community justice efforts may or may not be "restorative" and could be viewed as more of a process, while restorative justice is more of a philosophy that would affect the process as well as the end goal or purpose of the process. Restorative justice also includes the victim as a key focus of process and outcome, whether or not community based. *The philosophy would affect the process as well as the end goal or purpose of the process in restorative justice.*

Community justice and restorative justice are two approaches to the criminal justice system that aim to achieve a more just and equitable society. While there are some similarities between these approaches, there are also significant differences in their underlying philosophies and goals.

Community justice is a model of justice that emphasizes the importance of engaging the community in crime control and problem-solving efforts. It is a philosophy that recognizes that the criminal justice system cannot solve all of society's problems, and that community members must take an active role in addressing the underlying issues that contribute to crime. The primary goal of community justice is to mobilize communities to be active partners in crime control and problem-solving efforts. This approach is based on the idea that crime is a social problem that requires a community-level response. Community justice initiatives seek to facilitate the performance by private citizens of the functions that were once performed by the extended family, neighborhood, and school. This approach shifts the emphasis from individual incidents to systemic patterns, from individual conscience to social morals, and from individual good to the common good.

Restorative justice, on the other hand, is a paradigm of justice that emphasizes the importance of repairing the harm caused by crime. It views crime as more than just a violation of the law but as a harm to people, relationships, and the community. The restorative justice paradigm holds that justice must address both the harm caused by the crime and the wrongdoing itself. This approach is based on the idea that crime is an injury that requires healing and reconciliation. Restorative justice seeks to hold offenders accountable and make the victim the center of the criminal justice process. It emphasizes the importance of elevating the role of the crime victim and community members through more active involvement in the justice process. The primary goal of restorative justice is to create or restore equity, to make things right.

One of the key differences between community justice and restorative justice is their focus. Community justice is focused on mobilizing communities to be active partners in crime control and problem-solving efforts, while restorative justice is focused on repairing the harm caused by crime. Community justice initiatives seek to address the systemic issues that contribute to crime, such as poverty, inequality, and lack of access to education and employment opportunities. Restorative justice initiatives, on the other hand, seek to address the immediate harm caused by crime, such as physical, emotional, and psychological harm to victims.

Another key difference between community justice and restorative justice is their approach to accountability. Community justice emphasizes problem-solving and seeks to engage offenders and victims in a collaborative process to address the underlying issues that contribute to crime. Restorative justice emphasizes repairing the harm caused by crime and seeks to hold offenders accountable for their actions by requiring them to take responsibility and take action to repair the harm they have caused. This approach to accountability is redemptive rather than retributive, meaning that it aims to rehabilitate offenders and reintegrate them into society rather than punish them for their actions.

In conclusion, while community justice and restorative justice share some similarities, they are fundamentally different approaches to the criminal justice system. Community justice emphasizes the importance of engaging the community in crime control and problem-solving efforts, while restorative justice emphasizes repairing the harm caused by crime. Both approaches offer a more inclusive and collaborative way of thinking about justice that involves community-level outcomes and seeks to create a more just and equitable society.

26. Describe a restorative community justice paradigm.

A restorative community justice paradigm would have both of these approaches in mind – to involve the victim and community, to the end of repairing the harm to victim and community while holding the offender accountable.

A restorative community justice paradigm is a holistic approach to justice that focuses on repairing harm caused by criminal behavior while holding the offender accountable for their actions. It recognizes that crime is not just a violation of the law, but also a violation of people, relationships, and the community. The paradigm is grounded in the belief that justice is best achieved by actively involving those who have been harmed, the offender, and the community in the justice process.

Restorative community justice paradigms differ from traditional criminal justice systems in several key ways. Firstly, they prioritize the needs of the victim over punishment. The victim is seen as the central figure in the justice process, and their needs and desires are taken into account when determining the outcome of the case. This approach allows victims to have a voice in the process, to express their feelings, and to be heard. Victims are given the opportunity to participate in the process of healing and restoration, rather than simply being a witness or a passive recipient of punishment.

Secondly, restorative community justice paradigms aim to build stronger, more connected communities by involving community members in the process of justice. This means that community members are not only involved in responding to crime but also in preventing it. They are encouraged to take responsibility for their community's well-being, to identify problems, and to work together to find solutions. Community members are also involved in the rehabilitation of offenders, working closely with them to help them repair the harm they have caused and reintegrate back into society.

Thirdly, restorative community justice paradigms focus on repairing the harm caused by the offender. This means that the offender is held accountable for their actions and must take responsibility for repairing the harm they have caused. This may involve making restitution to the victim, performing community service, participating in therapy or counseling, or other forms of restorative justice. The goal is to address the root causes of the offender's behavior, to prevent future harm, and to restore the offender to their full potential.

In a restorative community justice paradigm, justice is seen as a process rather than an outcome. The process involves all stakeholders, including victims, offenders, and community members, in a collaborative effort to repair harm and prevent future harm. The emphasis is on restoring relationships and building stronger, more connected communities. This approach recognizes that justice cannot be achieved by punishment alone, but rather through a holistic approach that addresses the needs of all stakeholders involved.

In conclusion, a restorative community justice paradigm is a transformative approach to justice that seeks to repair harm caused by criminal behavior while holding the offender accountable for their actions. It is grounded in the belief that justice is best achieved through collaboration, community involvement, and the restoration of relationships. By prioritizing the needs of the victim, involving community members, and focusing on repairing harm, this paradigm offers a more effective and humane approach to justice.

27. Briefly explain why Restorative justice is a compilation of principles and practices that come together to form an approach that involves all parties – the offender, victim, and community – to achieve justice?

Restorative justice is an approach to justice that aims to address harm and restore relationships between the victim, offender, and community. It is based on the principle that crime is not just a violation of the law, but also a violation of people and relationships, and thus requires a response that focuses on repairing harm and rebuilding trust.

The restorative justice approach involves all parties affected by the harm, including the victim, offender, and community. It is based on a set of principles that emphasize accountability, repairing harm, and community involvement in the justice process.

One of the key principles of restorative justice is accountability. This means that the offender takes responsibility for their actions and works to repair the harm they have caused. This can include making restitution, performing community service, and taking steps to prevent similar harm in the future. The goal is to help the offender understand the impact of their actions and take steps to make things right.

Another important principle of restorative justice is repairing harm. This involves addressing the needs of the victim and working to restore the harm that has been caused. This can include providing support and resources to help the victim recover, as well as taking steps to address any damage or loss that has occurred.

Community involvement is also a key aspect of the restorative justice approach. This means that the community is involved in the justice process and works to support the victim and offender in their efforts to repair harm and rebuild relationships. Community members can provide support and resources, serve as mediators or facilitators, and help to hold the offender accountable for their actions.

Restorative justice practices can take many forms, including victim-offender mediation, family group conferencing, and community panels. These processes are designed to create a safe and supportive environment for all parties involved and to facilitate open and honest communication. They also provide an opportunity for the victim and offender to work together to develop a plan for repairing harm and preventing future harm.

Consequently, the restorative justice paradigm offers a new way of thinking about justice that focuses on repairing harm, restoring relationships, and involving the community in the process. It is based on a set of principles that emphasize accountability, repairing harm, and community involvement, and is designed to create a more just and equitable society. By bringing all parties together to work towards a common goal, restorative justice can help to build stronger and more resilient communities that are better equipped to address the complex challenges of our time.

28. Give a summary of the many principles and practices of restorative justice.:

    a) Crime is an offense against human relationships.

    b) Victims and the community are central to justice processes.

    c) The first priority of justice processes is to assist victims.

    d) The second priority is to restore the community, to the degree possible.

    e) The offender has personal responsibility to victims and to the community for crimes committed.

    f) Stakeholders share responsibilities for restorative justice through partnership for action.

    g) The offender will develop improved competency and understanding as a result of the restorative justice experience.

Furthermore, Restorative justice is a philosophy that aims to repair harm caused by criminal offenses by involving all parties – the offender, victim, and community – in the justice process. There are many principles and practices that make up the restorative justice approach, including:

1. Harm and Needs Assessment: This principle requires identifying the harm caused by the offense and the needs of the victim, offender, and community.
2. Victim-Centered Approach: Restorative justice emphasizes the needs of the victim and provides opportunities for them to have a voice in the process.
3. Offender Accountability: The offender is held accountable for their actions and is encouraged to take responsibility for repairing the harm caused.
4. Community Involvement: The community is involved in the justice process, providing support and resources for both the victim and offender.

5. Restitution and Reparation: Offenders are required to make amends and provide compensation for the harm caused.
6. Dialogue and Communication: Restorative justice encourages open and honest communication between the parties involved to promote understanding and healing.
7. Healing and Reconciliation: The ultimate goal of restorative justice is to promote healing and reconciliation between the parties involved.
8. Voluntary Participation: Participation in the restorative justice process is voluntary, allowing all parties to choose whether or not to participate.
9. Fairness and Equity: Restorative justice seeks to provide fairness and equity for all parties involved in the justice process.
10. Continuity of Care: The restorative justice process seeks to provide ongoing support and resources to all parties involved, promoting long-term healing and growth.

Accordingly, the principles and practices of restorative justice aim to promote healing and reconciliation, encourage accountability, involve the community, and provide a more equitable and just approach to the justice system.

29. Name some of the fundamental concepts that are common among restorative justice advocates.

Restorative justice is a theory of justice that emphasizes repairing the harm caused by criminal behavior. It is best accomplished through cooperative processes that include all stakeholders. This can lead to transformation of people, relationships and communities.

There are several fundamental concepts that are common among restorative justice advocates. Here are three:

1. Repairing harm: The central focus of restorative justice is repairing the harm caused by a crime. This includes not only repairing the tangible harm, such as property damage or financial loss, but also the intangible harm, such as emotional trauma and social disruption.
2. Inclusivity: Restorative justice emphasizes the importance of involving all parties affected by a crime, including the offender, victim, and community. It recognizes that crime is not just an individual act, but a violation of relationships and social bonds.
3. Responsibility and accountability: Restorative justice holds offenders accountable for their actions by requiring them to

take responsibility for the harm they have caused and to take action to repair that harm. At the same time, it recognizes that offenders are human beings with the potential for change and seeks to help them make amends and reintegrate into the community.

4. Crime is fundamentally a violation of people and interpersonal relationships.
5. Violations create obligations and liabilities.
6. Restorative justice seeks to heal and put right the wrongs.

30. Victim and the community have been harmed and need restoration.

Restorative justice emphasizes accountability, making amends, and — if the parties are interested — facilitated meetings between victims, offenders, and other persons.

In traditional criminal justice systems, the focus is often solely on the offender and punishing them for their actions. However, the restorative justice paradigm emphasizes that the victim and the community are also harmed by crime and need restoration.

When a crime is committed, the victim is left with physical, emotional, and psychological scars. They may feel violated, vulnerable, and may struggle with feelings of anger, fear, and distrust. The harm caused by the crime can affect the victim's relationships, work, and overall quality of life. Restorative justice seeks to address these harms by giving the victim a voice and an active role in the justice process. It creates an opportunity for the victim to express their needs, feelings, and concerns, and to have those needs heard and addressed. The process empowers the victim by giving them a sense of agency and control over what happens next, rather than leaving them feeling like a passive bystander.

In addition to the victim, the community is also affected by crime. When a crime occurs, it can create fear, mistrust, and division within a community. This can lead to a breakdown in social cohesion and a sense of disconnection and isolation. Restorative justice recognizes that crimes harm the social fabric of communities and seeks to repair this harm by involving the community in the justice process. This can include community members participating in conferences, circles, or other restorative justice practices to discuss the impact of the crime on the community and to work together to find ways to address the harm caused.

Restorative justice also recognizes that offenders are part of the community and that their actions have an impact on the community as a whole. Punishing offenders in isolation from the community does not address the root causes of crime or promote a sense of responsibility and accountability. By involving offenders in the restorative justice process, they can come face-to-face with the harm they have caused and take responsibility for their actions. This can lead to a deeper understanding of the impact of their actions on the victim and the community, and can encourage them to make amends and take steps to repair the harm caused.

Wherefore, restorative justice paradigm recognizes that crime is not just a violation of the law, but also a violation of relationships and communities. By involving the victim, the offender, and the community in the justice process, it seeks to restore these relationships and promote healing and repair.

31. Briefly explain why in restorative justice victims, offenders, and the affected communities are the key stakeholders in justice?

In restorative justice, the focus is on the harm that has been caused to the victim and the community, and on repairing that harm as much as possible. It recognizes that crime is not just a violation of the law, but also a violation of relationships and community values. Therefore, it involves the victim, offender, and affected community members as key stakeholders in the justice process.

The victim is central to the restorative justice process. Restorative justice aims to address the harm that has been done to the victim, rather than just punishing the offender. Victims are given the opportunity to tell their story, share their feelings, and have a say in the outcome of the process. They are also provided with the opportunity to receive restitution, which may include financial compensation or community service by the offender.

The offender is also a key stakeholder in restorative justice. Rather than being seen as a passive recipient of punishment, the offender is seen as an active participant in repairing the harm they have caused. The offender is encouraged to take responsibility for their actions, make amends to the victim and the community, and become a positive member of society.

The affected community is also an important stakeholder in restorative justice. Crime does not just affect the victim and offender, but also the broader community. Restorative justice seeks to involve the community in the process of repairing harm and preventing future harm. Community members are given the opportunity to participate in the justice process, to share their experiences, and to work together with the victim and offender to find a resolution.

Thence, restorative justice recognizes that crime is a complex issue that requires the involvement of multiple stakeholders in order to achieve true justice. By involving the victim, offender, and affected community members, restorative justice seeks to repair harm, restore relationships, and build stronger communities.

32. Describe the obligations created by violations in the community.:

a) Offender's obligations are to make things right as much as possible.

b) The community's obligations are to victims and the offenders and the general welfare of its members.

Obligations that follow from harm inflicted by crime should be related to making things right. The community helps victims of crime and support efforts to integrate offenders into the community

When violations occur in a community, various obligations are created for different stakeholders involved. For the offender, their obligation is to take responsibility for their actions and do what they can to make things right as much as possible. This can include acknowledging the harm caused, making amends to the victim or affected parties, and taking steps to prevent similar harm in the future.

For the community, there are also obligations that arise. Firstly, the community has a responsibility to the victim and the offender to ensure that justice is served in a fair and just manner. This includes providing support to the victim and ensuring that the offender is held accountable for their actions. Additionally, the community has an obligation to the general welfare of its members, which may include addressing underlying issues that contribute to crime and harm in the community, such as poverty, inequality, and lack of access to resources.

Overall, the obligations created by violations in the community are multifaceted and involve a range of stakeholders. Restorative justice principles emphasize the importance of all parties taking responsibility for their actions and working together to create a more just and equitable community.

33. What are some ways in which restorative justice seeks to heal and put right the wrongs?

Restorative justice theory and programs have emerged over the past 35 years as an increasingly influential world-wide alternative to criminal justice practices.

Restorative justice is a philosophy and practice that seeks to heal the harm caused by crime or wrongdoing by involving the victim, offender, and community in the justice process. It aims to create a space for dialogue, understanding, and accountability. Restorative justice recognizes that traditional criminal justice systems often fall short in addressing the needs of victims and communities affected by crime. As such, restorative justice seeks to heal and put right the wrongs in several ways:

a) The needs of victims for information, validation, vindication, restitution, testimony, safety, and support are the starting points of justice: The focus of restorative justice is on the harm caused by the offense, and how to repair that harm. The process of restorative justice aims to address the needs of the victim and create opportunities for them to receive information, validation, vindication, restitution, testimony, safety, and support. This approach is grounded in the idea that justice should not only be about punishing the offender but also about addressing the harm done to the victim.

b) The process of justice maximizes opportunities for the exchange of information, participation, dialogue, and mutual consent between victim and offender: Restorative justice creates opportunities for the victim and offender to come together in a safe and respectful environment, where they can communicate their needs and feelings. The goal is to create a dialogue that allows the victim to express the harm they have suffered and for the offender to take responsibility for their actions. This process can help both the victim and offender gain a better understanding of each other's perspectives and needs, which can lead to mutual consent and agreement on how to repair the harm caused.

c) Offender's needs and competencies are addressed: Restorative justice recognizes that the offender may have needs and competencies that need to be addressed to prevent future harm. This may involve addressing issues such as addiction, mental health, education, and employment. By addressing these underlying issues, restorative justice aims to reduce the likelihood of the offender re-offending.

d) The justice process belongs to the community: Restorative justice emphasizes the importance of involving the community in the justice process. The community is seen as a key stakeholder, and their involvement can help create a sense of accountability and responsibility. The community can also play a role in supporting the victim and offender as they work towards repairing the harm caused.

e) Justice is mindful of the outcomes, intended and unintended, of its responses to crime and victimization: Restorative justice recognizes that the criminal justice system can have unintended consequences, such as exacerbating harm, perpetuating inequality, or alienating the victim and offender. As such, the justice process aims to be mindful of these outcomes and work towards preventing them. This can involve taking steps such as reducing the use of incarceration or involving community members in decision-making processes.

In conclusion, restorative justice seeks to heal and put right the wrongs caused by crime or wrongdoing by involving the victim, offender, and community in the justice process. It aims to address the needs of the victim, provide opportunities for the offender to take responsibility for their actions, and involve the community in the process. Restorative justice recognizes that traditional criminal justice systems often fall short in addressing the needs of victims and communities affected by crime, and seeks to create a more equitable and compassionate approach to justice.

CHAPTER IV
CONCEPTUAL FRAMEWORKS OF
RESTORATIVE JUSTICE

---

1. Without question, our method of carrying out justice in the 21st century must be changed.

The traditional method of carrying out justice in the 21st century is rooted in punishment and retribution. The focus has been on punishing offenders for their crimes, often without considering the underlying causes of their behavior or the needs of victims and communities affected by the crime. However, it is becoming increasingly clear that this approach is not effective in reducing crime or addressing the harm caused by it. Therefore, a shift towards a more restorative and community-based approach to justice is needed.

Firstly, the current system of justice has failed to reduce crime rates. Despite the increasing number of people being incarcerated, the overall crime rates remain high. The punishment-focused approach to justice has not addressed the root causes of crime, such as poverty, lack of education, and mental health issues. Rather than addressing these issues, the current system has exacerbated them, leading to higher rates of recidivism and further harm to victims and communities.

Secondly, the current system is not victim-centered. Victims are often treated as secondary to the needs of the state and the offender. They are left out of the justice process and are not given a say in the outcome of their case. Victims' needs for information, validation, vindication, restitution, testimony, safety and support are often not addressed, which leaves them feeling ignored and disempowered.

Thirdly, the current system is costly, both financially and socially. The high costs of maintaining prisons and carrying out lengthy trials and appeals have drained resources from other important social programs. Additionally, the negative impact of incarceration on families and communities is immeasurable, leading to further social and economic costs.

Therefore, a shift towards a more restorative and community-based approach to justice is needed. This approach focuses on addressing the harm caused by the crime and repairing the relationships between the victim, offender, and community. It emphasizes the importance of including all stakeholders in the justice process, including victims, offenders, and community members. It aims to address the underlying causes of crime and promote social justice by providing opportunities for offenders to make amends for their actions and to become active members of their communities.

Restorative justice practices, such as victim-offender mediation, community conferencing, and family group conferencing, have been shown to be effective in reducing recidivism rates and promoting healing for victims and offenders. These practices provide a more holistic approach to justice, taking into account the needs of all stakeholders and the community as a whole.

In conclusion, the traditional method of carrying out justice in the 21st century must be changed. A shift towards a more restorative and community-based approach to justice is needed, one that addresses the root causes of crime, promotes healing for victims and offenders, and promotes social justice for all. It is time to prioritize the needs of victims and communities over punishment and retribution.

2. Briefly explain why Christie (criminologist) believes that crime serves as a catalyst which, if channeled properly, can provide the motivation to empower the community to take a fuller and more direct responsibility for crime?

Nils Christie, a Norwegian criminologist, introduced the concept of "conflict resolution through social discipline" as an alternative approach to traditional criminal justice. He believed that crime could serve as a catalyst for community empowerment and responsibility.

Christie's approach suggests that crime is not only an individual act but a social phenomenon, and that traditional criminal justice systems fail to address the root causes of crime. Instead of punishing offenders and relying on law enforcement, Christie proposed a restorative justice approach that focuses on community involvement and responsibility.

In this approach, the community is empowered to take a more active role in addressing crime and conflict. Restorative justice processes seek to repair the harm caused by the offense and restore relationships between the offender, victim, and community. Offenders are held accountable for their actions, but the goal is not punishment for its own sake but rather to promote healing and reconciliation.

Christie believed that crime can serve as a catalyst for community empowerment because it forces individuals to confront the impact of crime on their community and to take action to address it. In a restorative justice system, the community is seen as the primary stakeholder, and justice is based on restoring relationships and repairing harm rather than on punishing offenders.

This approach also emphasizes the importance of social discipline, which refers to the informal social controls that exist within a community. These controls can include family, friends, and other members of the community who hold each other accountable for their actions. Christie argued that social discipline can be a more effective form of control than formal criminal justice systems, as it is rooted in the community and based on shared values.

So, Christie's approach emphasizes the importance of community involvement and empowerment in addressing crime and conflict. By viewing crime as a social problem rather than an individual one, restorative justice seeks to create a more just and equitable society.

3. Name some of the popularized conceptual models which provide interesting frameworks to help develop and organize community-based practices in responding to crime.:

    a) Restorative Justice

    b) Community Justice

    c) Communitarianism

    d) Communities That Care Programs

    e) Community Policing

    f) Civic Responsibility

    g) Devolution

For example, "Communities That Care PLUS" is the product of years of prevention science research and collaboration with states and communities across the country. They help communities use the system, choose tested and effective programs tailored to the specific needs of that community, and track progress over time. Theirs is a social development strategy that fosters the success of young people through every stage of development.

There are several conceptual models that provide interesting frameworks for community-based practices in responding to crime. These models include Restorative Justice, Community Justice, Communitarianism, Communities That Care Programs, Community Policing, Civic Responsibility, and Devolution.

Restorative Justice is a philosophy that seeks to repair the harm caused by crime and conflict by involving all parties – the victim, offender, and community – in a process of dialogue, accountability, and restitution. The goal is to restore relationships and promote healing, rather than simply punishing offenders. Restorative justice programs often include victim-offender mediation, community conferencing, and other forms of dialogue and accountability.

Community Justice is a model that emphasizes the importance of involving the community in all aspects of the criminal justice system, from prevention and intervention to adjudication and reentry. The goal is to empower the community to take a more active role in addressing the root causes of crime and to promote community safety and well-being.

Communitarianism is a political philosophy that emphasizes the importance of community values, social responsibility, and civic engagement. Communitarians believe that individual rights must be balanced with the needs and interests of the community, and that communities must take an active role in shaping social norms and values.

Communities That Care Programs are community-based initiatives that seek to prevent crime and delinquency by identifying and addressing risk factors in young people's lives. The programs involve a range of stakeholders, including parents, schools, law enforcement, and community organizations, and focus on building protective factors and promoting positive youth development.

Community Policing is a law enforcement strategy that emphasizes the importance of partnerships between police and the community in preventing crime and promoting public safety. Community policing involves a range of activities, including problem-solving, community engagement, and collaborative problem-solving.

Civic Responsibility is the belief that individuals have a moral obligation to participate in the life of their community and to work for the common good. This includes participating in civic organizations, volunteering, voting, and taking an active role in community decision-making.

Devolution is the transfer of power and responsibility from the central government to local communities. Devolution seeks to empower local communities to take an active role in addressing social and economic issues, including crime and justice.

In summary, these conceptual models provide frameworks that can help guide community-based practices in responding to crime. They emphasize the importance of community involvement, restorative approaches, problem-solving, and social responsibility. By using these models to inform policy and practice, communities can work together to promote safety, prevent crime, and promote social justice.

4. Give a summary why crime-prevention through problem solving for the future is the main focus in restorative justice, rather than solely establishing blame for past criminal behavior?

The attitude behind crime prevention is: "Let's fix the problem so it doesn't happen again." Establishing blame is NOT crime prevention!

Introduction:

Restorative justice is a process of justice that aims to repair the harm caused by a crime by involving the offender, victim, and community in a collaborative process. It is a victim-centered approach that focuses on addressing the underlying causes of the crime and preventing it from happening in the future. This essay will discuss how crime prevention through problem solving is the main focus of restorative justice, rather than solely establishing blame for past criminal behavior.

Restorative Justice and Crime Prevention:

Restorative justice is a process that is focused on addressing the root causes of crime and preventing it from happening in the future. It is a proactive approach to justice that emphasizes crime prevention through problem solving. The aim of restorative justice is not just to punish offenders, but to rehabilitate them and help them to become responsible members of society.

Restorative justice recognizes that crime is not just a legal problem but a social problem that affects the community as a whole. It emphasizes the importance of addressing the underlying causes of crime, such as poverty, lack of education, and social inequality. By involving the community in the restorative justice process, it creates an opportunity for the community to address these underlying issues and work together to prevent future crime.

In restorative justice, the focus is on repairing the harm caused by the crime rather than just punishing the offender. This means that the victim is given a voice in the process and is able to express how the crime has affected them. The offender is also given an opportunity to take responsibility for their actions and make amends for the harm caused. By addressing the harm caused by the crime, restorative justice aims to prevent future crime by changing the behavior of the offender and creating a sense of accountability.

Restorative justice also emphasizes the importance of rehabilitation and reintegration. It recognizes that offenders are often products of their environment and that by providing them with the necessary support, they can become responsible members of society. By focusing on rehabilitation and reintegration, restorative justice aims to prevent future crime by addressing the root causes of criminal behavior.

Comparison with Retributive Justice:

Retributive justice, on the other hand, is focused on punishing offenders for their past criminal behavior. It is a reactive approach to justice that emphasizes punishment as a deterrent to future crime. Retributive justice does not address the underlying causes of crime or focus on preventing future crime.

Retributive justice is based on the principle of retribution, which means that offenders should receive punishment in proportion to the harm they have caused. This approach is based on the belief that punishment serves as a deterrent to future crime. However, research has shown that punishment alone is not an effective deterrent to future crime.

Conclusion:

Restorative justice is a victim-centered approach that focuses on addressing the harm caused by a crime and preventing future crime. It is a proactive approach to justice that emphasizes crime prevention through problem solving. By involving the community in the restorative justice process, it creates an opportunity to address the underlying causes of crime and work together to prevent future crime. Restorative justice recognizes the importance of rehabilitation and reintegration in preventing future crime. In contrast, retributive justice is focused solely on punishing offenders for their past criminal behavior and does not address the underlying causes of crime or focus on preventing future crime.

5. Briefly explain why in the restorative justice process, victims are given the opportunity for input and healing by gaining a better understanding of what happened to them?

Crime, which is viewed as a violation of one person by another, produces a wide range of emotions - anger bitterness, fear, confusion, etc... A victim's emotions resulting from crime are a major concern in the restorative justice process.

Restorative justice is an alternative approach to the traditional criminal justice system that emphasizes the importance of repairing harm caused by crime and promoting healing for all parties involved, including the victim. This essay will discuss how victims are given the opportunity for input and healing in the restorative justice process by gaining a better understanding of what happened to them.

Victim Input in Restorative Justice:

In the traditional criminal justice system, victims often feel left out of the process and not heard. Restorative justice recognizes that victims play a critical role in the process of repairing harm caused by crime and promotes their active participation. In the restorative justice process, victims are given a voice and an opportunity to share their experiences and express how the crime has affected them.

Victims are encouraged to participate in the process and provide input on how to address the harm caused by the crime. They may be asked to provide a victim impact statement, which is a written or oral statement that describes how the crime has affected them physically, emotionally, and financially. The impact statement is then shared with the offender and the community, allowing them to understand the full impact of the crime.

Victims may also participate in a face-to-face meeting with the offender, known as a restorative conference or circle. In this meeting, the victim has the opportunity to express how the crime has affected them directly to the offender. The meeting is facilitated by a trained restorative justice practitioner and includes both the victim and offender, as well as any other affected parties and community members. The goal is to promote healing for all parties involved and come up with a plan to repair the harm caused by the crime.

Healing Through Understanding:

In the restorative justice process, victims are given the opportunity to gain a better understanding of what happened to them. They may learn about the offender's motivations for committing the crime, as well as any underlying issues that contributed to their behavior. This understanding can be an important part of the healing process for the victim.

Victims may also learn about the criminal justice system and how it works, including the roles of the police, prosecutors, and judges. This can be important for victims who may feel frustrated or powerless by the system. Restorative justice provides an opportunity for victims to have a more active role in the process and feel that their voices are being heard.

In addition to gaining a better understanding of what happened, victims may also receive support and resources to help them cope with the trauma of the crime. This may include counseling, financial assistance, or referrals to other support services. By addressing the needs of the victim, restorative justice promotes healing and can help to prevent further victimization.

Conclusion:

Restorative justice emphasizes the importance of repairing harm caused by crime and promoting healing for all parties involved, including the victim. Victims are given the opportunity to provide input and participate in the process, including sharing their experiences and expressing how the crime has affected them. They are also given the opportunity to gain a better understanding of what happened and receive support and resources to help them cope with the trauma of the crime. By promoting healing and addressing the needs of the victim, restorative justice can help to prevent further victimization and promote a sense of community and accountability.

6. Briefly explain why understanding brings closure and enables the victims to move on with their lives?

A good formula for closure is understanding + venting + input = closure. It is imperative that the victim has a part in the justice process.

Victims of crime often experience feelings of anger, fear, and helplessness. These emotions can linger long after the crime has occurred and can have a significant impact on the victim's ability to move on with their life. In order to achieve closure, it is important for victims to gain a sense of understanding about the crime and its impact on their life. This essay will discuss how understanding brings closure and enables victims to move on with their lives.

Understanding:

One of the most important aspects of achieving closure is gaining a sense of understanding about the crime and its impact on the victim's life. This understanding can come from a variety of sources, including the restorative justice process. Restorative justice emphasizes the importance of understanding the harm caused by the crime and promoting healing for all parties involved, including the victim.

By participating in the restorative justice process, victims have the opportunity to learn about the offender's motivations for committing the crime, as well as any underlying issues that contributed to their behavior. This understanding can help the victim to see the offender as a person and not just as a criminal. It can also help the victim to let go of any feelings of anger or resentment towards the offender.

Venting:

In addition to gaining a sense of understanding, victims also need the opportunity to vent their emotions and express how the crime has affected them. This venting can take place in a variety of settings, including therapy, support groups, or the restorative justice process.

By venting their emotions, victims are able to release pent-up feelings of anger, frustration, and sadness. This can be an important step in the healing process and can help the victim to feel a sense of relief and catharsis.

Input:

Finally, victims need to have a part in the justice process. This means that they should have the opportunity to provide input on how to address the harm caused by the crime and what steps should be taken to prevent further victimization. This input can be provided through a victim impact statement, participation in a restorative conference or circle, or through advocacy efforts.

By having a part in the justice process, victims are able to regain a sense of control over their lives. They are able to play an active role in the process of repairing harm caused by the crime and in preventing further victimization.

Conclusion:

Achieving closure after a crime can be a difficult and complex process. However, understanding, venting, and input are all important components of achieving closure and moving on with one's life. Through the restorative justice process, victims have the opportunity to gain a sense of understanding about the crime and its impact on their life, to vent their emotions and express how the crime has affected them, and to provide input on the justice process. By participating in this process, victims are able to heal and regain a sense of control over their lives, enabling them to move on from the crime and towards a brighter future.

7. Briefly explain why in restorative justice, offenders are taught the real human impact of their criminal behavior and how to make restitution to victims?

Making amends to victims may also include restitution for any financial loss caused by the offender.

Offenders are held accountable for their actions and are given the opportunity to make amends to the victim and the community.

Traditionally, the criminal justice system has focused on punishment as a means of holding offenders accountable for their actions. However, restorative justice takes a different approach. It seeks to promote accountability through a process of repairing harm and restoring relationships.

Through the restorative justice process, offenders are given the opportunity to understand the real human impact of their criminal behavior. They may meet with the victim and hear firsthand about the harm that was caused. This can be a powerful experience, as it allows the offender to see the victim as a real person with feelings and emotions, rather than just as a faceless entity.

In addition to understanding the impact of their actions, offenders are also taught how to make restitution to the victim. This may involve financial compensation or community service, depending on the nature of the offense and the needs of the victim. By making restitution, offenders are able to take concrete steps to repair the harm that was caused and to demonstrate their commitment to making things right.

Restorative justice also emphasizes the importance of reintegrating offenders back into the community. Rather than simply punishing offenders and sending them to prison, restorative justice seeks to help offenders become responsible members of society. This may involve providing education or job training, counseling, or other forms of support.

Thus, the goal of restorative justice is to promote healing and repair harm, rather than simply punishing offenders. By teaching offenders, the real human impact of their criminal behavior and providing opportunities for restitution, restorative justice offers a more meaningful and effective form of accountability than traditional punishment-based approaches.

8. Within the restorative justice paradigm, the community plays a very crucial role by putting victim and offenders in active and interpersonal problem-solving roles.:

Restorative justice is based on the idea that crime is not just a violation of the law, but also a violation of relationships and communities. Therefore, the community plays a crucial role in the restorative justice paradigm by providing a supportive environment for victims and offenders to engage in active and interpersonal problem-solving.

One of the main goals of restorative justice is to repair the harm caused by the crime and to restore relationships between the victim, offender, and community. This can only be achieved through the active participation of all parties involved. By involving the community in the restorative justice process, victims and offenders are able to see the impact of their actions on a larger scale and to understand their roles within the community.

Through the restorative justice process, victims and offenders are able to work together to identify the harm that was caused and to develop a plan for repairing that harm. The community plays a crucial role in this process by providing a safe and supportive environment for this work to take place. This may involve bringing in community members to act as mediators or facilitators, or by providing resources and support for the victim and offender.

By involving the community in the restorative justice process, victims and offenders are also able to see the impact of their actions on the wider community. This can be a powerful motivator for change, as it helps offenders to understand the importance of taking responsibility for their actions and making amends to those they have harmed.

Therefore, the community plays a crucial role in the restorative justice paradigm by providing a supportive environment for victims and offenders to engage in active and interpersonal problem-solving. By working together to repair harm and restore relationships, the community helps to promote healing and create a stronger, more cohesive society.

9. Name some of the community's specific roles in a restorative justice paradigm.:

"Crime control needs to be understood as a community endeavor. Most crimes are problems between a perpetrator and a victim within the same community. In other words, most crimes of aggression are committed between persons living in the same community. It is, therefore, a problem that has to be coped with by all the members involved and not by professionals who are in fact outsiders."

The community plays a vital role in the restorative justice paradigm. Some of the specific roles of the community in this approach include:

a) Supporting crime victims: The community can provide support and resources to crime victims to help them heal from the harm caused by the crime. This may include counseling services, financial assistance, and emotional support.

b) Setting standards of conduct: The community can establish clear expectations for behavior and hold individuals accountable for their actions. This can help to prevent future crime by promoting a culture of respect and responsibility.

c) Providing opportunities for the offender to make amends: The community can provide opportunities for offenders to take responsibility for their actions and make amends to the victim and community. This may involve community service, restitution, or other forms of restorative justice.

d) Establishing community harmony: By promoting a sense of community and belonging, the community can help to reduce crime and create a more harmonious and peaceful society. This can be achieved through community-building activities, restorative justice programs, and other initiatives that bring people together.

Overall, the community plays a crucial role in the restorative justice paradigm by providing support and resources to victims, holding individuals accountable for their actions, providing opportunities for offenders to make amends, and promoting community harmony. By working together to promote healing and repair harm, the community helps to create a safer, more just, and more cohesive society.

10. Explain how will our elected officials serve the communities that elect them, by providing assistance, information, and funds for community programs?

Elected officials have an important role to play in serving the communities that elect them. One way they can do this is by providing assistance, information, and funds for community programs.

Elected officials have the ability to advocate for and allocate resources to support community programs that address issues such as crime prevention, education, job training, and social services. They can work with community leaders and organizations to identify needs and priorities, and to develop strategies for addressing them.

In addition, elected officials can serve as a liaison between the community and government agencies, helping to facilitate communication and access to services. They can also provide information and education to community members about government programs and policies, and advocate for their constituents' interests at all levels of government.

Through their role as elected officials, they have the ability to influence policy decisions that impact the well-being of their communities. They can work to promote policies that support community safety, economic development, and social justice.

Ultimately, elected officials have a responsibility to serve the communities that they represent. By providing assistance, information, and funds for community programs, they can help to build stronger and more resilient communities that are better equipped to address the challenges they face.

It should be noted that our elected officials serve the "loudest voice" in the community, therefore, we must band together when we seek assistance, information, and funds for community programs.

11. Briefly explain, how should the Community programs, and the efforts of organizing them, brings about familiarity, bonding, and trust within the community?

Over the past few years, the media has highlighted stories regarding unfortunate incidents between communities and law enforcement. When this is all the media chooses to focus on, it can paint a falsely negative and many times unfair picture of law enforcement, leading to a misplaced loss of trust by the public. While rebuilding that trust can be hard, it's not impossible, and community programs across the nation have taken measures to improve their relationships between law enforcement and the communities in which they serve.

Community programs are essential for building familiarity, bonding, and trust within a community. These programs bring together individuals who may not have had the opportunity to interact with each other before, creating opportunities for shared experiences, learning, and growth.

When community members come together to work on a shared goal, such as organizing a neighborhood watch program or a community garden, they are able to form connections based on common interests and values. This shared purpose creates a sense of camaraderie and trust among participants, who are more likely to support each other and work collaboratively in the future.

Community programs also provide opportunities for individuals to learn from each other and to develop new skills. For example, a neighborhood clean-up day may involve participants learning about recycling or waste reduction, while a community art project may involve learning new artistic techniques. As individuals learn and grow together, they become more invested in the success of the community and more willing to contribute to its improvement.

Another important benefit of community programs is that they help to build social capital, which refers to the networks, norms, and trust that exist within a community. By participating in community programs, individuals are able to build relationships and establish social connections with others in their community. These connections can lead to increased opportunities for civic engagement, as well as greater social and economic mobility.

Moreover, community programs provide a platform for community members to voice their opinions and concerns, and to participate in decision-making processes that impact their lives. This sense of empowerment and ownership over community issues leads to greater investment in the community and a stronger sense of belonging.

In addition, community programs can also help to promote cultural awareness and understanding. Programs that celebrate different cultural traditions or provide opportunities for cultural exchange can help to break down barriers and promote mutual respect and appreciation.

Hence, community programs play a critical role in building familiarity, bonding, and trust within a community. They provide opportunities for shared experiences, learning, and growth, while also building social capital and promoting civic engagement. By bringing community members together and creating a sense of purpose and investment in the community, these programs contribute to the overall health and well-being of the community.

12. Should the responsibility for managing crime conditions be assumed by the community?

While the community certainly has a role to play in managing crime conditions, it is not solely responsible for doing so. Crime management is a shared responsibility that involves a range of actors, including law enforcement agencies, local government, community organizations, and individual citizens.

Law enforcement agencies are responsible for enforcing the law and maintaining public safety. They play a critical role in preventing and responding to criminal activity, and in holding offenders accountable for their actions. In addition, local government has a responsibility to provide resources and support for crime prevention and intervention programs, as well as to develop and implement policies that promote public safety.

Community organizations and individual citizens also have a role to play in managing crime conditions. Community-based organizations can provide services and programs that address the root causes of crime, such as poverty, lack of education, and substance abuse. They can also help to build social connections and support networks that promote community safety and well-being.

Individual citizens can contribute to crime management by being vigilant and reporting suspicious activity to law enforcement. They can also take steps to prevent crime, such as securing their homes and vehicles, and by being proactive in their communities, such as organizing neighborhood watch programs or participating in community cleanup efforts.

Ultimately, crime management is a collaborative effort that requires the involvement of all members of the community. By working together, and by assuming responsibility for their individual roles in promoting public safety and well-being, community members can contribute to a safer and more secure environment for all.

13. Briefly explain, why the effects of crime on the community are evidenced by feelings of anger, anxiety, and fear?

Crime has a profound impact on the community, and the effects can be felt long after the crime has been committed. One of the most significant effects of crime on the community is the emotional toll it takes on individuals. Crime can create feelings of anger, anxiety, and fear among community members, which can have a range of negative consequences.

Anger is a common emotional response to crime, particularly when the crime is seen as a violation of community norms and values. Community members may feel angry that someone would commit a crime in their neighborhood or against someone they know. This anger can create a sense of frustration and helplessness, as community members struggle to come to terms with what has happened.

Anxiety is another common emotional response to crime. Community members may feel anxious about their own safety, particularly if the crime was violent or if they believe that they or their loved ones could be targeted. This anxiety can create a sense of hyper-vigilance, where community members are constantly on guard and may avoid certain areas or activities out of fear.

Fear is perhaps the most common emotional response to crime. When a crime is committed, community members may feel a sense of vulnerability and may worry that they or their loved ones could be the next victim. This fear can be particularly intense in communities that have experienced high levels of crime or have a reputation for being dangerous. Fear can create a sense of isolation, as community members may be hesitant to engage with their neighbors or participate in community activities out of concern for their safety.

The emotional effects of crime on the community can have a range of negative consequences, including reduced quality of life, decreased social cohesion, and increased stress and anxiety. These effects can be particularly pronounced in marginalized communities, where the impact of crime can be compounded by other social and economic challenges.

In order to address the emotional effects of crime on the community, it is important to provide support and resources for those who have been impacted. This may include counseling services for victims of crime and their families, as well as community-based programs and initiatives that promote safety and well-being. By working together to address the emotional toll of crime, communities can begin to heal and move forward.

Note: The wide range of emotions resulting from a violation of one's rights may include feelings of hatred, prejudice, depression, or even the need for revenge.

14. How have the negative feelings resulting from crime altered community behavior?

    a) Avoiding social activities

    b) Purchasing alarm systems

    c) Not leaving the house at night

    d) Watching children more closely

    e) Purchasing firearms

Have you ever driven through a neighborhood that has been violated by crime? You will notice tall fences, aggressive guard dogs, burglar bars on windows, and floodlights everywhere. Even the homeowners appear aggressive and unfriendly.

15. Is it true that the effect of crime has been illustrated as a tornado funnel having a type of "whirlwind effect."?

Yes, the effect of crime on a community has been compared to a tornado funnel with a whirlwind effect. Just as a tornado funnel can cause damage and destruction as it moves through a community, crime can have a similar impact, leaving a trail of physical and emotional damage in its wake.

At the center of the tornado funnel, there is a point of maximum destruction, where the most damage occurs. In the case of crime, this point of maximum destruction is typically the victim and their immediate family members. The victim may suffer physical injuries, financial losses, and emotional trauma as a result of the crime. Family members may also be impacted, as they provide support and care for the victim.

As the tornado funnel moves outward, the impact of the damage becomes more diffuse. In the case of crime, this means that the impact of the crime is felt by a wider circle of individuals and institutions. For example, neighbors and friends of the victim may feel a sense of fear and anxiety in the aftermath of a crime, as they worry about their own safety and the safety of their loved ones. Businesses in the area may also be impacted, as customers stay away from the area or are hesitant to spend money due to safety concerns.

The "whirlwind effect" of crime can also impact institutions such as schools, churches, and community organizations. These institutions may see a decline in attendance or participation following a crime, as community members are hesitant to engage in activities that take them out of their homes and into public spaces.

Overall, the impact of crime on a community can be far-reaching and long-lasting. It can create a sense of fear and anxiety, disrupt social and economic activity, and undermine trust and social cohesion. In order to address the impact of crime on a community, it is important to work together to provide support and resources for victims, strengthen community institutions, and promote safety and well-being for all members of the community.

16. Briefly describe the broad range of havoc created by a tornado.:

a) A tornado creates a broad range of havoc beginning with the spot where it touches the ground, causing the most damage.

b) Beyond the point of ground contact, the winds associated with the tornado have a far-reaching affect.

c) The tornado even produces fear and anxiety in areas away from its path.

A tornado creates a broad range of havoc with a destructive path that can be several miles long and hundreds of yards wide. At the point where the tornado touches the ground, it causes the most damage, with the potential to destroy buildings and homes, uproot trees, and overturn vehicles.

Beyond the point of ground contact, the winds associated with the tornado can have a far-reaching effect, causing damage to structures and landscapes even if they are not directly in the path of the tornado. The high winds can pick up debris and hurl it through the air, causing additional damage to buildings and homes. The tornado can also disrupt power lines and other infrastructure, leading to widespread power outages and communication disruptions.

In addition to the physical damage caused by the tornado, it can also have psychological effects on individuals and communities. The fear and anxiety created by the tornado can be felt not only in the immediate path of the storm but also in areas far away. People may feel vulnerable and uncertain in the aftermath of a tornado, and may require support and resources to cope with the trauma and disruption caused by the storm.

Hence, a tornado can create a broad range of havoc, with physical, economic, and psychological impacts that can be felt by individuals and communities alike.

17. The justice system has focused solely on the point of contact, the offender and to a degree the victim.

The justice system has traditionally focused primarily on the point of contact between the offender and the victim because its primary goal has been to punish offenders for their criminal behavior and ensure public safety. This approach is known as retributive justice, and it is based on the idea that individuals who commit crimes must be held accountable for their actions through punishment.

Under this approach, the offender is seen as the primary actor in the crime, and the victim's role is limited to that of a passive recipient of harm. The justice system's primary concern is to determine the guilt or innocence of the accused and to impose an appropriate punishment if the individual is found guilty. In this model, the focus is on establishing the facts of the case, determining who is responsible for the crime, and punishing the offender accordingly.

However, over time, there has been growing recognition that the traditional approach to justice may be incomplete, and that there are limitations to a focus on punishment alone. This has led to the development of alternative approaches to justice, such as restorative justice.

Restorative justice places greater emphasis on the needs of the victim, the offender, and the community as a whole. It seeks to address the harm caused by the crime by repairing relationships, promoting healing, and preventing future offenses. Restorative justice recognizes that crime is not just a violation of the law, but also a violation of people and relationships.

In contrast to retributive justice, which focuses on punishment, restorative justice seeks to provide opportunities for offenders to make amends and take responsibility for their actions. It also places greater emphasis on the role of the community in responding to crime, recognizing that community members can play an active role in preventing crime and promoting safety.

Wherefore, the justice system has historically focused on the point of contact between the offender and the victim because of its traditional emphasis on punishment and public safety. However, there is growing recognition that this approach may be incomplete, and that a more restorative approach that places greater emphasis on repairing relationships and promoting healing may be more effective in addressing the harm caused by crime.

18. Describe why the community has been widely ignored as both a key victim and a source of resolution?

The community has been widely ignored as both a key victim and a source of resolution for several reasons.

Firstly, the criminal justice system has traditionally viewed crime as a problem between an individual offender and victim, with little consideration given to the broader community impact of crime. This narrow focus has led to a neglect of the community's role in addressing crime, as the justice system has primarily focused on punishing offenders rather than preventing crime and addressing its underlying causes.

Secondly, the criminal justice system has often failed to engage with communities in a meaningful way, which has undermined trust and reduced the community's willingness to participate in justice processes. This has led to a perception that the criminal justice system is not interested in or responsive to community concerns, further reinforcing the marginalization of communities in the justice system.

Thirdly, there has been a lack of resources and support for community-based solutions to crime. In many cases, communities have been left to deal with the impact of crime on their own, with little support from government agencies or other organizations. This has limited the ability of communities to develop effective responses to crime and has contributed to a sense of powerlessness and disempowerment.

Finally, there has been a tendency to view crime as an individual problem rather than a social problem. This has led to a focus on punishing individual offenders rather than addressing the underlying social and economic factors that contribute to crime. By ignoring the broader community impact of crime and failing to address its root causes, the criminal justice system has perpetuated the marginalization of communities and failed to effectively address the harm caused by crime.

Overall, the community has been widely ignored as both a key victim and a source of resolution due to a range of factors, including the narrow focus of the criminal justice system, a lack of engagement with communities, a lack of resources and support for community-based solutions, and a failure to address the root causes of crime. To effectively address crime and its impact on communities, it is essential to adopt a more holistic and inclusive approach that recognizes the central role of communities in preventing crime and promoting safety.

19. What would restorative justice bring to the problem of crime within the community?

Restorative justice has the potential to bring resolution, healing, and reconciliation to the problem of crime within the community.

Firstly, restorative justice provides a framework for resolving conflicts in a way that is more responsive to the needs and concerns of victims and communities. Unlike traditional criminal justice processes that focus primarily on punishing offenders, restorative justice seeks to repair the harm caused by crime and restore relationships between offenders, victims, and the community. This can lead to a greater sense of resolution for victims, who may feel that their voices have been heard and that their needs have been taken into account.

Secondly, restorative justice can promote healing by providing victims with the opportunity to share their experiences and emotions in a safe and supportive environment. This can help victims to process their trauma and move forward with their lives, rather than feeling stuck in a state of fear, anger, or resentment. Through restorative justice, victims can also receive acknowledgement and validation for their experiences, which can be a powerful form of healing.

Thirdly, restorative justice can promote reconciliation by fostering a sense of community and shared responsibility for preventing and responding to crime. By engaging with offenders and encouraging them to take responsibility for their actions, restorative justice can help to create a sense of accountability and a commitment to making amends. This can lead to a greater sense of trust and cooperation within the community, which can help to prevent future crime and promote a greater sense of social cohesion.

Overall, restorative justice has the potential to bring resolution, healing, and reconciliation to the problem of crime within the community. By providing a more responsive and inclusive framework for addressing crime, restorative justice can help to repair the harm caused by crime and restore relationships between victims, offenders, and the community. This can lead to a greater sense of safety, trust, and social cohesion, which can help to prevent future crime and promote the well-being of the community as a whole.

Typical outcomes of restorative justice are:

- *Victim / offender conferencing and mediation*
- *Victim assistance*
- *Restitution*
- *Service by offenders to victims*
- *Community service by offenders*
- *Assistance to offenders*

CHAPTER V
PROMISING PRACTICES OF RESTORATIVE JUSTICE

1. Explain why the Community-based and restorative-minded practices seek to restore harmony at the community level, by directly involving the public in the justice process?

Community-based and restorative-minded practices aim to shift the focus of justice from punishment and retribution to repairing harm and restoring relationships. These approaches recognize that crimes and other harmful actions not only affect individuals, but also the wider community, and that addressing harm requires involvement from all stakeholders. By involving the public in the justice process, community-based and restorative-minded practices seek to restore harmony and prevent further harm.

Restorative justice is a prime example of a community-based and restorative-minded approach to justice. Restorative justice involves bringing together the victim, the offender, and members of the community affected by the crime to discuss the harm caused and how to make amends. The goal of restorative justice is to repair harm and restore relationships, rather than punish the offender. This approach is rooted in indigenous justice practices that emphasize the importance of community involvement in the resolution of conflicts.

Restorative justice has been shown to be effective in reducing recidivism rates and increasing victim satisfaction with the justice system. It also provides a more inclusive and transparent approach to justice, as it involves all stakeholders in the process. Restorative justice allows victims to have a voice and to have a say in how the harm caused by the crime is addressed. It also allows offenders to take responsibility for their actions and make amends for the harm caused.

Another community-based and restorative-minded approach to justice is community justice. Community justice involves the community in the decision-making process of the justice system. Community justice recognizes that crime and harm are not just individual issues, but also community issues that require community solutions. By involving the community in the decision-making process, community justice seeks to address the root causes of crime and prevent further harm.

Community justice programs can take many forms, such as community courts, community policing, and community mediation. Community courts involve community members in the sentencing and rehabilitation of offenders. Community policing involves police officers working closely with community members to address crime and disorder in a collaborative manner. Community mediation involves community members acting as mediators to resolve conflicts in a peaceful manner.

Community justice has been shown to be effective in reducing crime and increasing community engagement with the justice system. By involving the community in the decision-making process, community justice increases trust in the justice system and promotes a sense of ownership over community safety.

In conclusion, community-based and restorative-minded practices seek to restore harmony at the community level by involving the public in the justice process. These approaches recognize that crimes and other harmful actions have wider impacts on the community and require community solutions. By involving the public in the justice process, community-based and restorative-minded practices seek to repair harm and restore relationships, rather than simply punish offenders. Restorative justice and community justice are two examples of effective community-based and restorative-minded approaches to justice that have been shown to reduce crime, increase victim satisfaction, and promote community engagement with the justice system.

2. The goal of the restorative justice process is to bring the justice system to the community, rather than stripping them of this responsibility. Discuss:

Restorative justice is based on the principles of repairing harm and restoring relationships, and it seeks to involve all stakeholders in the justice process. This approach recognizes that crime and harm are not just individual issues, but also community issues that require community solutions. Therefore, the goal of the restorative justice process is to bring the justice system to the community, rather than stripping them of this responsibility.

In traditional criminal justice systems, the focus is often on punishment and retribution, with little regard for the needs and perspectives of victims and the community. This approach can be alienating for those who have been directly affected by the crime, as well as for the wider community who may feel disconnected from the justice process. By contrast, restorative justice seeks to involve all stakeholders in the process, including the victim, the offender, and the community. This approach allows for a more inclusive and transparent justice process that is better able to address the needs of all involved.

Restorative justice also recognizes that communities have a stake in the justice process and can play an important role in addressing harm and preventing further harm. Community members often have a unique understanding of the social and cultural context in which the harm occurred and can provide valuable insights into the needs and concerns of all involved. By involving the community in the restorative justice process, the justice system is able to draw on this knowledge and expertise to develop solutions that are more tailored to the specific needs of the community.

Moreover, by bringing the justice system to the community, restorative justice helps to promote a sense of ownership and accountability among community members. When community members are involved in the justice process, they are more likely to feel invested in the outcomes and to take an active role in preventing future harm. This can help to create a more cohesive and resilient community that is better able to address the underlying causes of crime and harm.

In conclusion, the goal of the restorative justice process is to bring the justice system to the community, rather than stripping them of this responsibility. By involving all stakeholders, including the victim, the offender, and the community, restorative justice seeks to repair harm and restore relationships in a way that is more inclusive, transparent, and effective. By promoting community involvement and accountability, restorative justice helps to create a more cohesive and resilient community that is better able to address the root causes of crime and harm.

3. List some of the features of a community-based and restorative approach.:

A community-based and restorative approach to justice involves several key features, including:

a) Providing full information to those affected by crime, including victims, offenders, and the wider community.

b) Giving full access to decision-making processes, allowing all stakeholders to participate in the development of solutions.

c) Using processes that are comfortable and understandable to those involved, such as dialogue, mediation, or circles.

d) Being consensual in nature, when necessary, with all parties agreeing to the terms of the restorative process.

e) Bringing together the community and the justice system to work collaboratively in addressing harm and preventing further harm.

f) Using the justice system to bring healing to the community, rather than just punishing offenders.

g) Being empowering in nature, allowing all stakeholders to have a voice and play an active role in the justice process.

Thus, a community-based and restorative approach prioritizes repairing harm, restoring relationships, and promoting community involvement and empowerment, rather than just punishing offenders.

4. The promising practices of restorative justice serve as bridges to connect the system and community objectives in such a way that they blend into one indistinguishable outcome, a better justice system.

Restorative justice is an approach to justice that focuses on repairing harm caused by crime or conflict and restoring relationships between individuals and the community. In contrast to the traditional punitive justice system, restorative justice seeks to involve all parties affected by a crime or conflict in a collaborative process to address the harm caused and find ways to prevent it from happening again.

The promising practices of restorative justice serve as bridges to connect the system and community objectives by creating a space for dialogue and collaboration between the justice system and the community. Restorative justice recognizes that the community is an important stakeholder in the justice system, and their involvement can lead to more effective and sustainable outcomes.

One of the key ways in which restorative justice practices connect the system and community objectives is by empowering community members to participate in the justice process. Restorative justice programs often involve community members as mediators, facilitators, and members of decision-making panels. This involvement not only gives community members a voice in the justice system but also helps to build trust and understanding between the justice system and the community.

Another way in which restorative justice practices serve as bridges is by addressing the root causes of crime and conflict. Restorative justice recognizes that crime and conflict are often the result of underlying issues such as poverty, trauma, and social inequality. By addressing these underlying issues, restorative justice can help to prevent crime and conflict from happening in the first place.

Restorative justice practices also help to promote accountability and responsibility among offenders. By involving offenders in the process of repairing harm caused by their actions, restorative justice provides them with a sense of ownership and responsibility for their behavior. This can help to prevent future offending and promote positive behavior change.

In summary, the promising practices of restorative justice serve as bridges to connect the system and community objectives by creating a collaborative process that involves all parties affected by a crime or conflict. By empowering community members, addressing the root causes of crime and conflict, and promoting accountability and responsibility among offenders, restorative justice can help to create a better justice system that is more effective, sustainable, and responsive to the needs of the community.

5. Name some of the many promising practices that are being developed as communities embrace the principles of restorative justice.:

a) Sentencing Circles

One of the best-known uses of the sentencing circle is the Hollow Water First Nations Community Holistic Healing Circle. Community members used circles to deal with the high level of alcoholism in Hollow Water. In the safety of those circles, many began to disclose experiences with sexual abuse. This led to development of healing circles as a way of dealing with the harm created by the offender, of healing the victim and of restoring the community.

b) Victim Impact Statements

Victim impact statements are written or oral information from crime victims, in their own words, about how a crime has affected them. All 50 states allow victim impact statements at some phase of the sentencing process. Most states permit them at parole hearings, and victim impact information is generally included in the pre-sentencing report presented to the judge.

Yes, those are all excellent examples of promising practices that are being developed as communities embrace the principles of restorative justice.

c) Community Restorative Boards: This is a process where trained community members come together to resolve conflicts and address harm caused by crime or conflict. The board helps to facilitate communication and decision-making between all parties involved.

d) Community Service: This is a process where individuals who have committed a crime are required to perform community service as a way of repairing harm caused by their actions. This can help to promote positive behavior change and reduce the likelihood of future offending.

e) Restitution: This is a process where individuals who have committed a crime are required to pay restitution to the victim as a way of repairing the harm caused by their actions. This can help to promote accountability and responsibility among offenders.

f) Victim Offender Mediation: This is a process where the victim and the offender meet face-to-face to discuss the harm caused by the offense and work together to find a way to repair the harm. This process can lead to greater understanding and empathy between the victim and offender and can promote healing.

g) Family Group Conferencing: This is a process where a group of family members and friends come together to discuss an issue or problem. The aim is to find a solution that works for everyone involved and to promote healing and understanding.

h) Victim Impact Panels: This is a process where victims of crime share their experiences with offenders. The aim is to promote understanding and empathy among offenders and to promote positive behavior change.

i) Victim Impact Class: This is a process where offenders attend a class or program designed to help them understand the impact of their actions on victims. The aim is to promote empathy and accountability among offenders and to promote positive behavior change.

Furthermore, there are many promising practices that have been developed as communities embrace the principles of restorative justice. Here are some examples:

1. Restorative Circles: This is a process where individuals gather in a circle to discuss a particular issue or problem. The process is guided by a facilitator and involves everyone taking turns to speak and listen. The aim is to build relationships, resolve conflicts, and promote healing.

2. Victim-Offender Mediation: This is a process where the victim and the offender meet face-to-face to discuss the harm caused by the offense and work together to find a way to repair the harm. This process can lead to greater understanding and empathy between the victim and offender and can promote healing.

3. Family Group Conferencing: This is a process where a group of family members and friends come together to discuss an issue or problem. The aim is to find a solution that works for everyone involved and to promote healing and understanding.
4. Community Reparations: This is a process where the community comes together to address harm caused by a particular issue or problem. The community works together to find ways to repair the harm, prevent future harm, and promote healing.
5. Restorative Justice in Schools: This is a process where restorative justice practices are used to address disciplinary issues in schools. This approach focuses on repairing harm caused by student behavior, promoting positive behavior change, and building a positive school community.

These are just a few examples of the many promising practices that have been developed as communities embrace the principles of restorative justice. Each practice is designed to promote healing, understanding, and accountability while addressing harm caused by crime or conflict.

6. What is a sentencing circle?

"A sentencing circle is a community-directed process, conducted in partnership with the criminal justice system, to develop an agreement on an appropriate sentencing plan that addresses the concerns of all interested parties."

A sentencing circle is a restorative justice practice that involves bringing together the victim, the offender, their families, and other community members to collectively determine an appropriate sentencing plan. The process is conducted in partnership with the criminal justice system, typically with the involvement of a judge or other legal official, but is community-directed and focused on repairing harm and promoting healing rather than solely on punishment.

The goal of a sentencing circle is to provide a space for all interested parties to come together to discuss the harm that has been caused by the crime, the needs of the victim, the responsibility of the offender, and the needs of the community. Through dialogue and discussion, the group works to develop an agreement on an appropriate sentencing plan that addresses the concerns of all parties involved.

The process typically involves several stages. First, the group establishes guidelines for the discussion, including a commitment to listening to one another with respect and empathy. Then, the victim and the offender are given the opportunity to share their perspectives on the crime, including how it has impacted them and their families. This is followed by a discussion among all participants about the harm that has been caused and the ways in which the offender can make amends.

The group then works together to develop a sentencing plan that addresses the needs of the victim, the responsibility of the offender, and the needs of the community. This can include a range of restorative measures, such as community service, restitution, counseling, and education. The plan is typically presented to a judge or other legal official, who has the final say in the sentencing, but the judge takes into account the recommendations of the group.

The benefits of sentencing circles are numerous. They provide an opportunity for the victim to have a say in the sentencing process and to receive restitution or other forms of amends from the offender. They also promote accountability and responsibility among offenders, and they can help to reduce recidivism rates by addressing the root causes of criminal behavior. Additionally, they can help to restore trust and build relationships within the community, as the group works together to develop a plan that addresses the needs of all parties involved.

In summary, a sentencing circle is a community-directed process that involves bringing together the victim, the offender, their families, and other community members to develop an appropriate sentencing plan that addresses the concerns of all interested parties. The process is conducted in partnership with the criminal justice system but is focused on repairing harm and promoting healing rather than solely on punishment. The benefits of this approach include increased victim participation, reduced recidivism rates, and stronger community relationships.

It should be noted that this is NOT a "lynch mob" but rather individuals who are truly concerned about developing the appropriate steps to promote the healing of all affected parties and to prevent future crimes.

7. Sentencing circles are structured to involve:

    a) The victim,

    b) Offender,

    c) Police,

d) Prosecutor,

e) Defense counsel,

f) Judge

g) and all interested community members.

Sentencing circles are a community-based restorative justice practice that is structured to involve the victim, offender, their families, and other interested community members in a process to develop an appropriate sentencing plan. The process is typically facilitated by a trained facilitator and conducted in partnership with the criminal justice system. In addition to the victim and offender, other stakeholders who may be involved in the process include police, prosecutors, defense counsel, judges, and community leaders. The goal of the process is to promote healing, accountability, and repair the harm caused by the crime, while also ensuring that the needs and concerns of all parties involved are addressed.

No one in the sentencing circle is a spectator. All are active participants in this justice process, with equal opportunity to offer input.

8. A successful sentencing circle encourages participants to:
    a) to resolve conflicts,
    b) share responsibility for outcomes,
    c) develop constructive relationships,
    d) enhance respect and understanding,
    e) and discover innovative solutions.

A successful sentencing circle encourages participants to resolve conflicts, share responsibility for outcomes, develop constructive relationships, enhance respect and understanding, and discover innovative solutions. By involving all parties in the process, sentencing circles provide an opportunity for the offender to take responsibility for their actions, make amends to the victim and community, and receive support to address underlying issues that may have contributed to their behavior. Similarly, victims have the opportunity to share their experiences and have their needs and concerns addressed. Through this process, participants can build understanding, empathy, and trust, leading to positive relationships and the potential for long-term healing and transformation. By engaging in a collaborative and community-directed process, participants can also develop innovative and effective solutions that may not have been possible through traditional justice processes.

9. Typically, a sentencing circle involves a multi-step procedure which includes:

Typically, a sentencing circle involves a multi-step procedure that includes:

a) The participation of the offender in the circle process: The offender is given the opportunity to take responsibility for their actions and address the harm they caused. They are also encouraged to identify and address any underlying issues that may have contributed to their behavior.

b) A healing circle for the victim: The victim is given the opportunity to share their experiences and have their needs and concerns addressed. This can help them to heal and move forward.

c) A healing circle for the offender: The offender is given the opportunity to receive support and guidance to address any underlying issues that may have contributed to their behavior.

d) A sentencing circle to develop an agreement on the elements of a sentencing plan: The circle process is used to develop an appropriate sentencing plan that addresses the needs and concerns of all parties involved. This can include elements such as restitution, community service, or other forms of accountability.

e) Follow-up circles to monitor the offender: The circle process may include follow-up circles to monitor the offender's progress and ensure that they are fulfilling the terms of their sentencing plan. This can help to ensure that the offender continues to take responsibility for their actions and work to repair the harm caused.

10. A community justice committee provides direction and leadership that decides which cases to accept, and establishes circles and support groups for the victim and offender.

A community justice committee (CJC) is a group of community members who come together to support and address the needs of individuals impacted by the criminal justice system. The committee provides direction and leadership by deciding which cases to accept, establishing circles and support groups for the victim and offender, and coordinating with the justice system. In this response, I will explain why a community justice committee is important and how it can benefit both the justice system and the community it serves.

Firstly, a community justice committee is important because it provides an opportunity for community members to take an active role in the justice system. By serving on a committee, community members can provide their perspectives and insights into the needs of the community and individuals impacted by the justice system. This can help to ensure that justice is delivered in a way that is responsive to the needs of the community, rather than being imposed from outside.

Additionally, a community justice committee can help to build trust and relationships between the justice system and the community it serves. By involving community members in the justice process, the committee can help to increase transparency and accountability, and demonstrate that the justice system is responsive to the needs of the community. This can help to reduce tension and conflict between the justice system and the community, and foster greater cooperation and understanding.

Furthermore, a community justice committee can help to address underlying issues that may contribute to criminal behavior. By establishing circles and support groups for the victim and offender, the committee can help to promote healing, accountability, and rehabilitation. This can help to address the root causes of criminal behavior, rather than simply punishing offenders. By providing support and guidance to offenders, the committee can help them to address the underlying issues that may have contributed to their behavior, and support them in making positive changes in their lives.

Moreover, a community justice committee can help to reduce the burden on the justice system. By diverting cases away from the traditional justice system, the committee can help to reduce the workload of courts and other justice system actors. This can free up resources to focus on more serious cases, and allow the justice system to operate more efficiently.

In conclusion, a community justice committee is an important tool for promoting justice and healing in the community. By providing direction and leadership, establishing circles and support groups, and working closely with the justice system, the committee can help to address the needs of the community, build trust and relationships between the justice system and the community, and promote healing and rehabilitation for those impacted by the justice system. As such, a community justice committee is an important component of a restorative justice approach, which seeks to build safer, healthier communities by addressing the root causes of criminal behavior and promoting healing and reconciliation.

11. Some of the key factors in determining whether a case is appropriate for the sentencing circle are:

Sentencing circles are typically reserved for cases where the offender is willing to take responsibility for their actions and work towards repairing the harm done to the victim and the community. Some of the key factors that are considered when determining whether a case is appropriate for a sentencing circle include:

1. The nature of the offense: Sentencing circles are typically used for non-violent offenses, such as property crimes or drug offenses, and may not be appropriate for crimes involving violence or sexual assault.

2. The willingness of the offender to take responsibility: The offender must be willing to admit their wrongdoing and take responsibility for their actions. If the offender denies the offense or shows no remorse, a sentencing circle may not be appropriate.

3. The victim's willingness to participate: The victim must also be willing to participate in the process and engage in dialogue with the offender.

4. The level of community support: The community must be willing to participate in the process and support the restorative justice approach. This includes the involvement of community members in the circle and their commitment to monitor the offender's progress and support their rehabilitation.

5. The availability of resources: A successful sentencing circle requires a significant number of resources, including trained facilitators, support services for the victim and offender, and follow-up support for the offender. If these resources are not available, a sentencing circle may not be appropriate.

Thus, the success of a sentencing circle depends on the willingness of all parties involved to participate in the process and work towards a restorative outcome. The community justice committee plays a key role in determining whether a case is appropriate for a sentencing circle and providing the necessary support and resources to ensure its success.

12. Representatives of the justice system must participate in circles, to ensure fair treatment of both victims and offenders.

The participation of representatives from the justice system, including police officers, prosecutors, defense attorneys, and judges, is an important aspect of ensuring fair treatment of both victims and offenders in sentencing circles.

Firstly, the presence of justice system representatives can help ensure that the process is conducted in a fair and impartial manner. These representatives can help ensure that the offender's rights are protected and that the victim's needs and concerns are addressed. The involvement of the justice system also helps ensure that the outcome of the circle is in compliance with the law.

Secondly, the participation of justice system representatives can help build trust between the community and the justice system. Restorative justice processes such as sentencing circles seek to promote community involvement and engagement in the justice system. By involving representatives from the justice system in the circle, it can help bridge the gap between the justice system and the community, and promote a greater sense of trust and understanding.

Thirdly, the involvement of justice system representatives can help educate the community on the legal process and the role of the justice system. By participating in the circle, justice system representatives can help explain legal concepts, such as the purpose of sentencing, to community members who may not be familiar with the legal system. This can help promote greater understanding and acceptance of the legal system in the community.

However, it is important to ensure that the justice system representatives participating in the circle do so in a way that is supportive of the restorative justice approach. This means that they must be willing to embrace the principles of restorative justice, including the focus on repairing harm and the involvement of all parties in the process. If justice system representatives approach the circle with a punitive mindset, it can undermine the effectiveness of the restorative justice approach.

In conclusion, the participation of justice system representatives in sentencing circles is important to ensure fair treatment of both victims and offenders, build trust between the community and the justice system, and educate the community on the legal process. However, it is important to ensure that justice system representatives approach the circle with a restorative mindset and embrace the principles of restorative justice.

13. Some of the goals of the sentencing circle are to:
1. Encouraging dialogue: The circle process is designed to encourage open dialogue between the victim, offender, and

community members. The goal is to create a safe space where all parties can share their perspectives and concerns, and work together to find a resolution that is acceptable to everyone.

2. Developing a fair and just sentencing plan: The circle process is intended to create a sentencing plan that addresses the harm caused by the offense and takes into account the needs of the victim, the offender, and the community. The goal is to create a plan that is fair and just for all parties involved.

3. Promoting healing and restoration: Sentencing circles are designed to promote healing and restoration for all parties involved. The circle process can help the victim to feel heard and understood, and can help the offender to take responsibility for their actions and make amends. The goal is to help everyone involved to move forward in a positive way.

4. Reducing recidivism: By focusing on the underlying causes of the offense and addressing the harm caused, the circle process can help to reduce the likelihood of the offender reoffending in the future. The goal is to create a plan that promotes accountability and helps the offender to make positive changes in their life.

5. Building community relationships: Sentencing circles are designed to promote community involvement and engagement in the justice system. By involving community members in the circle process, it can help to build stronger relationships between the community and the justice system. The goal is to create a more collaborative and effective justice system that works for everyone.

In summary, the goals of a sentencing circle are to encourage dialogue, develop a fair and just sentencing plan, promote healing and restoration, reduce recidivism, and build community relationships.

14. Through a VIS, the victim offers a description of the crime, and how it affected his/her life and the lives of their loved ones.

A Victim Impact Statement (VIS) is a written or oral statement prepared by a victim of a crime, or their family members, that describes the impact the crime has had on their lives. It is an opportunity for victims to share their experiences with the court and provide information that may be considered during the sentencing process.

The VIS is an important tool in the criminal justice system because it provides a voice for victims who may otherwise feel unheard.

It allows them to express their feelings, thoughts, and concerns about the impact of the crime on their lives. The VIS also helps the court to understand the emotional and physical harm caused by the offense, which can be used to determine an appropriate sentence.

The VIS typically includes a description of the crime, the physical and emotional impact of the crime on the victim and their loved ones, and a statement about the victim's opinions and recommendations regarding the sentence. The victim may also describe any financial losses, such as medical expenses or lost income, that resulted from the crime.

The VIS can be given in either written or oral form. In some jurisdictions, victims may have the option to read their statement out loud in court, while in others, the statement may be read by a victim advocate or the prosecutor. Regardless of the form it takes, the VIS is a powerful tool that can have a significant impact on the sentencing process.

The VIS serves a number of important purposes in the criminal justice system. First, it helps to ensure that victims are heard and their experiences are taken into account during the sentencing process. This can provide victims with a sense of closure and validation, and can help them to feel more empowered in the aftermath of the crime.

Second, the VIS can help to humanize the victim in the eyes of the court and the defendant. It can help the defendant to understand the harm they have caused and the impact of their actions on others. This can be an important factor in promoting empathy and accountability, and can help to reduce the likelihood of recidivism.

Finally, the VIS can help to promote transparency and accountability in the criminal justice system. By providing victims with an opportunity to share their experiences with the court, it can help to build trust between victims and the justice system, and can promote greater public understanding of the impact of crime.

In summary, the Victim Impact Statement is an important tool in the criminal justice system. It provides victims with an opportunity to share their experiences with the court, helps to humanize victims in the eyes of the court and the defendant, promotes transparency and accountability in the criminal justice system, and can have a significant impact on the sentencing process. The VIS is an important step towards promoting healing and restoration for victims, and towards creating a more just and compassionate justice system.

15. The victim impact statement provides authorities with vital information during:

The victim impact statement (VIS) is a crucial document that provides important information to authorities during various stages of the criminal justice process.

During the pre-sentencing investigation phase, the VIS is used by the probation officer or other officials to prepare a pre-sentencing report for the judge. The VIS helps to inform the judge about the impact of the crime on the victim, including emotional, physical, and financial harm. The information in the VIS can influence the judge's decision on the appropriate sentence for the offender, taking into account the harm caused to the victim and the community.

During the sentencing phase, the VIS is often read aloud in court, allowing the victim to share their story directly with the judge and the offender. This can have a powerful impact on both the offender and the judge, as they hear firsthand the effects of the crime on the victim and their loved ones.

The VIS can also be used as part of pre-parole investigations, which are conducted before an offender's release from prison to determine if they are suitable for release and to establish conditions of parole. The VIS can inform the parole board about the ongoing impact of the crime on the victim and their need for protection and support. It can also inform the board about the offender's level of remorse and rehabilitation efforts, which can be taken into account when deciding whether to grant parole.

Finally, the VIS can be used in parole revocation hearings, which are held when an offender violates the conditions of their parole. The VIS can inform the parole board about the ongoing impact of the crime on the victim and their continued need for protection and support, as well as the offender's lack of compliance with the conditions of their release.

In all of these stages, the VIS plays an important role in ensuring that the voice of the victim is heard and taken into account. It provides a platform for victims to share their experiences and the impact of the crime on their lives, and helps to ensure that the criminal justice system considers the harm caused to victims and their ongoing needs for support and protection.

These methods are used to reveal and record information during sentencing investigations, sentencing, pre-parole investigations and parole revocations.

16. In what ways can a restorative practice, such as victim impact panels, be an assistance?

a) Help offenders understand the impact of their crimes on victims and communities.

b) Provide victims with a structured, positive outlet to share their personal experiences and to educate offenders, justice professionals, and others about the physical, emotional and financial consequences of crime.

c) Build partnership among victim service providers and justice agencies that can raise the individual and community awareness of the short and long-term impacts of crime.

Victim impact panels are restorative justice programs that provide a platform for victims of crimes to share their experiences and the impact the crimes have had on their lives. These panels are usually held for a group of offenders who have committed similar crimes, such as drunk driving or drug offenses, and are required to attend as part of their sentence or rehabilitation program. The panels typically consist of several victims or family members who speak to the offenders about how the crimes affected them personally, emotionally, and financially.

One way in which victim impact panels can be helpful is by allowing victims to express their feelings and experiences in a safe and supportive environment. Many victims of crimes, especially those who have suffered from violent crimes or sexual assault, often feel isolated and unable to discuss their experiences with others. Victim impact panels provide a forum for these individuals to express their emotions and share their stories with others who have experienced similar situations.

Another benefit of victim impact panels is that they can be a powerful tool for changing offender behavior. By hearing firsthand from victims about the impact of their crimes, offenders can gain a deeper understanding of the harm they have caused and the long-term consequences of their actions. This can help to promote empathy and accountability, which are essential components of restorative justice.

Victim impact panels can also help to promote healing and closure for victims and their families. By providing an opportunity to share their experiences and feelings with others, victims can begin to process their trauma and move forward in their recovery. In addition, the panels can help victims to feel empowered by giving them a voice in the criminal justice system and the opportunity to make a positive impact on others.

Finally, victim impact panels can be an effective way to educate offenders about the impact of their crimes on the broader community. By hearing from a variety of victims and family members, offenders can gain a broader perspective on the harm caused by their actions and the need to take responsibility for their behavior. This can help to promote community safety by reducing the likelihood of recidivism and promoting positive behavior change.

In conclusion, victim impact panels are an important restorative justice practice that can provide a range of benefits to victims, offenders, and the broader community. By providing a safe and supportive environment for victims to share their experiences, promoting empathy and accountability among offenders, and promoting healing and closure, victim impact panels can help to create a more just and compassionate society.

Victim Impact Panels (VIPs) were introduced by Mothers Against Drunk Driving (MADD) in 1982 and have since spread throughout the United States in an attempt to reduce drunk driving. The objective of a VIP is to expose DUI offenders to the pain and suffering caused by drunk driving without necessarily condemning the DUI offender.

17. What are some things that need to be done in order for a victim impact statement (VIS) to be an effective tool?

The purpose of a victim impact statement is to present the victim's perspective to the sentencing authority as part of the sentencing process.

a) Prosecutors need to inform victims of their right to submit a VIS.

For a victim impact statement (VIS) to be an effective tool, several things need to be done, including:
1. Proper notification: Victims should be informed about their right to make a VIS and the opportunity to present it at the appropriate stage of the criminal justice process. Notification should be provided in a timely manner, and victims should receive assistance in preparing their statements if needed.

2. Confidentiality and safety: Victims should be assured that their VIS will be treated with confidentiality and not disclosed to the public or the media. They should also be provided with adequate protection and support during the process, especially if they fear retaliation or intimidation.

3. Clarity and accuracy: The VIS should be written in a clear and concise manner, using simple language that is easy to understand. The victim should describe the impact of the crime on their life and the lives of their family members or loved ones in a factual and objective way, avoiding emotional or inflammatory language. The statement should be based on accurate and verifiable information, supported by evidence or documentation if possible.

4. Focus on impact: The VIS should focus on the harm caused by the crime rather than on the offender's character or motives. The victim should describe how the crime has affected their physical, emotional, and financial well-being, as well as their sense of security, trust, and dignity. They should also address the impact of the crime on their relationships, work, and community involvement.

5. Respectful and constructive tone: The VIS should be written in a respectful and constructive tone, acknowledging the offender's right to a fair trial and due process, while expressing the victim's perspective and feelings in a non-confrontational way. The statement should aim to educate and sensitize the court or the parole board about the human cost of crime and the need for accountability, restitution, and rehabilitation.

6. Follow-up and feedback: Victims should be informed about the outcome of the case and the use of their VIS in the decision-making process. They should also be offered the opportunity to provide feedback on their experience of making a VIS and the support they received from the criminal justice system. This feedback can be used to improve the quality and accessibility of victim services and to enhance the effectiveness of restorative justice practices.

b): Probation officials must diligently seek to locate victims and document VIS information as part of the pre-sentencing investigations c): Correction officials need to maintain records of the VIS for review by parole authorities and notify victims of their right to VIS input at parole hearings.

d): Parole boards should encourage the use of VIS by victims for parole hearings and revocation proceedings.

18. The use of the victim's VIS in the justice process reportedly has increased their satisfaction with the entire criminal justice system.

Not only does the victim's VIS increase their satisfaction of the entire criminal justice system, it also promotes healing in the aftermath of crime.

The use of victim impact statements (VIS) in the criminal justice process has become more widespread in recent years. VIS are written or oral statements made by crime victims or their loved ones, describing the physical, emotional, and financial impact of the crime on their lives. The statements are provided to the court during the sentencing process, and can also be used during pre-sentencing investigations, parole hearings, and other legal proceedings.

One of the primary benefits of VIS is that they give victims a voice in the criminal justice process. Prior to the widespread use of VIS, victims often felt ignored or powerless in the face of a justice system that was focused on punishing offenders. By allowing victims to describe the impact of the crime on their lives, VIS validate the experiences and emotions of victims, and give them a sense of control over the process.

Research has shown that the use of VIS can have a positive impact on victims' satisfaction with the criminal justice system. Victims who are allowed to provide a VIS are more likely to report feeling that the court process was fair and just, and that their voice was heard. They are also more likely to feel that they received a measure of justice and closure, even if the sentence was not as severe as they had hoped.

In addition to improving victim satisfaction, the use of VIS can also have a positive impact on the sentencing process itself. Judges and other legal professionals are often limited in their understanding of the full impact of a crime on a victim's life. VIS provide a more complete picture of the harm caused by the crime, and can help judges make more informed decisions about appropriate sentences.

However, for VIS to be an effective tool, there are some key considerations that must be taken into account. First, victims must be given the opportunity to provide a statement, and must feel safe and supported in doing so. This may require providing victims with information about the process, and offering emotional support and other resources.

Second, VIS must be taken seriously by judges and other legal professionals. They must be viewed as a vital part of the sentencing process, and not just a perfunctory exercise. Judges must be willing to consider the full impact of the crime on the victim, and take this into account when determining an appropriate sentence.

Finally, VIS must be used in a way that is fair and equitable for all parties involved. They should not be used to inflame passions or encourage harsher sentences than are warranted by the crime. Instead, they should be viewed as a tool for understanding the full impact of the crime on the victim, and ensuring that the sentence takes this impact into account.

In conclusion, the use of victim impact statements in the criminal justice system can have a positive impact on victim satisfaction, as well as on the sentencing process itself. However, in order for VIS to be effective, they must be taken seriously by legal professionals, and used in a way that is fair and equitable for all parties involved. When used appropriately, VIS can provide victims with a sense of empowerment and closure, and help to ensure that justice is served in a way that reflects the true impact of the crime.

19. What four factors increase the victim's overall satisfaction with the justice system and reduce victim trauma?

    a) Being taken seriously

    b) Being believed

    c) Being informed

    d) Being involved in key justice proceedings related to their cases.

Furthermore, research suggests that four factors can increase the victim's overall satisfaction with the justice system and reduce victim trauma. These factors are:

1. Participation and involvement: Victims who are actively involved in the justice process, such as through the use of victim impact statements or other restorative practices, are more likely to feel that their voices are heard and that they have some control over the outcome of the case. This can lead to increased satisfaction with the justice system and a reduction in trauma.

2. Empathy and understanding: When victims feel that justice system professionals, including judges, prosecutors, and police

officers, are empathetic and understanding, they are more likely to feel supported and less traumatized by the experience. This can be achieved through training for justice system professionals and by ensuring that victims are treated with respect and dignity throughout the process.

3. Timeliness: Victims who experience a timely resolution to their case are more likely to feel satisfied with the justice system and less traumatized by the experience. Delays in the justice process can cause additional stress and trauma for victims, particularly if they are required to attend multiple court hearings or if the case drags on for months or even years.

4. Communication and information: Victims who are kept informed about the progress of their case and the decisions made by justice system professionals are more likely to feel satisfied with the justice system and less traumatized by the experience. This can be achieved through regular updates, clear communication, and providing victims with information about their rights and the options available to them.

Hence, these factors highlight the importance of a victim-centered approach to the justice system, which prioritizes the needs and experiences of victims in order to promote their healing and well-being. When victims are treated with respect and empathy, and are given opportunities to participate in the justice process, they are more likely to feel satisfied with the outcome and less traumatized by the experience.

20. What are the two main goals of VIS?

The two main goals of a victim impact statement (VIS) are:

1. To provide the victim with an opportunity to describe the impact of the crime on their lives, and the lives of their loved ones, in their own words. This allows the victim to have a voice in the justice process, and to express their emotions, feelings, and concerns about the crime.

2. To provide the court with information about the harm caused by the crime, which can be used to determine an appropriate sentence for the offender. The VIS can help the court to understand the full extent of the harm caused by the crime, and to make a more informed decision about the sentence.

21. A strategy for involving the community in the justice process would be through the establishment of community reparation boards, which would primarily be used with offenders convicted of non-violent crimes and minor offenses.

It is not accurate to say that community reparation boards would only be used with offenders convicted of non-violent crimes and minor offenses. Reparation boards can be established to address a wide range of offenses, including serious and violent crimes. The focus of community reparation boards is to involve the community in the justice process and provide opportunities for offenders to make amends for their actions by completing meaningful acts of reparation.

Community reparation boards typically consist of community members who work with offenders to identify appropriate acts of reparation that will benefit both the offender and the community. These acts of reparation may include community service, restitution, and other forms of restorative justice. By involving the community in the process, community reparation boards aim to increase public trust in the justice system and provide a more balanced and restorative approach to justice.

The use of community reparation boards can also help to address underlying issues that may have contributed to the offender's behavior, such as substance abuse or mental health issues. By involving the community in the process, community reparation boards can provide a more holistic approach to addressing crime and helping offenders to reintegrate into society.

In summary, community reparation boards can be an effective strategy for involving the community in the justice process and providing opportunities for offenders to make amends for their actions. While they may be used primarily with non-violent and minor offenses, they can also be used to address more serious and violent crimes. The focus is on providing a more restorative and community-centered approach to justice that benefits both the offender and the community.

22. Describe the function of a community reparation board.

A community reparation board is a restorative justice approach that involves community members in the rehabilitation of an offender who has committed a non-violent crime or a minor offense. The board is made up of volunteers from the local community who work with the offender to develop a plan of action to make amends for their actions.

The function of a community reparation board is to provide a forum for the offender to take responsibility for their actions and make amends for the harm they have caused to the community. The board works with the offender to develop a reparation plan that is designed to repair the harm caused by the offender's actions.

The reparation plan can include a variety of activities such as community service, financial restitution, or education and training programs. The board also monitors the offender's progress in carrying out their reparation plan and provides support and guidance as needed.

The community reparation board provides an opportunity for the offender to engage with the community and to make meaningful contributions to the community. It also helps to build trust and understanding between the offender and the community.

The community reparation board serves as an alternative to traditional forms of punishment such as incarceration, which can be costly and often do not address the root causes of the offender's behavior. By involving the community in the rehabilitation process, the community reparation board can provide a more effective and sustainable solution to non-violent crime and minor offenses.
a) Conduct one-on-one meetings with offenders sentenced by the court to participate in the
b) The board members and the offender discuss the nature of the crime, its impact on the victim and community, and its consequences.
c) The board members develop a set of proposed sanctions which are presented to the offender.
A community restoration board may also address the root causes of the crime and offer instruction/education on the matter. For instance, a drug dealer may not recognize that he has a lazy spirit and that the responsible thing for him to do is get a job.

23. List the factors that have been determined as important elements of implementing a successful community-driven reparation board program.:

Some of the factors that have been determined as important elements of implementing a successful community-driven reparation board program are:

a): Cooperation of the criminal justice system - In order for a community reparation board program to be effective, there needs to be cooperation and coordination with the criminal justice system, including law enforcement, prosecutors, and judges. This ensures that the program operates within the legal framework of the justice system, and that offenders are held accountable for their actions.

b): Well trained staff that is committed - Staff who are trained in restorative justice principles and practices, as well as in the specific procedures of the reparation board program, are essential to the success of the program. Staff members must be committed to the goals of the program, and must be able to work effectively with both offenders and community members.

c): Working with victim organizations, and ensuring that victims are represented and provided adequate opportunity to participate - Victims must have a voice in the reparation board process, and their input must be taken into account when developing agreements. Victim organizations can help to ensure that victims are informed about the program and have access to support services.

d): Processing cases expeditiously and in a manner that is simple for the community members to understand - Cases must be processed in a timely manner, and the procedures of the program must be clear and easy to understand for all participants. This helps to ensure that the program operates efficiently, and that community members feel that their time and efforts are valued.

e): Facilitating a positive experience for board members - Board members must have a positive experience in the reparation board process, so that they will be willing to participate in future cases. This includes providing training and support for board members, and ensuring that their contributions are recognized and appreciated.

f): Supporting the program with adequate resources - Adequate resources, including funding, staff, and facilities, are essential for the success of the program. Without sufficient resources, the program may not be able to operate effectively, or may not be able to serve all of the cases that are referred to it.

g): Striving for success and healing for victims, community and offender participants - The ultimate goal of the reparation board program is to achieve success and healing for all participants, including victims, offenders, and the community as a whole. This requires a commitment to restorative justice principles, and a willingness to work collaboratively towards a shared goal.

24. Experiential and anecdotal information show much promise for community reparation boards as an effective response to non-violent crime.:

Community reparation boards have shown great promise as an effective response to non-violent crimes through experiential and anecdotal information. These boards are an innovative way to involve the community in the criminal justice process, and they offer an alternative to traditional forms of punishment.

One of the key advantages of community reparation boards is that they allow community members to be actively involved in the resolution of crime. This participation can lead to greater community ownership of the justice process and a deeper sense of responsibility for addressing crime. Additionally, community reparation boards can help to restore trust between offenders and their community, creating a greater sense of accountability.

Furthermore, community reparation boards can offer a more effective and efficient way of resolving non-violent crimes. By involving community members in the resolution of these cases, it can reduce the burden on the criminal justice system and can save valuable resources. Also, this alternative approach can help reduce the likelihood of recidivism and prevent the escalation of minor offenses to more serious crimes.

Community reparation boards can provide a safe and supportive environment for victims to be heard and have their needs met. This approach can help to restore the harm caused by the offender, promote healing, and help the victim move forward with their lives. Additionally, community reparation boards provide an opportunity for offenders to take responsibility for their actions and make amends directly to those they have harmed.

However, the implementation of community reparation boards requires careful consideration and attention to detail. It is essential to ensure that the community members participating in the board have adequate training and support. Also, it is important to establish clear guidelines and procedures for the handling of cases to ensure fairness and consistency.

In conclusion, the experiential and anecdotal information of community reparation boards shows much promise as an effective response to non-violent crimes. While this approach requires significant effort and resources to implement, the potential benefits for victims, offenders, and communities make it a valuable alternative to traditional forms of punishment.

25. What are the goals of community restorative boards?

a) Promote citizen ownership of the criminal justice system by involving them directly in the justice process.

b) Provide opportunities for victims and community members to confront offenders in a constructive manner about their criminal behavior.

c) Provide opportunities for offenders to take personal responsibility and be held directly accountable for the harm caused to victims and communities.

d) Generate meaningful "community-driven" consequences for criminal behavior that reduce a costly reliance on formal criminal justice processing.

Furthermore, the community restorative boards aim to accomplish several goals, including:

1. Encouraging offender accountability: By involving the offender in the process, the board aims to encourage them to take responsibility for their actions and work towards repairing the harm they caused to the victim and the community.
2. Empowering victims: The board provides victims with an opportunity to participate in the justice process and have a say in the outcome of the case. It also aims to provide them with support and resources to aid in their healing process.
3. Building community relationships: The board aims to foster positive relationships between the offender, victim, and the community. It encourages community members to work together to find solutions to issues caused by non-violent crime.
4. Reducing recidivism: By providing offenders with a more meaningful and restorative consequence for their actions, the board hopes to reduce the likelihood of them reoffending.
5. Providing a cost-effective alternative to traditional justice systems: Community reparation boards are often less costly than traditional court proceedings, making them an attractive option for jurisdictions facing budget constraints.

Hence, community restorative boards aim to promote a more collaborative and community-focused approach to justice that prioritizes healing and rehabilitation over punishment.

Note: The main focus in this intervention measure is the satisfaction of the victim.

26. Community service is a restorative practice that offers a way an offender can be held accountable to repair some of the harm caused by their criminal behavior.

Community service should NOT be a practice sanctioned to humiliate the offender. The programs should be meaningful and contribute to the community's improvement.

27. What is community service?

Community service is a form of restorative justice that involves an offender performing a set number of hours of unpaid work for the benefit of the community. This work is typically performed as part of a court-ordered sentence or as a condition of probation or parole. The goal of community service is to provide offenders with a way to make amends for their actions and to give back to the community that was affected by their wrongdoing.

Community service can take many different forms, including picking up litter, cleaning up parks, volunteering at a local charity, or assisting with community events. The type of service is usually determined by the nature of the offense and the needs of the community. The number of hours an offender is required to perform is also typically based on the severity of the offense and the discretion of the sentencing judge or probation officer.

Community service is often seen as a more rehabilitative form of punishment compared to incarceration or fines. It allows offenders to take responsibility for their actions, make amends, and develop a sense of civic responsibility. Additionally, it can provide offenders with valuable job skills and work experience, which can help them secure future employment and reduce their likelihood of reoffending.

However, it is important to note that community service is not a one-size-fits-all solution and may not be appropriate for all offenders or offenses. It is also important to ensure that community service does not become a form of exploitation or a way to exploit free labor from offenders. Proper oversight and monitoring are necessary to ensure that community service is carried out in a fair and equitable manner, and that offenders are given meaningful opportunities to make amends and give back to the community.

28. Briefly explain why a successful community service program requires a close partnership between justice officials and community members?

Yes, a successful community service program requires a close partnership between justice officials and community members. Justice officials play a critical role in setting up the program, identifying appropriate projects, and monitoring compliance. Community members also play a vital role in identifying needs and opportunities for service projects, providing supervision and support for offenders, and evaluating the impact of the program on the community. Close collaboration between these two groups is necessary to ensure that the program is effective, sustainable, and meets the needs of both the justice system and the community. Additionally, effective communication and trust-building between justice officials and community members are essential to overcome any potential barriers or challenges in implementing the program.

29. Give some examples of community service.:

Community service can take various forms, including but not limited to:

1. Cleaning up litter from public areas like parks, beaches, and streets.
2. Planting trees or beautifying public spaces with gardening.
3. Serving food at a soup kitchen or food bank.
4. Helping out at a homeless shelter.
5. Assisting with the care of animals at an animal shelter.
6. Assisting at a nursing home or hospital.
7. Tutoring or mentoring children in schools or after-school programs.
8. Assisting with disaster relief efforts.
9. Helping with youth sports programs or other community events.
10. Performing administrative work for non-profit organizations.
11. Assisting with community recycling programs.
12. Providing support at community centers or libraries.
13. Painting or refurbishing community buildings or structures.
14. Assisting with community clean-up efforts after natural disasters.
15. Helping to maintain community gardens or urban farming projects.

These are just some examples, and community service opportunities can vary widely depending on the needs of the community and the interests and skills of the offender.

Community service programs began in the United States with female traffic offenders in Alameda County, California in 1966, and local initiatives followed in several counties throughout the United States.

In the United Kingdom, Parliament enacted legislation in the early 1970's giving the courts specific powers to order community service as a sentencing sanction, and not just a condition of probation.

30. What are some of the goals of community service?

a) Hold offenders accountable for the harm they have caused to victims and the community.

b) Provide communities with human resources that can improve the quality of life in public environments.

c) Help offenders develop new skills through supervised work activities.

d) Allow victims a voice in the type of community service performed.

In addition:

1. Providing restitution to the community: Community service is often viewed as a way for offenders to give back to the community they have harmed through their criminal behavior.
2. Encouraging responsibility: Community service is designed to help offenders take responsibility for their actions and make amends.
3. Promoting personal growth and development: Community service can be an opportunity for offenders to develop new skills, gain work experience, and build self-confidence.
4. Fostering community involvement: Community service encourages offenders to become more involved in their community, promoting a sense of belonging and connection.
5. Reducing recidivism: Community service can be used as a means of reducing recidivism by providing offenders with a positive outlet for their time and energy, and by helping them to build positive relationships with community members.
6. Community service can also help the offender develop better work habits.

31. Community service is effectively used in all states, and at the federal level as a component of criminal sentences involving diversion, probation, and parole because Community service is a form of punishment that requires offenders to perform unpaid work in their local communities as a way of repaying society for their crimes. It has been effectively used in all states and at the federal level as a component of criminal sentences involving diversion, probation, and parole.

One of the benefits of community service as a form of punishment is that it allows offenders to give back to the community and make amends for their actions. It can also provide a sense of accomplishment and self-worth to those who are completing the work. Additionally, community service can help offenders build new skills, develop a sense of responsibility and accountability, and gain valuable work experience, which can help them to become more employable in the future.

At the state level, community service is often used as an alternative to traditional incarceration, especially for low-level offenders who do not pose a serious threat to public safety. In many cases, community service can be more cost-effective than incarceration, and it can also help to reduce overcrowding in prisons and jails.

At the federal level, community service is often used as a component of criminal sentences involving diversion, probation, and parole. Diversion programs are designed to divert nonviolent offenders away from the criminal justice system and into community-based programs that address the root causes of their criminal behavior. Probation and parole programs are designed to provide supervision and support to offenders who are returning to the community after serving time in prison.

Thus, community service has proven to be an effective form of punishment that benefits both the offender and the community. By requiring offenders to give back to their communities, community service can help to reduce recidivism rates and promote public safety. Additionally, it can provide offenders with valuable skills and work experience that can help them to successfully reintegrate into society.

32. Briefly explain why Restitution is a restorative process by which offenders are held accountable for the financial losses they have caused the victims of their crime?

Restitution is a restorative process that holds offenders accountable for the financial losses they have caused to the victims of their crime. This process involves the offender making financial payments or providing other forms of compensation to the victim as a way of repairing the harm that was done.

Restitution can be a powerful tool in the criminal justice system as it helps to ensure that offenders are held accountable for their actions and that victims receive some form of justice. It can also be an important part of the healing process for victims, as it can provide a sense of closure and help them to recover from the financial losses that were incurred.

One of the key benefits of restitution is that it allows offenders to take responsibility for their actions and make amends for the harm they have caused. By requiring offenders to pay restitution, it sends a message that their actions have consequences and that they are accountable for the financial losses they have caused.

Restitution can also be beneficial for offenders, as it can provide them with a sense of accomplishment and help them to make positive changes in their lives. By making financial payments and taking steps to repair the harm they have caused, offenders may gain a sense of self-worth and personal responsibility that can help them to avoid future criminal behavior.

Additionally, restitution can be an effective alternative to traditional forms of punishment, such as incarceration or fines. Restitution can be less costly to the criminal justice system and can also be a more effective way of reducing recidivism rates by addressing the underlying issues that led to the offender's criminal behavior.

Accordingly, restitution is a restorative process that can be a powerful tool in the criminal justice system. By holding offenders accountable for the financial losses, they have caused and providing compensation to victims, restitution can help to promote justice, healing, and rehabilitation.

33. Appropriate restitution orders are based on information gathered through either victim impact statements or pre-sentencing investigations. Briefly explain:

Appropriate restitution orders should be made after a careful assessment of the victim's losses and the offender's earning capacity.

Restitution orders are an important part of the criminal justice system, as they require offenders to compensate their victims for the financial losses they have caused. In order to ensure that restitution orders are appropriate and based on accurate information, the criminal justice system relies on either victim impact statements or pre-sentencing investigations.

Victim impact statements are written or oral statements made by victims or their family members about the physical, emotional, and financial impact of the crime on their lives. These statements provide important information to judges and prosecutors about the harm that was caused by the crime and the financial losses that were incurred. This information can be used to determine the appropriate amount of restitution that the offender should be required to pay.

Pre-sentencing investigations, also known as PSI reports, are conducted by probation officers and provide judges with detailed information about the offender's background, criminal history, and current circumstances. These reports can also include information about the financial losses that were incurred by the victim as a result of the crime. Based on this information, judges can make informed decisions about the appropriate amount of restitution that the offender should be required to pay.

Both victim impact statements and pre-sentencing investigations are important tools in ensuring that restitution orders are appropriate and based on accurate information. By gathering information about the harm caused by the crime and the financial losses incurred by the victim, judges can make informed decisions about the appropriate amount of restitution that should be ordered.

In some cases, there may be disputes about the amount of restitution that should be ordered. In these cases, judges may hold hearings to gather additional information and make a determination about the appropriate amount of restitution. This process helps to ensure that restitution orders are fair, accurate, and based on the best available information.

34. Why is Restitution considered to be an essential victim's right, which helps victims reconstruct their lives in the aftermath of a crime?

Restitution is considered to be an essential "victims' right" because it helps victims to recover financially from the harm caused by a crime and to reconstruct their lives in the aftermath of the crime. When a crime is committed, victims can suffer significant financial losses, such as medical expenses, lost wages, and property damage. Restitution provides a way for victims to recover these losses and to receive compensation for the harm that was caused.

In addition to providing financial compensation, restitution also serves an important psychological function for victims. It can help victims to feel that they have regained some control over their lives and that justice has been served. It can also help victims to feel that they have been heard and that their experiences have been taken seriously.

Furthermore, restitution is often seen as a more just and equitable form of punishment than fines or other forms of financial penalties. Fines are typically paid to the government, while restitution is paid directly to the victim. This helps to ensure that the victim is compensated for their losses and that the offender is held accountable for the harm they have caused.

Finally, restitution can be an important tool in reducing recidivism rates. By requiring offenders to take responsibility for their actions and to make amends for the harm they have caused, restitution can help to prevent future criminal behavior. This can ultimately lead to safer communities and a more effective criminal justice system.

Wherefore, restitution is considered to be an essential "victims' right" because it helps victims to recover financially, psychologically, and emotionally from the harm caused by a crime. It is also an important tool for holding offenders accountable, promoting justice, and reducing recidivism rates.

35. Receiving restitution payment can make a victim feel that the justice system is working on their behalf to ensure that they are justly compensated for their losses.

Yes, receiving restitution payment can make a victim feel that the justice system is working on their behalf to ensure that they are justly compensated for their losses. Restitution is an important component of the criminal justice system that provides victims with a sense of justice and accountability. When offenders are required to pay restitution, it sends a message that they are being held responsible for the harm they have caused and that the justice system is taking steps to address the victim's financial losses.

Victims who receive restitution payments can also feel a sense of closure and satisfaction, knowing that they have been compensated for the harm they have suffered. This can help to ease their financial burdens and allow them to move forward with their lives.

However, it is important to note that not all victims will receive restitution payments. In some cases, offenders may not have the financial means to make restitution payments, or they may refuse to pay. In these situations, victims may need to seek alternative forms of compensation, such as civil lawsuits or victim compensation programs.

Despite these challenges, restitution remains an important component of the criminal justice system that helps victims to recover financially and to feel that justice has been served.

In its traditional sense, restitution has been defined as a monetary payment by the offender to the victim for the harm reasonably resulting from the offense. Restitution can be either or both monetary payments and in-kind services to the victim. The main purpose of institutionalized restitution was to prevent retaliatory violence for wrongdoing, providing a more "civilized" means of reparation.

36. Remedies for non-compliance to restitution orders may include ....:

Remedies for non-compliance to restitution orders may include:

a) Converting restitution orders to civil judgments, which allows the victim to pursue collection through civil court.

b) Extending sentence periods until restitution is paid, which means that the offender will remain under supervision until the restitution is fully paid.

c) Forfeiture of assets, which means that the offender's assets, such as property or vehicles, can be seized and sold to pay the restitution.

d) Income garnishment orders, which means that a portion of the offender's wages can be withheld and applied towards the restitution.

e) Revocation of the offender's driver's license, which can serve as a deterrent and incentive for the offender to comply with the restitution order.

f) Revocation of probation and parole, which means that the offender may be returned to prison for violating the terms of their release.

It is important to note that the specific remedies for non-compliance to restitution orders may vary depending on the jurisdiction and the nature of the offense. In some cases, additional penalties or sanctions may be imposed, such as fines or community service. The goal of these remedies is to ensure that the offender is held accountable for their actions and that the victim receives the compensation they are owed.

37. What are the goals of restitution?

Providing financial compensation: The primary goal of restitution is to provide financial compensation to the victim(s) of a crime. This includes reimbursement for expenses related to medical treatment, property damage, lost wages, and other financial losses.

1. Holding offenders accountable: Restitution is also a way to hold offenders accountable for their actions. By requiring them to pay restitution, they are taking responsibility for the harm they have caused and working to make things right.

2. Deterrence: Restitution can act as a deterrent to future criminal behavior. Knowing that they will be required to pay restitution

if they commit a crime can discourage some offenders from engaging in criminal activity.

3. Restoration: Restitution can be part of a restorative justice approach, which aims to restore the harm caused by a crime. By compensating victims for their losses, restitution can help to restore their sense of security and well-being.

4. Promoting justice: Restitution can be seen as a way to promote justice and fairness in the criminal justice system. It ensures that offenders are held accountable for their actions and that victims are compensated for the harm they have suffered.

Accordingly, the goals of restitution are to provide financial compensation to victims, hold offenders accountable, deter future criminal behavior, restore the harm caused by the offense, and promote justice and fairness in the criminal justice system.

38. Victim offender mediation provides interested victims the opportunity to meet their offender in a safe, structured and supervised setting, to engage in meaningful mediated discussion of the crime.:

Yes, victim offender mediation provides interested victims the opportunity to meet their offender in a safe, structured, and supervised setting to engage in meaningful mediated discussion of the crime. This type of mediation is a form of restorative justice that is based on the principles of healing, reconciliation, and accountability.

The goal of victim offender mediation is to provide victims with a voice in the justice system and to promote healing and closure for both the victim and the offender. Through mediated discussions, victims are able to express how the crime has impacted their lives and to ask questions of the offender. Offenders are also given the opportunity to take responsibility for their actions and to make amends for the harm they have caused.

The mediation process is structured and supervised to ensure the safety and well-being of all participants. Mediators are trained professionals who facilitate the discussion and ensure that both parties have an opportunity to be heard. The process is voluntary, and both the victim and the offender must agree to participate.

Research has shown that victim offender mediation can have positive outcomes for both victims and offenders. Victims who participate in mediation may experience a sense of empowerment, healing, and closure. Offenders may gain a greater understanding of the harm they have caused and may be more likely to take responsibility for their actions and make amends.

Hence, victim offender mediation is a valuable tool in the criminal justice system that can help to promote healing, reconciliation, and accountability.

Note: This program should not be court ordered but voluntary for both the victim and offender. The success of this service will largely depend on the willingness of the victim and offender to settle the issues resulting from the crime.

39. The victim offender mediation program operates on a referral system by:

The victim offender mediation program typically operates on a referral system, which means that the program is not open to all victims and offenders, but rather only those who are referred by a judge, prosecutor, or other criminal justice official. The referral process typically involves the following steps:

1. Identification: Criminal justice officials identify cases that may be appropriate for victim offender mediation. This may include cases in which the offender has admitted guilt, the victim is interested in participating, and there is no history of violence or abuse.
2. Assessment: The victim and offender are assessed to determine their suitability for mediation. This may involve interviews with both parties to assess their willingness and ability to participate in the process.
3. Referral: If both parties are found to be suitable for mediation, they are referred to a trained mediator who will facilitate the process.
4. Mediation: The mediator facilitates a face-to-face meeting between the victim and offender in a safe and structured environment. During the mediation, the parties discuss the offense and its impact on the victim, and the offender takes responsibility for their actions and makes amends.
5. Follow-up: After the mediation, the parties may be required to follow up with the mediator or other criminal justice officials to ensure that the terms of the agreement are being met.

By operating on a referral system, the victim offender mediation program is able to ensure that only cases that are appropriate for mediation are referred to the program. This helps to ensure the safety and well-being of all participants and to promote positive outcomes for both victims and offenders.

40. What are the goals of victim offender mediation?

a) Support the healing process, by providing a safe controlled setting for them to meet and speak with the offender on a strictly voluntary basis.

b) Allow the offender to learn about the impact of the crime on the victim and to take direct responsibility for their behavior.

c) Provide an opportunity for the victim and offender to develop a mutually acceptable plan that addresses the harm caused by their crime.

In addition, the goals of victim offender mediation are to provide a safe, structured, and supervised setting for victims and offenders to meet and discuss the crime and its impact, and to promote healing, accountability, and reconciliation. More specifically, some of the goals of victim offender mediation include:

1. Empowering victims: Victim offender mediation provides victims with an opportunity to be heard, to express how the crime has affected them, and to ask questions of the offender. This can help victims feel more empowered and in control of their lives.

2. Holding offenders accountable: By meeting face-to-face with the victim, offenders are encouraged to take responsibility for their actions and to make amends for the harm they have caused. This can help to hold offenders accountable and to prevent future offenses.

3. Promoting healing and closure: Victim offender mediation can help victims to heal from the emotional and psychological harm caused by the crime. It can also provide both victims and offenders with a sense of closure and resolution.

4. Restoring relationships: Victim offender mediation can help to restore relationships between victims and offenders by promoting understanding, empathy, and forgiveness.

5. Reducing recidivism: By addressing the underlying issues that led to the offense and promoting accountability and responsibility, victim offender mediation may help to reduce the likelihood of future offenses by the offender.

Hence, victim offender mediation is a form of restorative justice that seeks to promote healing, accountability, and reconciliation for all parties involved.

41. Family group conferencing is a process of intervention whereby the community members most affected by the crime came together to meet with the victim and the offender to discuss the resolution of the criminal incident.

This particular intervention process can have a great impact on the offender who is sensitive to the voice of family members and relatives because Family group conferencing is a process of intervention that brings together the community members most affected by a crime, including the victim, offender, and their families, to discuss the resolution of the incident. The purpose of the conference is to provide a forum for open dialogue and problem-solving, and to create a plan for repairing the harm caused by the crime.

While family group conferencing is often used in cases involving juvenile offenders, it can also be used in cases involving adult offenders. The process typically involves the following steps:

1. Referral: The case is referred to a family group conferencing coordinator, who assesses whether the case is appropriate for family group conferencing and, if so, invites the relevant parties to participate.
2. Preparation: The coordinator meets with each participant individually to explain the process and their role in it, and to address any concerns they may have.
3. Conference: The conference is held in a neutral setting, and is facilitated by the coordinator. Each participant is given the opportunity to speak and to share their perspective on the crime and its impact. The group then works together to develop a plan for repairing the harm caused by the crime.
4. Follow-up: After the conference, the plan is implemented, and the coordinator follows up with each participant to ensure that the plan is being carried out.

The goals of family group conferencing are similar to those of victim offender mediation, and include empowering victims, holding offenders accountable, promoting healing and closure, restoring relationships, and reducing recidivism. Family group conferencing is based on the principles of restorative justice, and seeks to create a sense of community involvement and responsibility for addressing crime and its impact.

42. The conferencing group may include:

The conferencing group in family group conferencing may include:

1. The victim: The person who was directly harmed by the crime.
2. The offender: The person who committed the crime.
3. Family members or support persons of the victim: This may include parents, siblings, partners, or friends of the victim who can provide emotional support and guidance during the conference.
4. Family members or support persons of the offender: This may include parents, siblings, partners, or friends of the offender who can provide support and guidance during the conference.
5. Community members: This may include representatives from the local community who have been affected by the crime or who can provide support and guidance to the victim and offender.
6. Conference facilitator: A neutral third party who guides the conference process and ensures that everyone has an opportunity to speak and be heard.

The specific makeup of the conferencing group may vary depending on the case and the preferences of the participants. The goal is to create a safe and supportive environment where everyone has a voice and is able to contribute to the resolution of the crime.

43. Who runs the conferencing group?

The family group conferencing process is typically facilitated by a trained facilitator or coordinator who is neutral and impartial. The coordinator is responsible for guiding the conference process and ensuring that everyone has an opportunity to speak and be heard. The coordinator may be a trained mediator, social worker, or other professional with experience in restorative justice practices. In some cases, the coordinator may be a member of the community or a volunteer who has been trained to facilitate family group conferences. The coordinator's role is to ensure that the conference is conducted in a safe and respectful manner, and that the needs of all participants are taken into consideration.

44. Describe how is the conference beings?

The conference typically begins with the offender admitting guilt and accepting responsibility for their actions.

Yes, that is correct. In a family group conference, the offender is typically asked to admit guilt and accept responsibility for their actions. This is an important step in the restorative justice process, as it allows the victim and the community to see that the offender is taking responsibility for their behavior and is committed to making things right. By admitting guilt, the offender acknowledges the harm they have caused and signals a willingness to work towards repairing the harm. This can be an important first step in the process of healing and restoration for all parties involved.

Conferencing is used only when the offender admits guilt (or in some jurisdictions, admits liability or declines to deny guilt). It is not used to determine guilt, and at any time during the process the offender may choose to bring the conference to a halt and proceed to court for a traditional determination of guilt or innocence.

45. How does a successful family group conference end?

A successful family group conferencing session ends when participants reach and sign an agreement outlining their expectations and commitments.

The goal of a family group conference is to come to a resolution that is satisfactory to all participants, including the victim, the offender, and the community. This resolution is typically outlined in a written agreement that is signed by all parties involved.

The agreement may include a range of commitments and expectations, such as:

1. Restitution: The offender may agree to make restitution to the victim, either through monetary payments or through other means such as community service.

2. Apology: The offender may agree to apologize to the victim for their behavior, either in writing or in person.

3. Counseling or therapy: The offender may agree to participate in counseling or therapy to address the underlying issues that contributed to their behavior.

4. Future behavior: The offender may agree to avoid certain behaviors in the future, or to take specific steps to prevent similar incidents from occurring.

5. Community service: The offender may agree to participate in community service as a way of making amends to the community.

Once the agreement has been reached and signed, the coordinator or facilitator will typically follow up with all participants to ensure that the commitments outlined in the agreement are being fulfilled. This follow-up process is an important part of the restorative justice process, as it helps to ensure that the resolution reached in the family group conference is meaningful and effective for all parties involved.

Note: Family Group Conferencing is a means of involving family members, including extended family and friends, in decision making and planning for children about whom concerns have been expressed in relation to their safety or well-being.

46. Family group conferencing is currently used in:

    a) Schools,

    b) Police departments,

    c) Probation offices

    d) and neighborhood groups

47. What are the benefits of family group conferencing?

Studies have shown that family group conferencing can be an effective way of building community skills in conflict resolution and participatory decision-making. By involving members of the community in the process of resolving conflicts and addressing criminal behavior, family group conferencing can help to strengthen social ties and promote a sense of collective responsibility for maintaining safe and healthy communities.

One of the key benefits of family group conferencing is that it allows all participants to have a voice in the decision-making process. By bringing together the victim, the offender, and members of the community, family group conferencing encourages open and honest dialogue, and provides an opportunity for all parties to be heard. This can be a powerful tool for building community cohesion and promoting positive social interactions.

In addition to promoting community skills in conflict resolution and decision-making, family group conferencing has been shown to have a number of other benefits as well. For example, it can be an effective way of reducing recidivism rates among offenders, as it provides a more holistic approach to addressing criminal behavior. By focusing on the underlying causes of criminal behavior and working to repair harm to the victim and the community, family group conferencing can help to break the cycle of crime and reduce the likelihood of future offenses.

Accordingly, family group conferencing is a valuable tool for promoting restorative justice and building stronger, more resilient communities. By involving all stakeholders in the process of resolving conflicts and addressing criminal behavior, family group conferencing can help to create a sense of shared responsibility and promote positive social change.

48. What are the goals of family group conferencing?

a) Provide an opportunity for the victim to be directly involved in the discussion of the offense and in decisions regarding appropriate sanctions to be placed on the offender.

b) Increase the offender's awareness of the human impact of their behavior and provide an opportunity to take full responsibility for it.

c) Engage the collective responsibility of the offender's support system for making amends and shaping the offender's future behavior.

d) Allow both offender and victim to reconnect to key community support systems.

In addition, the goals of family group conferencing are to promote accountability, responsibility, and healing for all parties involved in a crime or conflict. These goals are achieved through the following:

1. Encouraging open and honest dialogue: Family group conferencing provides a safe and structured environment for all parties to discuss the impact of the crime and work towards a resolution. This encourages open and honest dialogue and helps to build understanding and empathy among participants.

2. Restoring harm: Family group conferencing aims to repair harm caused by the crime to the victim and the community. This can involve developing a plan to make restitution, apologizing for the harm caused, or taking other steps to make things right.

3. Empowering participants: Family group conferencing empowers all participants to be actively involved in the process of resolving the conflict. By providing a forum for all voices to be heard, family group conferencing helps to promote participation, decision-making, and ownership of the outcome.

4. Reducing recidivism: Family group conferencing is aimed at reducing the likelihood of future offending by addressing the underlying causes of criminal behavior. By working to address

these root causes, family group conferencing can help to break the cycle of offending and promote positive social change.

5. Strengthening relationships: Family group conferencing helps to build and strengthen relationships among participants. By encouraging open and honest dialogue, promoting accountability and responsibility, and focusing on healing and restoration, family group conferencing can help to build stronger, more resilient communities.

49. Victim impact panels are designed to educate offender groups about the negative consequences and impact of criminal behavior on their lives and on the lives of their families, friends, and other members of the community. Discuss:

Victim impact panels are an important component of many criminal justice systems and are designed to educate offender groups about the negative consequences and impact of criminal behavior on their lives and on the lives of their families, friends, and other members of the community. Some key points to consider when discussing victim impact panels include:

1. Purpose and structure: Victim impact panels are typically structured as educational sessions where offenders hear from victims or family members of victims who have been impacted by crime. These sessions may take place in-person or online and are often mandatory for offenders as part of their sentence or as a condition of their release.

2. Education and awareness: The primary goal of victim impact panels is to educate offenders about the real-world consequences of their criminal behavior. This can include hearing about the physical, emotional, and financial impact of crime on victims, as well as the broader impact on families, friends, and the community as a whole. By increasing awareness and empathy, victim impact panels can help to deter future criminal behavior and promote positive social change.

3. Victim participation: Victim impact panels rely on the participation of victims or their family members to share their experiences and provide a personal perspective on the impact of crime. This participation is entirely voluntary and victims are typically given support and guidance throughout the process to ensure their comfort and safety.

4. Effectiveness: While the effectiveness of victim impact panels can be difficult to measure, many studies have shown that they

can be a powerful tool for reducing recidivism and promoting offender accountability. By providing a human face to the impact of criminal behavior and increasing awareness of the real-world consequences of crime, victim impact panels can help to promote positive behavioral change and reduce the likelihood of future offending.

Accordingly, victim impact panels play an important role in the criminal justice system by providing a forum for victims to share their experiences and educating offenders about the impact of their actions on others. By promoting empathy, awareness, and accountability, victim impact panels can help to reduce recidivism and build stronger, more resilient communities.

Note: Victim impact panels offer the offender groups a wide range of views or perspectives on the type of crime being discussed. A panel group speaking collectively can have a greater chance of impacting the offenders.

50. The victim impact panel has been used with crimes such as:
Victim impact panels have been used in a wide range of criminal cases, including but not limited to:

1. Robbery
2. Assault
3. Domestic violence
4. Child abuse
5. Elder abuse
6. DUI/DWI
7. Manslaughter
8. Homicide
9. Sexual assault
10. Hate crimes
11. White-collar crime
12. Property crimes

The purpose of a victim impact panel is to provide a forum for victims or their family members to share the impact of the crime on their lives with offenders. This can help to increase offender awareness of the human impact of their actions, promote empathy, and reduce the likelihood of future offending.

51. How is the victim impact panel utilized?
a) In jail and in prison settings,
b) Treatment programs,

c) Defensive driving schools

d) Youth education programs

e) Training forums for criminal justice professionals to help them better understand the scope

f) and trauma of victimization.

Furthermore, Victim impact panels are typically utilized as a component of a criminal sentence or as part of a diversion or rehabilitation program. Offenders who are required to attend a victim impact panel may be mandated to do so by a judge, as a condition of probation, or as part of a plea agreement.

During the panel, victims or their family members share their personal experiences of victimization and the impact it has had on their lives. The panel may also feature presentations from law enforcement officials, victim advocates, or other experts on the effects of crime on individuals and communities.

The goal of the victim impact panel is to provide a powerful and emotional reminder to offenders of the harm that their actions have caused. By hearing directly from those who have been affected by crime, offenders may be more likely to take responsibility for their behavior, show remorse, and commit to making positive changes in their lives. The panel also serves as a form of community education, helping to raise awareness of the impact of crime on victims and the community as a whole.

52. What are the goals of victim impact panels?

The goals of victim impact panels can be summarized as follows:

1. To increase offender awareness: Victim impact panels are designed to increase the awareness of offenders about the human impact of their actions. By hearing directly from victims or their family members, offenders may be more likely to understand the harm they have caused and the need to take responsibility for their behavior.

2. To promote empathy: Victim impact panels aim to promote empathy in offenders, encouraging them to see the world from the victim's perspective. This can help to reduce the likelihood of future offending by encouraging offenders to consider the impact of their actions on others.

3. To facilitate healing: For victims or their family members, the victim impact panel can be a cathartic experience that provides an opportunity to express their feelings about the crime and its impact on their lives. The panel can help to facilitate the healing

process by providing a supportive environment for victims to share their experiences.

4. To raise community awareness: The victim impact panel also serves as a form of community education, helping to raise awareness of the impact of crime on victims and the community as a whole. By bringing victims and offenders together, the panel can help to foster a sense of community responsibility for preventing crime and supporting victims.

Thus, the goals of victim impact panels are to promote accountability, responsibility, and understanding, while also providing a platform for healing and community education.

53. The victim impact class is an educational program designed to teach offenders the human consequences and impact of crime.

It is possible that the term "victim impact class" is being used interchangeably with "victim impact panel" or "victim impact program." However, in general, a victim impact class refers to a specific type of educational program that is designed to provide offenders with a deeper understanding of the impact of their crimes on victims and society.

The goal of a victim impact class is to help offenders develop empathy and understanding for their victims, as well as a sense of accountability for their actions. These classes typically involve lectures, videos, and other interactive activities that are intended to demonstrate the real-world consequences of criminal behavior.

Offenders who are required to attend a victim impact class may do so as a condition of their sentence or as part of a diversion or rehabilitation program. The specific content and format of the class may vary depending on the jurisdiction and the type of crime committed.

In summary, a victim impact class is an educational program that aims to teach offenders about the human consequences and impact of crime, with the goal of promoting accountability and empathy.

Note: The main focus in victim impact classes is on how the crime affected the victim and the victim's family.

54. What types of crimes are addressed in the curriculum of the victim impact class?

    a) Property crimes,

    b) Sexual assault,

    c) Domestic violence,

    d) Child abuse and neglect,

e) Elder abuse and neglect,

f) Drunk driving,

g) Drug-related crimes,

h) Gang violence,

i) Homicide.

The curriculum of a victim impact class can vary depending on the jurisdiction and the type of crime committed by the offender. However, in general, victim impact classes are designed to address a wide range of crimes, including:

1. Property crimes such as theft, burglary, and vandalism.
2. Drug offenses such as possession and distribution.
3. Crimes of violence such as assault, battery, and domestic violence.
4. Sexual offenses such as sexual assault and rape.
5. Driving under the influence (DUI) and other traffic offenses.

In addition to these specific types of crimes, victim impact classes may also address broader topics such as the impact of crime on victims and their families, the criminal justice system, and the role of rehabilitation and treatment in preventing recidivism.

The curriculum of a victim impact class is designed to help offenders understand the consequences of their actions and to promote empathy and accountability. By educating offenders about the impact of their crimes, victim impact classes aim to prevent future criminal behavior and promote community safety.

55. The success of a victim impact class program depends largely on the strong support and involvement from:

a) crime victims,

b) victim service providers,

c) and community members.

But it's a two-way street. I think the success of the program also depends on criminals' willingness to acknowledge the effects that their actions had on the victim and the victim's family. and how it damaged the community's sense of security.

The success of a victim impact class program depends largely on the strong support and involvement from various stakeholders, including:

1. Criminal justice professionals: Judges, prosecutors, defense attorneys, and probation officers play a critical role in referring offenders to victim impact classes, monitoring their progress, and ensuring compliance with program requirements.

2. Victim advocates: Victim advocates may assist with program administration and provide support to victims who participate in the program.

3. Program facilitators: Trained professionals who facilitate victim impact classes are essential to the success of the program. These facilitators are often licensed counselors or social workers with expertise in trauma-informed care and group therapy.

4. Offenders: The active participation of offenders is crucial to the success of the program. Offenders who are willing to engage in the program, listen to victims' stories, and reflect on the impact of their behavior are more likely to benefit from the program and reduce their risk of reoffending.

5. Victims: Victims who participate in the program play a critical role in educating offenders about the impact of their crimes and promoting accountability and empathy. The involvement of victims in the program also provides an opportunity for them to share their experiences and to heal from the trauma of their victimization.

6. Community organizations: Community organizations, such as victim service agencies and faith-based groups, can also provide support for victim impact class programs. These organizations may assist with program promotion, volunteer recruitment, and fundraising.

56. In what settings is the victim impact class currently being implemented?

a) Diversion,

b) Probation,

c) Prison,

d) Pre-release,

e) Detention,

f) and parole supervised setting.

The victim impact class is currently being implemented in a variety of settings, including probation and parole agencies, correctional facilities, and court systems. It is often used as a condition of probation or parole, and may also be required as part of a court-ordered sentence for certain crimes. Additionally, some schools and community organizations offer victim impact classes as a preventative measure to educate youth about the impact of crime and encourage pro-social behavior.

57. What are the goals of victim impact classes?

a) To teach offenders about the short- and long-term trauma of victimization.

b) Increase offenders' awareness of the negative impact of their crime on victims and other community members.

c) Encourage offenders to accept responsibility for their past criminal behaviors.

d) Provide victims and victim service providers with a forum to educate offenders about the consequences of their criminal actions, with the hope that it will help to prevent future offending.

e) Building linkages between criminal justice agencies, victims and victim service organizations.

The goals of victim impact classes are to educate offenders about the impact of their criminal behavior on the victims and the broader community, and to encourage them to take responsibility for their actions. Some specific goals of victim impact classes may include:

1. Increasing awareness and empathy: Offenders may not fully understand the physical, emotional, and financial toll that their actions have on victims and their families. Victim impact classes aim to increase offenders' awareness of these impacts and promote empathy for those affected by crime.

2. Encouraging accountability: Offenders may not always take responsibility for their actions. Victim impact classes aim to encourage offenders to take accountability for their behavior and to understand that they have a responsibility to repair the harm they have caused.

3. Reducing recidivism: Offenders who understand the impact of their actions on victims and the community may be less likely to reoffend. Victim impact classes may help to reduce recidivism rates by promoting pro-social behavior and encouraging offenders to make amends for their actions.

4. Promoting healing: Victim impact classes can provide a space for victims to share their experiences and for offenders to understand the harm that they have caused. This can promote

healing and closure for victims, and may help offenders to better understand the consequences of their actions.

Hence, the goal of victim impact classes is to promote understanding, empathy, accountability, and positive behavior change among offenders, while also providing healing and closure for victims. *Victim Impact Classes assist offenders in learning the true nature of crime and how crime harms and damages real people and communities.*

58. How do the following restorative-minded practices connect the criminal justice system and the public?

Restorative-minded practices aim to promote healing, accountability, and community involvement in the criminal justice system, bridging the gap between the criminal justice system and the public. Here is how some of the practices connect the criminal justice system and the public:

1. Victim Offender Mediation (VOM): VOM provides an opportunity for victims to meet their offender in a safe and structured setting to discuss the impact of the crime and work towards a resolution. By involving victims and offenders in the process, VOM promotes communication and empathy, which helps to rebuild relationships between the two parties. This process can also help to restore trust and confidence in the criminal justice system and promote community involvement in the justice process.

2. Family Group Conferencing (FGC): FGC brings together the community members most affected by a crime to discuss a resolution of the incident. This process allows community members to participate in decision-making and helps to build community skills in conflict resolution and participatory decision-making. FGC encourages community involvement in the justice process, promoting transparency and accountability in the criminal justice system.

3. Victim Impact Panels (VIP): VIP is an educational program designed to teach offenders the impact of their crimes on victims and the community. By providing offenders with a better understanding of the harm they have caused, VIP promotes empathy, accountability, and responsibility. VIP also promotes community involvement by bringing victims and offenders together, creating opportunities for dialogue, and increasing public awareness of the impact of crime.

4. Victim Impact Classes (VIC): VIC is an educational program designed to teach offenders the human consequences and impact of crime. By providing offenders with an understanding of the impact of crime on victims and society, VIC promotes empathy and accountability. VIC also promotes community involvement by educating offenders on the impact of crime, which can reduce recidivism and help build safer communities.

a) Community Policing: Community policing involves the establishment of "mini-stations" in neighborhoods and the assignment of law enforcement officers to a specific geographic area.

In cities and towns across the country, the recent, tragic deaths of black youths in confrontations with police have sown a wave of distrust for law enforcement. This perception is not fair to the vast majority of dedicated, well-meaning law enforcement officers, but it has shaken the connection between law enforcement agencies and the neighborhoods they serve.

The concept of community policing isn't a new one. In fact, an estimated 58% of law enforcement agencies reported having dedicated community-oriented officers back in 2003. Since then, many more have adopted a more transparent model for the organization of community programs that involve neighborhood businesses, nonprofits, media outlets, and other community groups directly in the process of keeping their municipality safe.

b) Neighborhood Probation: Neighborhood probation is similar to community policing whereby probation officers are assigned to specific geographic areas instead of having dispersed caseloads. These probation officers establish community partnerships in which they join the area neighborhoods in working with offenders to prevent recidivism, deal with community "hot spots", gang intimidation, drug houses, and other community concerns. Efforts are also made to collaborate with other service agencies, such as public health, social services, churches, etc.

c) School Based Probation: School based probation involves placing juvenile probation officers in schools who are assigned to the same geographic area as the schools. These officers are to provide problem solving assistance to the school for those students on probation. The objective is to monitor probationers while seeking ways to increase the likelihood of school success through improved grades, reduction in truancy and expulsion, and increase high school graduation.

d) Community Prosecution: Community prosecution helps communities resolve crime related problems identified by the residents, using prosecutors who have been assigned to specific neighborhoods. This intervention practice can also assist communities by explaining legal constraints that prevent law enforcement from acting, and devising alternative tools citizens and police can use when conventional ones fail.

e) Community Defense: Accessible community-based defense attorneys represent individuals accused of crime. They also represent clients before an arrest is made in an effort to avoid problems. The main objective is to provide legal services for the purpose of solving problems that foster crime and injustice before crime occurs. Furthermore, it seeks to address structural problems that are in existence in many communities. Assistance is offered to families and community members who are experiencing difficulties that can be addressed, in part, with legal assistance.

f) Community Courts: Community courts are established in neighborhoods as a response to the need to be closer to community needs. By decentralizing court facilities, the community citizens are permitted access to many remote locations where they can file forms, pay fines, and participate in the court process more conveniently. Court decentralization, also known as devolution, requires collaboration between the court and one or more community groups in order to forge a more broadly based connection between the court and community.

CHAPTER VI
SHOULD THE CHURCH GET
INVOLVED IN RESTORATIVE JUSTICE?

---

1. God has selected the Church as His primary instrument of restorative justice, and has given it a clear mandate to do criminal justice ministry.

I agree. In Matthew 25:36 Jesus clearly taught that it is His will for the Church to minister in prison: "I was in prison and you visited Me." This mandate has been reaffirmed in Hebrews 13:3: "Remember them that are in bonds, as bound with them."

The Bible clearly teaches that Christians are called to minister to those who are in prison or in other forms of confinement. In addition to the verses you mentioned, there are many other passages in the Bible that emphasize the importance of caring for prisoners and those who are marginalized or oppressed.

For example, in Isaiah 61:1, the prophet declares that God has anointed him to "preach good tidings unto the meek; he hath sent me to bind up the brokenhearted, to proclaim liberty to the captives, and the opening of the prison to them that are bound." Similarly, in Matthew 5:7, Jesus says, "Blessed are the merciful, for they shall obtain mercy."

Throughout the New Testament, we see examples of Christ's compassion for prisoners and his call to his followers to care for them. For example, in Acts 16, we read about how Paul and Silas were thrown into prison for preaching the gospel. Rather than being discouraged or bitter, they used their time in prison to worship and pray, and their witness led to the conversion of their jailer and his family.

In addition to ministering to prisoners themselves, the Church also has an important role to play in advocating for criminal justice reform and promoting restorative justice practices. The Church can provide a powerful witness to the world by modeling forgiveness, reconciliation, and healing, even in the midst of brokenness and injustice.

2. What are some questions that are raised by the mandate to do criminal justice ministry?

a) Is my view of justice consistent with the biblical view?

b) Does a commitment to restorative justice suggest that I do not support retributive efforts to administer justice?

c) What should be my goal and from what perspective do I view my work within the criminal justice system?

d) Do I preach Jesus only and leave past behavior alone, or do I deal with both behavior and faith, and, in dealing with both, in what sequence do I approach the two?

The mandate to do criminal justice ministry raises several questions, including:

1. What specific actions should the Church take to fulfill this mandate?
2. How can the Church balance its role as a spiritual institution with the practical aspects of criminal justice ministry?
3. How can the Church work collaboratively with the criminal justice system, while also advocating for systemic change?
4. What types of support and resources are necessary for the Church to effectively carry out its mandate?
5. How can the Church ensure that its criminal justice ministry is inclusive and equitable, and does not perpetuate systemic biases or discrimination?
6. How can the Church help to address the root causes of crime, such as poverty, inequality, and lack of access to education and employment opportunities?
7. How can the Church support both victims and offenders in the restorative justice process, while also upholding the principles of accountability and justice?

3. Restorative justice is a Biblical-based paradigm, that is founded in a call to the ministry of reconciliation.

2 Corinthians 5:18 refers to the ministry of reconciliation, assigned to all believers. The message we must declare is that we can have a restored relationship with God through Jesus. The verse says this: "All this is from God, who reconciled us to himself through Christ and gave us the ministry of reconciliation."

Restorative justice is indeed founded on a Biblical-based paradigm that emphasizes the importance of reconciliation, healing, and restoration. The concept of restorative justice is rooted in the biblical principles of forgiveness, mercy, and justice. In the Old Testament, the concept of justice is central to God's character and His relationship with His people. Justice is not only about punishment, but also about restoring relationships, reconciling people to God and each other, and making things right.

In the New Testament, Jesus taught and modeled restorative justice in His interactions with individuals who were considered outcasts by society, such as the woman caught in adultery and the tax collector Zacchaeus. He demonstrated compassion and forgiveness, and He challenged the religious leaders of the time to consider the importance of mercy and grace.

The Apostle Paul also emphasized the importance of reconciliation and restoration in his letters to the early Christian communities. He called on them to forgive one another, to reconcile their differences, and to work together for the common good.

Restorative justice seeks to build on these biblical principles by providing a framework for addressing harm, restoring relationships, and promoting healing and reconciliation. Rather than focusing solely on punishment and retribution, restorative justice encourages offenders to take responsibility for their actions, to make amends for the harm they have caused, and to work toward repairing the harm done to the victim and the community.

In summary, restorative justice is grounded in the biblical call to the ministry of reconciliation, which emphasizes the importance of forgiveness, mercy, and justice in addressing harm and restoring relationships.

4. The ministry of reconciliation requires that we view man through the eyes of Jesus, rather than as the World views him.:

Jesus made the statement (John 3:17) that "God did not send His Son into the world to condemn the world, but that the world through Him might be saved." When He comes again, He will come in judgment upon those who refuse His offer of salvation. Until then, we must remember that mankind is so important to Jesus that He died for them (John 3:16).

The ministry of reconciliation is grounded in the belief that human beings are created in the image of God and that their worth and dignity must be recognized and affirmed. This means that we must view individuals through the eyes of Jesus, who saw them as valuable and worthy of love and redemption, regardless of their past actions.

In contrast, the world often views individuals based on their actions or social status, and can stigmatize and marginalize those who have been involved in the criminal justice system. This can create a cycle of shame and despair that can hinder their ability to make positive changes and reintegrate into society.

The restorative justice paradigm seeks to shift the focus from punishment and retribution to healing and restoration, both for victims and offenders. This requires us to see individuals not just as perpetrators of crime, but as human beings who have the potential to change and be restored to their communities.

By viewing individuals through the eyes of Jesus and embracing the restorative justice paradigm, we can promote healing, reconciliation, and transformation for all those impacted by crime.

5. As a result of his sin, what has Adam passed on to the human race?

"Physical and spiritual death for everyone."

Death has three distinct manifestations: 1) spiritual death or separation from God (Eph. 2:1,2; 4:18); 2) physical death (Heb. 9:27); and 3) eternal death (also known as the second death), which includes not only eternal separation from God, but eternal torment in the lake of fire (Rev. 20:11-15).

In Christian theology, it is believed that as a result of Adam's sin, he passed on the state of sinfulness to all of humanity. This state of sinfulness is commonly referred to as "original sin." The idea of original sin is based on the biblical account in the book of Genesis where Adam and Eve disobeyed God by eating the forbidden fruit from the tree of the knowledge of good and evil.

The concept of original sin teaches that as a result of Adam's disobedience, human nature has been corrupted and inclined towards sin. This means that all human beings are born with a natural tendency towards sin and a predisposition to rebel against God. This sin nature is said to affect every aspect of human life, including thoughts, emotions, and actions.

The Bible teaches that the only way to overcome this state of sinfulness is through faith in Jesus Christ. Through his death and resurrection, Jesus provides a way for human beings to be reconciled to God and to be set free from the power of sin. Restorative justice, therefore, is seen as a means of embodying the ministry of reconciliation by extending forgiveness and restoration to those who have committed offenses, just as Christ has done for us.

6. Although punishment is deserved, Jesus, the Great Mediator between God and man, brings restorative justice to the earth.

Rather than condemn the world "God was in Christ reconciling the world to Himself, not imputing their trespasses to them (2 Corinthians 5:19).

As the Bible teaches, all humans have sinned and fall short of the glory of God (Romans 3:23). The punishment for sin is death (Romans 6:23), but God, in His love and mercy, provided a way for humans to be reconciled to Him through the sacrifice of His son Jesus Christ (John 3:16).

Jesus' death on the cross provided a way for humans to be forgiven of their sins and restored to a right relationship with God. Through faith in Jesus, individuals can receive the forgiveness and reconciliation that He offers (Romans 5:10-11, 2 Corinthians 5:18-19).

In this sense, Jesus brings restorative justice to the earth by reconciling individuals to God and restoring relationships that have been broken by sin. This restorative justice is not limited to the spiritual realm, but can also be extended to the earthly realm through practices such as forgiveness, reconciliation, and restoration. In this way, restorative justice can be seen as an expression of Jesus' love and mercy towards humanity, as well as a way to bring healing and wholeness to broken individuals and communities.

7. The new justice of God is not retributive in nature, but redemptive because:

God's new justice does bring healing because of its redemptive nature. Notice how Paul described God's redemptive justice in Titus 2:14: "Our great God and Savior Jesus Christ, who gave Himself for us, that He might redeem us from every lawless deed and purify for Himself His own special people..."

The concept of restorative justice emphasizes repairing the harm caused by a crime rather than merely punishing the offender. In contrast to traditional retributive justice, which focuses on punishing the offender for breaking the law, restorative justice seeks to restore the harm caused by the offender's actions and promote healing and reconciliation between the offender, victim, and community.

In this sense, the new justice of God is not retributive but redemptive. The Bible teaches that God's justice is rooted in His love and mercy for humanity. Instead of simply punishing humanity for their sins, God seeks to redeem them through His Son Jesus Christ. Through His death and resurrection, Jesus paid the penalty for humanity's sins and offers the gift of salvation to all who repent and believe in Him.

As followers of Christ, we are called to imitate His example of restorative justice. This involves seeking the good of all parties involved, including the offender, victim, and community. Restorative justice recognizes the humanity of all individuals, including those who have committed crimes, and seeks to help them become fully restored members of society. This approach acknowledges that all individuals have inherent value and are capable of change and growth.

In summary, the new justice of God is redemptive, seeking to restore and reconcile all parties involved in a crime. This approach emphasizes love, mercy, and the potential for growth and transformation, rather than punishment and retribution.

8. God's new justice brings healing to relationships with God and the Community of man.

God's new justice, which is restorative in nature, seeks to bring healing and reconciliation to relationships between God and humanity, as well as among people. This is reflected in the life and teachings of Jesus, who taught his followers to love one another, to forgive their enemies, and to seek reconciliation with those they had wronged.

Through Jesus' death and resurrection, he made it possible for humanity to be reconciled to God and to one another. This reconciliation is not simply a matter of forgiving sins and moving on, but of restoring broken relationships and building new ones based on love, trust, and mutual respect.

In this way, restorative justice seeks to bring healing to the harm caused by crime, rather than simply punishing the offender. It recognizes the dignity and worth of every human being, and seeks to restore the harm done to the victim, the offender, and the community as a whole.

Restorative justice practices, such as victim-offender mediation and family group conferencing, provide opportunities for those affected by crime to come together, share their experiences, and work towards healing and reconciliation. These practices seek to empower victims, hold offenders accountable, and promote community healing and restoration.

Ultimately, the goal of restorative justice is not simply to punish offenders, but to create a more just and peaceful society, where relationships are characterized by love, forgiveness, and mutual respect, and where harm is transformed into healing and growth.

9. The restorative justice paradigm suggests that crime is an injury to:

The restorative justice paradigm suggests that crime is an injury to God, individuals, relationships, and the community, rather than just a violation of laws and rules. It views crime as a harm done to people and relationships, rather than simply as a violation of the state's laws and rules. It emphasizes repairing the harm done to victims and restoring relationships between the offender, victim, and the community, rather than focusing solely on punishing the offender.

In addition, crime causes injury to the criminal him/herself, when you consider all the opportunity costs associated with the criminal's choice to engage in illegal rather than legal and productive activities.

10. What is the goal of restorative justice?

The goal of restorative justice is to repair the harm caused by the crime, promote healing for the victim and community, and hold the offender accountable while giving them an opportunity to make amends and reintegrate into society. It focuses on addressing the root causes of the crime and finding ways to prevent future harm, rather than just punishing the offender. Restorative justice seeks to restore relationships and promote reconciliation between the parties involved, and to empower individuals and communities to take an active role in resolving conflicts and repairing harm.

11. Who accepts the responsibility for the administration of justice in the indigenous communities around the world?

In indigenous communities around the world, the responsibility for the administration of justice is often held by the community itself, rather than by external authorities. This approach to justice is rooted in the community's traditions, values, and cultural practices. Indigenous communities view justice not only as a response to crime or wrongdoing but also as a way of restoring relationships and promoting harmony within the community.

In these communities, the administration of justice is often carried out by a council of elders or other community members who are respected for their wisdom, knowledge, and experience. These individuals are selected based on their understanding of the community's customs and values and their ability to make fair and just decisions. The council may also include representatives from the victim's family and the offender's family, as well as other members of the community who are affected by the incident.

The process of administering justice in indigenous communities often involves dialogue and consensus-building rather than punishment. The goal is to restore the relationships that have been damaged by the wrongdoing and to find a resolution that benefits everyone involved. This may involve restitution, compensation, or other forms of reparation, as well as efforts to address the root causes of the problem and prevent similar incidents from occurring in the future.

However, the acceptance of the responsibility for the administration of justice in indigenous communities is not without its challenges. The traditional methods of justice often conflict with the legal systems imposed by colonial powers, leading to a lack of recognition and support from the government. Additionally, the use of traditional practices may not always be accepted by younger generations who have been exposed to different ways of thinking and may not fully understand the cultural significance of these practices.

Hence, the responsibility for the administration of justice in indigenous communities is an important aspect of maintaining cultural identity and promoting social harmony. It serves as a reminder that justice is not just about punishing offenders but also about healing relationships and promoting community well-being.

12. The community facilitates the healing process between the broken relationship caused by crime.

In the restorative justice paradigm, the community plays a critical role in facilitating the healing process between the broken relationship caused by crime. Rather than leaving the criminal justice process solely to the legal system, the community takes responsibility for addressing the harm caused by crime and promoting healing.

The community's involvement in the restorative justice process is important for several reasons. First, it helps to rebuild trust between the victim, offender, and the community. When the community comes together to address the harm caused by the crime, it sends a powerful message of solidarity and support to both the victim and offender. This can help to promote a sense of community and foster a sense of accountability for everyone involved.

Second, the community's involvement in restorative justice can help to promote healing and closure for the victim. In traditional criminal justice systems, victims are often left feeling isolated and powerless. However, when the community comes together to support the victim and hold the offender accountable, it can help the victim to regain a sense of control over their life and promote healing.

Finally, the community's involvement in restorative justice can help to reduce recidivism rates. By providing the offender with support and guidance, the community can help to address the underlying issues that may have contributed to their criminal behavior. This can help to reduce the likelihood of future offenses and promote rehabilitation.

Thus, the community's involvement in restorative justice is critical for promoting healing, accountability, and rehabilitation. By working together to address the harm caused by crime, the community can play an important role in building a safer and more just society.

13. Punishment is not restorative if it is done out of revenge or through retribution.

Restorative justice focuses on repairing harm and restoring relationships between victims, offenders, and the community. Punishment, on the other hand, often focuses on retribution and deterrence rather than restoration. Punishment can be a necessary response to criminal behavior, but it is not inherently restorative.

When punishment is done out of revenge or a desire for retribution, it can perpetuate cycles of harm and violence. Instead of addressing the root causes of the behavior and working to repair the harm done, punitive responses may simply escalate the conflict and create new victims. Punishment that is not focused on restoration can also perpetuate societal inequalities and injustices by disproportionately affecting marginalized and oppressed populations.

Restorative justice, on the other hand, offers an alternative to punitive responses by prioritizing the needs of the victim, the offender, and the community. This approach seeks to understand the underlying causes of criminal behavior and to address the harm done through a process of dialogue, accountability, and repair.

Restorative justice can provide healing and closure for victims, as they are given the opportunity to share their experiences and have a say in the resolution of the harm done to them. Offenders are also given the chance to take responsibility for their actions and to make amends for the harm they have caused. The community is involved in the process, and is given the opportunity to address underlying issues and to work towards preventing future harm.

In conclusion, punishment is not restorative if it is done out of revenge or through retribution. Restorative justice offers an alternative approach that focuses on repairing harm, restoring relationships, and preventing future harm.

14. What are some of the questions that can be addressed in a restorative justice paradigm for ministry?

a) What is God's view of justice? a) The concept of justice is central to the character of God as described in the Bible. According to the Bible, God's view of justice is that it is impartial, fair, and righteous. God's justice is not influenced by any human biases or prejudices, and it is based on his unchanging moral standards. God's justice is also described as restorative, meaning that it seeks to repair the damage caused by wrongdoing and restore right relationships.

b) What does He expect of us? b) God expects us to pursue justice and righteousness in all areas of our lives. This includes treating others fairly, advocating for the oppressed and marginalized, and working towards systems and structures that promote justice and equity. The Bible also emphasizes the importance of mercy and forgiveness, even in the context of justice.

How should we view the unrighteous acts of the offenders?

c) As Christians, we are called to hate sin but love sinners. This means that we should condemn and resist unrighteous acts, but also seek to offer grace, forgiveness, and the opportunity for redemption to those who have committed them. We should strive to see offenders through God's eyes, recognizing that they too are made in his image and are in need of his love and mercy.

d) Does biblical justice include something other than punishment of wrongs committed against God and man? d) Yes, biblical justice includes more than just punishment for wrongs committed against God and man. It also includes restorative justice, which seeks to repair the harm caused by wrongdoing and restore relationships between the offender and the victim. Restorative justice emphasizes the importance of accountability, but also focuses on healing and reconciliation.

e) How do I minister through a biblical paradigm of justice? e) To minister through a biblical paradigm of justice, it is important to first cultivate a deep understanding of God's character and his view of justice. This can be done through prayer, study of scripture, and engagement with the broader Christian community. From there, it is important to seek out opportunities to advocate for justice and mercy in our communities and to work towards building systems and structures that reflect God's vision of justice. This can involve supporting organizations that are doing this work, volunteering time and resources, and engaging in advocacy and activism. Ultimately, ministering through a biblical paradigm of justice involves a commitment to love, mercy, and restoration, even in the face of great injustice and pain.

Furthermore,

Restorative justice is a framework for addressing harm and promoting healing in relationships, communities, and systems. In a ministry context, restorative justice can be applied to a variety of situations, such as:

1. How can we respond to harm caused within our faith community in a way that promotes accountability, healing, and reconciliation?
2. How can we address the root causes of injustice in our society and work towards systemic change?
3. How can we create a culture of empathy, compassion, and forgiveness within our faith community?
4. How can we support those who have experienced trauma and help them to find healing and wholeness?
5. How can we engage in dialogue with those who hold different beliefs or have been harmed by our community, with a focus on understanding and relationship-building?
6. How can we integrate restorative justice principles into our worship and spiritual practices, such as confession, forgiveness, and reconciliation?
7. How can we work towards repairing harm caused by historical injustices, such as colonization or racism?
8. How can we support individuals who have been impacted by the criminal justice system, including those who have been incarcerated and their families?
9. How can we promote a restorative approach to conflict resolution within our faith community and in our wider society?
10. How can we work collaboratively with other organizations and faith communities to promote restorative justice principles and practices in our communities?

15. What did Job discover about the nature of God's justice?

Apparently, Job discovered that God's justice was more complicated than simply receiving punishment for wrongs he had done and blessings for living a righteous life.

Job is a book in the Hebrew Bible that tells the story of a man named Job who experiences great suffering and loss. Throughout the book, Job struggles to understand why he is suffering and questions the justice of God. In the end, Job has an encounter with God that leads him to a deeper understanding of God's justice.

One of the key things that Job discovers is that God's justice is not always predictable or easily understood. Job had assumed that if he was righteous, he would be rewarded, and if he sinned, he would be punished. However, his suffering seemed to contradict this understanding of justice. Through his conversations with his friends and with God, Job begins to realize that God's justice is more complex than a simple cause-and-effect relationship between behavior and outcome.

Job also discovers that God's justice is rooted in God's wisdom and sovereignty. Job realizes that God's ways are beyond his understanding, and that God is not obligated to explain or justify his actions. Job humbly submits to God's authority, recognizing that God's justice is ultimately trustworthy and good, even if it is not always easy to understand.

Consequently, Job's experience leads him to a deeper appreciation of God's justice, which is not simply about rewarding the righteous and punishing the wicked, but is rooted in God's wisdom, sovereignty, and goodness.

16. Discover within Job 40:8 two questions that God asked Job that suggest he knew little about the justice of God?

a) Wilt thou also disannul my judgment?

b) Wilt thou condemn Me?

In Job 40:8, God speaks to Job and says, "Would you discredit my justice? Would you condemn me to justify yourself?" These two questions suggest that Job had a limited understanding of the justice of God and that he had been trying to justify himself rather than trust in God's wisdom and sovereignty.

The first question, "Would you discredit my justice?", implies that Job may have been questioning the fairness or goodness of God's justice. Job had experienced great suffering and loss, and he may have been struggling to reconcile his understanding of justice with his own experiences. God's question challenges Job to trust in God's justice, even when it is difficult to understand.

The second question, "Would you condemn me to justify yourself?", suggests that Job may have been trying to justify his own righteousness in the face of his suffering. Job had maintained his innocence throughout his trials, and he may have been tempted to criticize God's justice in order to make his own case. God's question challenges Job to trust in God's righteousness and sovereignty, even when it challenges his own sense of justice.

Together, these two questions remind Job that God's justice is not limited by human understanding or perspective. Job is called to trust in God's wisdom and righteousness, even when it challenges his own assumptions and beliefs.

17. How did Job respond after God revealed His concept of justice in chapter 42?

In the book of Job, after Job had endured immense suffering and loss, he questioned God's justice and righteousness. He had argued with his friends and challenged God to explain his situation. God finally responded to Job's challenge by speaking to him directly out of a whirlwind in chapters 38-41, revealing His power, knowledge, and wisdom.

In chapter 42, Job responds to God's revelation by acknowledging his own limited understanding and submitting to God's sovereignty. He says, "I know that you can do all things, and that no purpose of yours can be thwarted... I had heard of you by the hearing of the ear, but now my eye sees you" (Job 42:2,5). Job confesses that he had spoken without understanding and repents in dust and ashes.

God then rebukes Job's friends for their misguided attempts to explain Job's suffering and instructs them to offer burnt offerings and have Job pray for them, indicating that Job's faithfulness and repentance had led to his restoration.

Hence, Job's response to God's concept of justice is one of humility and submission, acknowledging that he did not fully comprehend God's ways and trusting in His sovereignty.

Job did repent and admit that he did not understand or know God's concept of justice.

18. When Job saw the righteousness of God, he also saw the justice of God.

Job's story is one of suffering, loss, and ultimately, redemption. Throughout his trials, Job never lost his faith in God, but he did question the justice of his situation. He demanded an explanation for his suffering, and his friends offered various theories, including that Job must have sinned and brought his misfortune upon himself.

However, in the end, God spoke directly to Job and revealed his ultimate plan and purpose. Job was humbled by the experience and realized that he could not fully comprehend the justice and righteousness of God. He acknowledged that God's ways were beyond his understanding and that he had spoken about things he did not understand.

Therefore, when Job saw the righteousness of God, he also saw the justice of God. He recognized that God's justice was not necessarily based on the human understanding of fairness and punishment. Instead, God's justice was rooted in his ultimate plan and purpose, which was beyond human comprehension.

Job's story demonstrates that justice is not always straightforward, and the human understanding of justice is limited. Ultimately, justice is grounded in the divine plan and purpose, and it is only through faith and trust in God that we can truly understand it.

19. It is important to know that God's attributes are one.

In Christianity, God's attributes are often described as being unified or inseparable. This means that each attribute, such as God's love, mercy, justice, and righteousness, are not separate or distinct qualities, but rather they are interconnected and flow from God's essential nature.

For example, God's justice is not arbitrary or separate from God's love and mercy. Instead, God's justice is grounded in his love and mercy and works in harmony with these attributes. God's justice is not punitive, but restorative and seeks to bring about the healing and redemption of individuals and society.

Similarly, God's righteousness is not a separate attribute from his justice, but rather flows from it. God's righteousness is the standard by which justice is measured and the foundation of his dealings with humanity.

Thus, the unity of God's attributes is a fundamental concept in Christian theology and helps to shape our understanding of God's character and actions in the world.

20. In scripture, Jesus is spoken of both, the justice and righteousness of God.

In scripture, Jesus is referred to as both the justice and righteousness of God because he embodies these attributes in his teachings and actions. Jesus taught about the importance of justice and how it should be carried out with compassion and mercy. He challenged the corrupt authorities of his time and defended the marginalized and oppressed.

Jesus also lived a life of perfect righteousness, obeying God's laws and fulfilling the prophecies of the Old Testament. Through his death and resurrection, Jesus provided a way for humanity to be reconciled with God and receive salvation. This act was both just and righteous, as it fulfilled the requirement of justice for sin while demonstrating God's love and mercy for his creation.

Therefore, when Jesus is referred to as the justice and righteousness of God, it highlights the fact that he embodies these attributes fully and perfectly. It also emphasizes the importance of justice and righteousness in the Christian faith and how they are central to understanding God's character and plan for humanity.

21. When justice came to the nations, it brought the righteousness of God, which reconciles those who receive Jesus Christ as Savior.

The concept of justice and righteousness is a common theme throughout the Bible, both in the Old and New Testaments. The justice of God is often described as a characteristic that is synonymous with righteousness, mercy, and compassion. In the Old Testament, justice was typically administered through the law, and the consequences of disobedience were severe. However, God's ultimate goal was always to restore and reconcile His people to Himself.

In the New Testament, the justice and righteousness of God were fully revealed through Jesus Christ. Jesus came to fulfill the law and to reconcile sinners to God through His death on the cross. The Apostle Paul wrote in Romans 3:21-26, "But now apart from the law the righteousness of God has been made known, to which the Law and the Prophets testify. This righteousness is given through faith in Jesus Christ to all who believe. There is no difference between Jew and Gentile, for all have sinned and fall short of the glory of God, and all are justified freely by his grace through the redemption that came by Christ Jesus. God presented Christ as a sacrifice of atonement, through the shedding of his blood—to be received by faith. He did this to demonstrate his righteousness, because in his forbearance he had left the sins committed beforehand unpunished— he did it to demonstrate his righteousness at the present time, so as to be just and the one who justifies those who have faith in Jesus."

Through faith in Jesus Christ, God's justice and righteousness are revealed in a way that reconciles us to Him. This reconciliation brings about a transformation of our lives, as we are empowered to live in a way that is pleasing to God and brings about justice and righteousness in our relationships and communities. Ultimately, the justice and righteousness of God are inseparable and are fully revealed through Jesus Christ.

22. Discover within 2 Corinthians 5:18 the responsibility of every believer.

2 Corinthians 5:18 states, "All this is from God, who reconciled us to himself through Christ and gave us the ministry of reconciliation." This verse highlights the responsibility of every believer to be involved in the ministry of reconciliation.

The passage emphasizes that it is God who has initiated reconciliation through Jesus Christ. As believers, we have received this gift of reconciliation and are now called to extend it to others. This involves actively participating in the work of bringing people into a restored relationship with God and with one another.

The phrase "ministry of reconciliation" means that believers are called to be ambassadors of Christ, working towards the restoration of relationships and the healing of brokenness. This can take many forms, including sharing the gospel with others, seeking to reconcile broken relationships, working for social justice, and demonstrating love and compassion towards others.

The responsibility of every believer is not just to receive the gift of reconciliation but to actively participate in extending it to others. This requires a commitment to living out our faith in practical ways, both individually and collectively as the body of Christ. It is a call to be agents of change in a broken world, working towards the restoration of all things through the power of the Holy Spirit.

Furthermore, we have been given the ministry of reconciliation. In other words, as ambassadors for Christ, we have the responsibility of bringing others to Christ so they can reconcile with God.

23. Restoration is reflected in the Law that was given in the Old Testament, and the new commandment Jesus gave in the New Testament.

In the Old Testament, the Law included provisions for restitution and restoration for victims of crime. For example, Exodus 22:1 state, "If a man steals an ox or a sheep and slaughters it or sells it, he must pay back five head of cattle for the ox and four sheep for the sheep." This shows that the offender had to not only return the stolen property but also provide additional compensation for the harm caused to the victim.

In the New Testament, Jesus gave a new commandment to his disciples in John 13:34, "A new commandment I give to you, that you love one another: just as I have loved you, you also are to love one another." This commandment emphasizes the importance of love and forgiveness in relationships, and is reflected in the principles of restorative justice which aim to repair harm and restore relationships.

Furthermore, the ultimate act of restoration is seen in the death and resurrection of Jesus Christ. Through his sacrifice, he made it possible for individuals to be restored to a right relationship with God, and to experience healing and reconciliation in their relationships with others. This concept is central to the Christian faith and underlies the principles of restorative justice, which seek to restore broken relationships and promote healing and reconciliation.

24. What purpose did the Law serve? (Galatians 3:24):

Wherefore the law was our schoolmaster to bring us unto Christ, that we might be justified by faith

Galatians 3:24 states, "So the law was our guardian until Christ came that we might be justified by faith." The purpose of the Law was to serve as a guardian or tutor, guiding the Israelites and teaching them about God's standards of righteousness. The Law revealed God's moral and ethical standards and demonstrated humanity's inability to perfectly keep them. It exposed the need for a savior and pointed towards Jesus Christ, who fulfilled the Law and made a way for justification by faith. The Law also served as a temporary measure until the coming of Christ, who established a new covenant and fulfilled the requirements of the Law. Therefore, the Law served to reveal humanity's need for redemption, guide them in righteousness, and ultimately point towards Jesus Christ as the solution to the problem of sin.

A schoolmaster/tutor in ancient Greek culture would accompany the children in his care, instructing and disciplining them when necessary. The law was like a schoolmaster/tutor which, by showing us our sins, was escorting us to Christ.

25. When the Word of God became flesh and lived among us, the consummation of the justice of God in the earth yielded righteousness.

The statement highlights the idea that when Jesus Christ, who is referred to as the "Word of God," came to live among human beings, it marked the ultimate fulfillment of God's justice on earth. In other words, God's justice was made complete and perfect through Jesus Christ, who through his life, death, and resurrection, reconciled humanity to God and made it possible for people to receive forgiveness and salvation.

The justice of God is a fundamental aspect of God's character, which requires that all wrongdoing is punished and righteousness is upheld. The law of God, as revealed in the Old Testament, serves as a standard for righteousness and justice, but it also highlights the impossibility of human beings being able to perfectly keep the law. As a result, humanity became separated from God due to sin and was in need of redemption.

Through Jesus Christ, however, God's justice was satisfied, and the gap between humanity and God was bridged. Christ's death on the cross paid the penalty for sin, and his resurrection defeated death, which is the ultimate consequence of sin. As a result, those who believe in Jesus Christ and follow him can experience the righteousness of God and be reconciled to God.

In summary, the statement implies that the justice of God finds its ultimate fulfillment in the person of Jesus Christ, who through his life, death, and resurrection, reconciled humanity to God and made it possible for people to experience the righteousness of God.

26. The law of "lex talionis" was given to limit the revenges of a people without Christ.

The "lex talionis" is a Latin term that translates to "law of retaliation" or "law of retribution." It is often associated with the Old Testament law of "an eye for an eye, a tooth for a tooth" found in Exodus 21:24, Leviticus 24:20, and Deuteronomy 19:21. This law was given to the ancient Israelites to regulate the concept of justice in their society, particularly in relation to crimes committed against one another.

The law of "lex talionis" sought to limit the revenge of a people without Christ by instituting a proportionate punishment for the harm done. In essence, it prevented individuals from taking excessive vengeance on others and encouraged them to seek justice through legal means. For example, if someone caused harm to another person, they were required to compensate them in a proportionate manner, rather than inflicting greater harm or taking excessive revenge.

However, the "lex talionis" was not perfect, and it had limitations. It did not address the underlying causes of the crimes committed or seek to restore relationships between offenders and victims. It was primarily concerned with ensuring justice was served by punishing the offender.

With the coming of Christ, the concept of justice was transformed from retribution to restoration. Jesus taught the importance of forgiveness, mercy, and love, and He demonstrated these qualities in His own life and ministry. Through His death and resurrection, Jesus provided a way for all people to be reconciled with God and with one another.

In summary, while the "lex talionis" served a purpose in regulating justice in ancient Israel, it was limited in its ability to address the underlying issues and restore relationships. Through Christ, the concept of justice was transformed into one of restoration, emphasizing forgiveness, mercy, and love as the means to bring about reconciliation between individuals and with God.

27. The law of retaliation began to teach that revenge was not part of God's justice, and that punishment did not yield righteousness.

The law of retaliation, also known as "lex talionis," was a principle of justice that was common in many ancient cultures, including the ancient Near East. It was a law that allowed for retaliation in kind, that is, "an eye for an eye" and "a tooth for a tooth." This law was given to limit the revenges of a people without Christ and to ensure that justice was served in a fair and proportionate manner.

However, with the coming of Christ, the law of retaliation began to be seen in a new light. Jesus taught that revenge was not part of God's justice and that punishment did not yield righteousness. Instead, He called for forgiveness and reconciliation, and taught that the greatest commandment was to love God and love our neighbors as ourselves.

The apostle Paul also emphasized the importance of forgiveness and reconciliation in his teachings. In his letter to the Romans, he wrote, "Do not repay anyone evil for evil. Be careful to do what is right in the eyes of everyone. If it is possible, as far as it depends on you, live at peace with everyone" (Romans 12:17-18). Paul also wrote to the Corinthians that "God was reconciling the world to himself in Christ, not counting people's sins against them" (2 Corinthians 5:19).

In light of these teachings, it is clear that the law of retaliation was given to limit revenge in a world without Christ, but that the coming of Christ brought a new way of thinking about justice and righteousness. Forgiveness and reconciliation became the central focus, and the law of retaliation was seen as a limited and imperfect means of achieving justice.

28. Jesus came to fulfill the Law, and to provide a higher standard for those needing restoration.

The concept of restoration has been a part of God's plan since the beginning of time, as seen in the Law given to the Israelites in the Old Testament. However, the people's inability to keep the Law perfectly revealed the need for a higher standard and a means of true restoration. This is where Jesus Christ comes in.

Jesus came not to abolish the Law, but to fulfill it (Matthew 5:17). He provided the perfect example of righteousness and obedience to God's will, serving as the ultimate sacrifice for the forgiveness of sins and offering a path to true restoration. Through faith in Jesus, believers can experience reconciliation with God and the transformation necessary to live a life of righteousness.

Furthermore, Jesus elevated the concept of restoration beyond just physical or material compensation to include emotional and spiritual healing. In the Sermon on the Mount, He taught that those who have been wronged should not seek revenge but rather seek to love and serve their enemies (Matthew 5:43-48). He also emphasized the importance of forgiveness, instructing His followers to forgive others as they have been forgiven by God (Matthew 6:14-15).

In this way, Jesus provided a higher standard of justice and restoration that goes beyond mere legalistic compliance with the Law. He showed that true restoration involves not only the settling of debts and the restoration of relationships but also the healing of emotional and spiritual wounds. Through faith in Him, believers can experience the transformative power of God's love and grace, leading to true restoration and righteousness.

29. The fulfillment of justice was not intended to give offenders what they deserved, but to move them towards restoration through the power of love.

Romans 6:23 describes two inexorable absolutes: 1) spiritual death is the paycheck for every man's sin; and 2) eternal life is a loving free gift God gives undeserving sinners who believe in His Son.

The concept of justice in Christianity is closely related to restoration, which involves the transformation of the offender and the healing of the community affected by the offense. Jesus came to fulfill the law of justice, not by simply punishing offenders, but by providing a higher standard for restoration. The ultimate goal of justice, therefore, is not to give offenders what they deserve, but to restore them through the power of love.

Jesus demonstrated this approach to justice in his teachings and actions. For example, when the Pharisees brought to him a woman caught in adultery and asked if she should be stoned according to the Law of Moses, Jesus did not condemn her, but instead offered forgiveness and restoration (John 8:1-11). He also taught that forgiveness should be offered not just seven times, but seventy-seven times (Matthew 18:21-22).

Furthermore, Jesus' death and resurrection provided the ultimate demonstration of restorative justice. Through his sacrifice, he provided a way for offenders to be reconciled to God and restored to their rightful place in the community. This is exemplified in 2 Corinthians 5:18-19, which states, "All this is from God, who reconciled us to himself through Christ and gave us the ministry of reconciliation: that God was reconciling the world to himself in Christ, not counting people's sins against them."

In summary, the fulfillment of justice in Christianity is not about punishment or revenge, but about restoration through love and forgiveness. This approach requires a shift in focus from the offender to the victim and the community, and a willingness to work towards healing and reconciliation.

30. What is the goal of restorative justice ministry?

Most ministries today do NOT address all the parties that are affected by the crime. They either focus on the offender while neglecting the victim and community or they focus only on the victim. Complete healing and restoration only occur when the injuries to all parties are addressed.

The goal of restorative justice ministry is to promote healing, reconciliation, and restoration for all parties affected by crime or harm. This approach recognizes that crime is not just a violation of law, but a violation of relationships and the community. Therefore, restorative justice ministry seeks to repair the harm caused by crime by bringing together the victim, the offender, and the community to address the needs of all involved.

Restorative justice ministry aims to shift the focus from punishment to restoration, offering a more holistic approach to justice that takes into account the emotional, psychological, and spiritual needs of all parties involved. This involves creating a safe space for open dialogue, empathy, and understanding, and facilitating a process of healing and transformation that leads to greater accountability, responsibility, and meaningful restitution.

The goal of restorative justice ministry is not just to resolve conflicts, but to promote social justice and community well-being. This means addressing the root causes of crime and working towards systemic change that promotes equity, fairness, and respect for all individuals. Restorative justice ministry also seeks to empower individuals and communities to take an active role in shaping the justice system and promoting a more compassionate and restorative approach to justice.

Therefore, the goal of restorative justice ministry is to foster healing, reconciliation, and restoration for all involved, promoting a more just and peaceful society for all.

31. God requires that we love one another, as Jesus loved us, and to love our neighbor as ourselves.

This statement is derived from two key teachings of Jesus. In John 13:34-35, Jesus says, "A new commandment I give to you, that you love one another: just as I have loved you, you also are to love one another. By this all people will know that you are my disciples, if you have love for one another." This commandment to love one another is rooted in Jesus' own love for his disciples, which was selfless, sacrificial, and unconditional.

The second teaching comes from Mark 12:31, where Jesus answers a question about which commandment is the most important. He replies, "The most important is, 'Hear, O Israel: The Lord our God, the Lord is one. And you shall love the Lord your God with all your heart and with all your soul and with all your mind and with all your strength.' The second is this: 'You shall love your neighbor as yourself.' There is no other commandment greater than these."

Together, these teachings call us to love others with the same love that God has shown us, and to love our neighbors as ourselves. This love is not based on merit or worthiness, but is a reflection of the unconditional love that God has for all people. As Christians, we are called to live out this love in our relationships with others, seeking to show kindness, compassion, and forgiveness to all, regardless of their background, beliefs, or actions. Ultimately, the goal of this love is to bring healing, restoration, and reconciliation to broken relationships and a hurting world.

32. Our neighbor is the prisoner who offended, the victim who is brokenhearted, and the community which was blinded by a need for revenge.:

In the Bible, Jesus tells us to love our neighbor as ourselves. This commandment includes all people, even those who have committed crimes and are incarcerated. When we show love and compassion to those who have offended, we are fulfilling this commandment and demonstrating the love of Christ.

The victim of a crime is also our neighbor, and we are called to show them love and support as they heal from the trauma they have experienced. Restorative justice seeks to bring healing to both the offender and the victim, recognizing that both have been affected by the crime in different ways.

Furthermore, when a community is affected by crime, it is important to remember that the members of that community are also our neighbors. Restorative justice principles aim to involve the community in the process of addressing the harm caused by the crime and developing solutions that promote healing and prevention.

Ultimately, restorative justice ministry recognizes that all people are created in the image of God and have inherent dignity and worth. By loving our neighbor, including those who have offended, those who have been victimized, and the wider community, we can work towards a more just and compassionate society.

33. Biblical justice is restoration through righteousness to all who receive Christ.

Paul described this view in Romans 3:22: " ... the righteousness of God, through faith in Jesus Christ, to all and on all who believe."

Biblical justice can be defined as the restoration of what is broken or wrong, to bring about righteousness in all aspects of life. The ultimate source of justice is God, and He has revealed His perfect standard of justice in the Bible. The Bible teaches that justice is an important part of God's character, and that He desires justice for all people. This includes both the victim and the offender.

Restoration is the key to biblical justice. When a wrong has been committed, restoration involves making things right between the offender and the victim, and also between the offender and God. This restoration is made possible through the sacrifice of Jesus Christ, who paid the penalty for our sins and made it possible for us to be reconciled to God.

Restorative justice ministry, therefore, seeks to bring about this restoration through various means such as restitution, reconciliation, and rehabilitation. It seeks to involve all parties affected by the crime, including the offender, the victim, and the community.

The goal of restorative justice ministry is not only to hold offenders accountable for their actions but also to bring about healing and reconciliation for all involved. It aims to address the root causes of crime and to provide opportunities for offenders to take responsibility for their actions, make amends, and move towards a better future.

In summary, biblical justice is about restoring what is broken or wrong to bring about righteousness for all involved, and this is made possible through the sacrifice of Jesus Christ. Restorative justice ministry seeks to bring about this restoration by involving all parties affected by the crime and providing opportunities for healing, reconciliation, and rehabilitation.

34. Which epistle of the Apostle Paul serves as a fine example of restorative justice? Philemon

Paul's letter to Philemon serves as a fine example of restorative justice.

The epistle of Philemon serves as a fine example of restorative justice. In this letter, Paul writes to Philemon, a slave owner, regarding his slave Onesimus who had run away and then come to faith in Christ through Paul's ministry. Paul writes to appeal to Philemon to receive Onesimus back not just as a slave, but as a brother in Christ.

Paul could have simply ordered Philemon to release Onesimus, or could have taken legal action against him for mistreating his slave. Instead, Paul takes a restorative justice approach by appealing to Philemon's Christian values and urging him to do what is right, not just what is legally required.

In his letter, Paul acknowledges that Onesimus had wronged Philemon, and offers to make things right by paying for any damage caused by his escape. He also reminds Philemon that they are brothers in Christ, and that he should receive Onesimus back as he would receive Paul himself.

This approach emphasizes reconciliation and restoration rather than punishment and retribution. It shows how restorative justice can be applied even in situations that involve societal structures of oppression, such as slavery.

35. List the concepts found in the epistle to Philemon that demonstrate the principles of restorative justice.:

a) the concepts of rehabilitation (vs. 10, 16),

b) restoration (vs. 17),

c) and restitution (vs. 18-19).

Until I read this letter to Philemon, I didn't' realize what a talented leader Paul was. I knew he was a great theologian, an incredible author, a successful businessman (tentmaker) and church planter, and a compelling speaker.

But in this letter, we see his leadership skills as he competently addressed the situation. He left the decision completely up to Philemon, and didn't trample all over his rights as the slave's owner. And yet, as we see throughout this letter, Paul arranged things so it would be very difficult for Philemon to say no without losing face among his brothers and sisters in Christ.

The epistle to Philemon demonstrates several principles of restorative justice, including:

1. Forgiveness - Paul encourages Philemon to forgive his runaway slave, Onesimus, who has since become a Christian.
2. Reconciliation - Paul writes to Philemon, asking him to receive Onesimus back as a brother in Christ, rather than as a slave.
3. Restitution - Paul offers to pay any debts or damages owed by Onesimus to Philemon, as a way of making things right between them.
4. Healing - Paul acknowledges the hurt and pain caused by Onesimus' actions, but seeks to bring healing and restoration through forgiveness and reconciliation.
5. Community involvement - Paul asks the church in Colossae to support Philemon and Onesimus in their journey towards reconciliation, showing the importance of community involvement in restorative justice.

Thus, the epistle to Philemon demonstrates how restorative justice principles can be applied in personal relationships, leading to reconciliation and restoration.

36. What crime did the slave, Onesimus, commit against his owner, Philemon? Onesimus stole from his master and ran away.

This very heart-warming letter was written by Paul for the purpose of interceding for the runaway slave who had become a faithful Christian. He not only was pleading for mercy for him from his master, Philemon - he was also reminding Philemon of his duty as a fellow Christian toward this man.

37. What course of action did Paul recommend to Onesimus after he became a Christian?

It was agreed that Onesimus would return to Philemon to make amends, even though under Roman law he could face the death penalty.

In the Epistle to Philemon, Paul recommended that Onesimus should return to his master, Philemon, and reconcile with him. Paul urged Philemon to welcome Onesimus back not as a slave, but as a brother in Christ. He offered to personally pay for any wrong that Onesimus had committed, and asked Philemon to receive him with forgiveness and love. Paul's message was that true restoration and justice can only be achieved through forgiveness and reconciliation, rather than punishment and retribution.

This was a volatile situation. Onesimus was a changed man, but he must have been nervous about going back to Philemon. After all Roman law gave slave owners the right to brand the forehead of runaway slaves, lock them in chains, or simply execute them. Onesimus knew he deserved any one of these punishments because he had not only run away from Philemon, but had stolen from him as well. Anything could happen.

38. The Epistle to Philemon is Paul's plea that Onesimus no longer be viewed as a runaway slave, but rather as a brother beloved.

If a man is a stranger, I might make him my slave. But how can I make my brother be my slave? In this relationship as brothers and not slaves, Paul effectively abolished the sting of the "master-slave" relationship.

In the ancient Roman world, slavery was a common institution and it was not uncommon for slaves to run away from their masters. When Onesimus, a slave of Philemon, ran away and later met Paul, he became a Christian and a changed man. Paul recognized that Onesimus was now a brother in Christ and not just a slave, and as such, he encouraged Philemon to see him in the same light.

In his letter to Philemon, Paul writes in verse 16, "no longer as a slave but more than a slave, a beloved brother, especially to me but how much more to you, both in the flesh and in the Lord." This statement makes it clear that Paul is urging Philemon to see Onesimus as more than just a slave, but as a fellow Christian and beloved brother.

Furthermore, Paul also offered to take responsibility for any debt that Onesimus owed to Philemon, indicating that he was willing to make things right between them and reconcile them as brothers in Christ.

Thence, Paul's message in the Epistle to Philemon is one of reconciliation and restoration, urging Philemon to see Onesimus not as a slave who had wronged him, but as a brother who had been transformed by the power of Christ.

39. While the world pursues power and glory, Christians are to pursue the way of the Cross — the way of forgiveness, restoration and love.

The way of the Cross, as exemplified by Jesus Christ, is a way of sacrificial love and humility. It is a path that goes against the values of the world, which often prioritize power, prestige, and personal gain. Instead of seeking these things, Christians are called to imitate Christ by putting the needs of others before their own and seeking restoration and reconciliation rather than revenge.

Forgiveness is a key aspect of the way of the Cross. Just as Christ forgave those who crucified Him, Christians are called to forgive those who have wronged them. This does not mean that justice should not be sought or that wrongs should be ignored, but rather that forgiveness should be extended even to those who do not deserve it. In this way, forgiveness can lead to restoration and healing, both for the individual who forgives and for the one who is forgiven.

Restoration is also a crucial aspect of the way of the Cross. Rather than seeking revenge or punishment, Christians are called to seek restoration and reconciliation with those who have wronged them. This means working towards repairing relationships and restoring the dignity of those who have been hurt. Restoration requires humility and a willingness to admit fault and seek forgiveness.

Love is the foundation of the way of the Cross. Christ's sacrificial love on the Cross is the ultimate example of love in action, and Christians are called to love others in the same way. This means seeking the good of others, even at personal cost, and putting the needs of others before one's own desires. Love is a transformative force that can bring healing, restoration, and reconciliation.

In summary, the way of the Cross is a path of forgiveness, restoration, and love. It is a way that goes against the values of the world, but leads to true healing and transformation. As Christians, we are called to imitate Christ in all things, including the way we interact with others. By following the way of the Cross, we can be agents of God's love and restoration in the world.

40. No matter what a person has done in the past, God calls them to Himself and offers them the hope of restorative justice.

Paul recognized this fact when he recorded these words in First Timothy 1:15: "Christ Jesus came into the world to save sinners, of whom I am chief." Paul had been a persecutor and murderer of the followers of Christ, but God called him to Himself and offered him the hope of restorative justice.

The message of the gospel is one of hope and redemption. It is a message that God loves us, despite our failures and sins, and desires to restore us to a right relationship with Him. This hope is available to all people, no matter what they have done in the past.

Throughout the Bible, we see examples of individuals who were given a second chance by God. David, for example, committed adultery and murder, but when he repented, God forgave him and restored him to his position as king. The apostle Paul, who persecuted Christians before his conversion, went on to become one of the greatest evangelists in history.

God's desire for restorative justice is seen in His provision of a way for our sins to be forgiven through Jesus Christ. When we repent and turn to Him, He forgives us and begins the process of restoring us to a right relationship with Him. This process may involve discipline and correction, but it is ultimately for our good and His glory.

As Christians, we are called to extend this message of restorative justice to others. We are called to love our neighbors and to seek to restore those who have been broken by sin and injustice. This may involve advocating for the rights of the oppressed, providing support to victims of crime, and working towards reconciliation between offenders and their victims.

In all of our efforts towards restorative justice, we must remember that it is only through the power of God's love and grace that true restoration can take place. We are not called to be judges or to seek revenge, but to extend the same forgiveness and mercy that we have received from God to others.

41. The forgiveness granted by God and by others is what makes restoration possible.

Forgiveness is an essential component of restorative justice because it allows for healing and reconciliation to take place. When someone has wronged another person, the relationship between them is damaged, and forgiveness is necessary for that relationship to be restored. Without forgiveness, the wronged person may hold onto anger, bitterness, and resentment towards the offender, preventing any chance of restoration.

God's forgiveness is offered freely to all who come to Him in repentance, acknowledging their wrongdoing and asking for His forgiveness. This forgiveness is not based on our own merit or worthiness but on God's grace and love for us. Similarly, when someone wrongs us, forgiving them is an act of grace and love, not based on their merit or worthiness, but on our desire to restore the relationship and move forward in love and reconciliation.

In the context of restorative justice, forgiveness allows both the offender and the victim to move towards healing and restoration. The offender can acknowledge their wrongdoing, seek forgiveness, and work towards making amends and rebuilding trust. The victim can choose to forgive and release their anger and bitterness towards the offender, allowing them to move forward in healing and reconciliation. Overall, forgiveness is a crucial aspect of restorative justice as it allows for the possibility of restoration and healing for all parties involved.

CHAPTER VII
THE RESTORATIVE JUSTICE MINISTRY
PARADIGM

1. Although the primary goal of restorative justice ministry is the regeneration of the offender, other issues concerning their crime and the impact of that behavior need to be addressed.

Most regenerated offenders who come out of prison without having addressed the impact of their criminal behavior will often believe that society owes them something. Crime and the impact of that behavior needs to be addressed in order to eliminate this misconception and because it is vital to the restorative justice process.

Restorative justice is a multifaceted approach to crime that focuses on healing and restoration, rather than solely on punishment. While the regeneration of the offender is a primary goal of restorative justice ministry, it is not the only issue that needs to be addressed.

When a crime is committed, it affects not only the offender but also the victim and the community. Therefore, restorative justice also seeks to address the harm caused by the crime and to make amends for the damage done. This includes addressing issues of accountability and responsibility, repairing harm, and reconciling relationships.

Restorative justice ministry recognizes that offenders must be held accountable for their actions and that they must make amends for the harm they have caused. This can take various forms, such as restitution, community service, or counseling. Additionally, offenders must acknowledge their responsibility for their actions and express remorse for the harm they have caused.

Restorative justice ministry also recognizes the importance of supporting the victim and addressing their needs. This can involve providing emotional support, financial assistance, or other forms of restitution. Victims must also be given a voice in the process, allowing them to express their feelings and concerns and to participate in the restoration process.

Finally, restorative justice ministry recognizes that crimes have a broader impact on the community as a whole. Therefore, the restoration process must involve the community, including community leaders and other stakeholders, in addressing the root causes of crime and working together to promote healing and reconciliation.

In conclusion, while the regeneration of the offender is an important goal of restorative justice ministry, it is only one aspect of a broader process that seeks to address the harm caused by the crime and to promote healing and restoration for all parties involved.

2. When you minister to the needs of the offender, you must not forget that one of their needs is to be healed of the injury of the crime through:

When ministering to the needs of an offender in a restorative justice context, it is important to acknowledge and address the harm that their actions have caused to others. This requires a focus not only on the offender's rehabilitation and restoration, but also on the needs of the victim and the wider community.

The offender may need to make amends for their actions, both through restitution and through actions that seek to repair the harm caused. This may involve making reparations to the victim, such as paying for damages or providing other forms of compensation. It may also involve participating in community service or other activities that benefit those affected by their behavior.

Additionally, the offender may need to address any underlying issues that contributed to their behavior, such as addiction, mental health problems, or a history of trauma. This may involve connecting them with appropriate resources and support, such as counseling, treatment programs, or support groups.

Overall, a restorative justice approach seeks to address the needs of all parties involved, with a focus on healing and restoration rather than punishment and retribution. By ministering to the needs of the offender in a holistic way, we can work towards building a more just and compassionate society.

3. What marks the beginning of the restorative justice process in the offender's life?

Part of that healing process is to right the wrongs as much as it is in the power of the offender to do so.

The beginning of the restorative justice process in the offender's life is when they take responsibility for their actions and show genuine remorse for the harm they have caused. This may involve admitting guilt, making restitution, and seeking forgiveness from those affected by their actions. It is important for the offender to acknowledge the harm they have caused and to take steps towards making things right. Only then can the process of restoration begin.

4. In a restorative justice paradigm, the offender at some point recognizes the hurt he has caused, and experiences shame for his actions, a shame and sorrow which leads to repentance.

Correct. In 2 Corinthians 7:10, Paul explained that repentance is a result of "godly sorrow", which is very different from human remorse that has no redemptive capability. Human remorse is nothing more than the wounded pride of getting caught in a sin and having one's lusts go unfulfilled. This kind of sorrow leads only to guilt, shame, despair, depression, self-pity, hopelessness and death.

In a restorative justice paradigm, the offender is not only held accountable for their actions, but is also given the opportunity to take responsibility for their actions and make amends. This can only happen when the offender recognizes the harm they have caused and experiences genuine remorse for their actions.

This recognition and remorse often come through a process of deep reflection and self-examination. The offender may be encouraged to acknowledge the full extent of the harm they have caused, and to understand how their actions have affected not only their victim, but also their family, their community, and themselves. Through this process, the offender may come to understand the gravity of their actions and the need for accountability.

This recognition and remorse can lead to genuine repentance, which involves not only feeling sorry for one's actions, but also taking concrete steps to make things right. This can include making restitution to the victim, participating in counseling or treatment programs to address underlying issues that led to the offense, and engaging in community service or other activities to make amends for the harm caused.

In short, the beginning of the restorative justice process in the offender's life is marked by a genuine recognition of the harm caused, a deep sense of remorse, and a willingness to take responsibility for one's actions and make things right.

5. Repentance goes far beyond accepting Christ as one's personal Savior; it is a decision to change behavior, attitudes, and beliefs that are not in agreement with the Word of God.

Repentance is a crucial aspect of the Christian faith and a necessary step in the process of restorative justice. It is a decision to turn away from one's old way of life and turn towards God's way of living. It involves a change in behavior, attitudes, and beliefs that are not in agreement with the Word of God.

True repentance is not just about feeling sorry for one's actions; it is a genuine desire to change and make amends for the harm caused. In the context of restorative justice, repentance is the first step towards making things right with the victim and the community. It is a recognition that one's actions have hurt others and a willingness to take responsibility for the harm caused.

Repentance involves confessing one's wrongdoing and seeking forgiveness from God and those who have been hurt. It requires humility, vulnerability, and a willingness to face the consequences of one's actions. It is only through genuine repentance that the offender can begin the process of restoration and reconciliation.

In summary, repentance is a vital part of the restorative justice process. It is a decision to turn away from one's old way of life and turn towards God's way of living. It involves a change in behavior, attitudes, and beliefs that are not in agreement with the Word of God. Repentance is the first step towards making things right with the victim and the community and is necessary for true restoration and reconciliation to take place.

6. The restorative justice paradigm suggests that the offender not only has to be restored through repentance, but also must become a restorer through restorer.

It is very common for even regenerated offenders to harbor bitterness, hatred, and resentment toward members of the criminal justice community. They may even view this as a right resulting from the way they were treated while serving time. According to Hebrews 12:15, these types of feelings "cause trouble"; therefore, the offender must learn to forgive.

Restorative justice is a philosophy and approach to justice that focuses on repairing harm caused by criminal behavior rather than punishing the offender. It seeks to restore relationships between the offender, victim, and community, rather than simply punishing the offender. One of the key principles of restorative justice is the idea that the offender should not only be restored through repentance, but also become a restorer through restoration.

Restoration in the context of restorative justice involves repairing the harm caused by the offense. This can involve several steps, including acknowledging the harm done, taking responsibility for the offense, making amends to the victim, and working to prevent similar harm from occurring in the future. Restoration aims to bring about healing and reconciliation between the offender, victim, and community.

The idea that the offender should become a restorer through restoration means that the offender must not only be restored but also play an active role in restoring the harm they caused. This involves taking steps to make amends, such as apologizing to the victim, offering restitution, or engaging in community service. It also involves working to prevent future harm by addressing the underlying causes of the offense and taking steps to avoid similar behavior in the future.

By becoming a restorer through restoration, the offender can demonstrate their commitment to repairing the harm they caused and to making positive changes in their life. This can help to rebuild trust between the offender, victim, and community and can contribute to a sense of justice and healing.

In conclusion, the restorative justice paradigm suggests that the offender not only has to be restored through repentance, but also must become a restorer through restoration. This involves taking responsibility for the harm caused, making amends, and working to prevent future harm. By becoming a restorer, the offender can demonstrate their commitment to repairing the harm and making positive changes in their life, which can contribute to healing and reconciliation.

7. Ministry from a restorative justice paradigm has to address the issues concerning the injury to the victim of the offense(s).

Restorative justice is a philosophy and approach to justice that focuses on repairing harm caused by criminal behavior rather than punishing the offender. It seeks to restore relationships between the offender, victim, and community, rather than simply punishing the offender. One of the key principles of restorative justice is the idea that ministry from this paradigm must address the issues concerning the injury to the victim(s) of the offense(s).

When ministry is approached from a restorative justice paradigm, the needs of the victim(s) are given priority. This involves addressing the injury caused by the offense(s) and working to repair the harm. The goal of restorative justice ministry is to bring about healing and reconciliation between the offender, victim, and community.

To address the issues concerning the injury to the victim(s) of the offense(s), restorative justice ministry may involve several steps. These may include:

1. Acknowledging the harm done: This involves recognizing and acknowledging the impact of the offense(s) on the victim(s). It involves listening to their experiences and feelings, and validating their pain.

2. Offering support and care: Restorative justice ministry must provide care and support to the victim(s). This can include emotional support, practical assistance, and access to resources to help them heal.

3. Facilitating communication: Restorative justice ministry can facilitate communication between the offender and victim(s). This can help the offender to take responsibility for their actions, apologize for the harm caused, and work to make amends.

4. Providing opportunities for the victim(s) to participate in the justice process: Restorative justice ministry can provide opportunities for the victim(s) to participate in the justice process. This can include offering input on the terms of restitution or community service, or participating in a restorative justice conference or circle.

5. Supporting the victim(s) throughout the process: Restorative justice ministry must continue to support the victim(s) throughout the process of healing and reconciliation. This can involve follow-up care, ongoing support, and advocacy for their needs.

In conclusion, ministry from a restorative justice paradigm must address the issues concerning the injury to the victim(s) of the offense(s). This involves prioritizing the needs of the victim(s), acknowledging the harm done, providing support and care, facilitating communication, providing opportunities for the victim(s) to participate in the justice process, and supporting them throughout the process. By addressing the needs of the victim(s), restorative justice ministry can contribute to healing and reconciliation between the offender, victim(s), and community.

8. The victim cannot be the system or the State, which are only abstractions.

In the context of restorative justice, the victim is the person who has been directly harmed or affected by the offense committed by the offender. This can be an individual, a group, or a community. The focus of restorative justice is on repairing the harm caused by the offense and restoring the relationships between the offender, victim(s), and the community.

The system or the state, on the other hand, are abstractions that do not have feelings, emotions, or experiences. While the justice system and the state may have a role in responding to crime and addressing harm, they cannot be the victim(s) of the offense(s). Rather, they are responsible for upholding the law and administering justice in a fair and impartial manner.

It is important to recognize the difference between the victim(s) and the justice system or state in the context of restorative justice. By focusing on the needs of the victim(s), restorative justice seeks to provide a more human-centered approach to justice that prioritizes repairing harm and restoring relationships. This approach recognizes the emotional and psychological impact of crime on individuals and communities, and seeks to address these impacts through a process of healing and reconciliation.

In conclusion, the victim cannot be the system or the state, which are only abstractions. Rather, the focus of restorative justice is on repairing the harm caused to the victim(s) and restoring relationships between the offender, victim(s), and community. By recognizing the difference between the victim(s) and the justice system or state, restorative justice provides a more human-centered approach to justice that seeks to address the emotional and psychological impact of crime.

9. Crime has an impact on human beings, who have feelings and emotions.

Crime has an impact on human beings who have feelings and emotions because it involves the violation of one's physical or psychological integrity, sense of safety, and personal autonomy. When a person becomes a victim of crime, they may experience a range of emotions, including fear, anger, sadness, and anxiety.

For example, if someone is physically assaulted, they may suffer physical injuries and trauma, which can lead to pain, fear, and a loss of sense of control over their own body. Similarly, if someone's property is stolen or damaged, they may feel violated and experience a sense of loss or grief.

In addition to the direct impact on the victim(s), crime can also have an impact on their family, friends, and community. The fear of crime can lead to a loss of trust, a sense of vulnerability, and a decreased quality of life. It can also affect people's sense of safety and well-being, leading to social isolation, anxiety, and depression.

The emotional and psychological impact of crime is often long-lasting, and can have a significant impact on a person's quality of life.

Restorative justice recognizes the importance of addressing these impacts and seeks to provide a more human-centered approach to justice that focuses on repairing harm and restoring relationships between the offender, victim(s), and community.

In conclusion, crime has an impact on human beings who have feelings and emotions because it involves the violation of one's physical or psychological integrity, sense of safety, and personal autonomy. The emotional and psychological impact of crime can be long-lasting, and can have a significant impact on a person's quality of life. Restorative justice seeks to address these impacts by providing a more human-centered approach to justice that focuses on repairing harm and restoring relationships.

10. Whenever there is a direct victim, their pain needs to be addressed so the offender can see how his/her actions affected and damaged the lives of other people.:

"This step is so vital because it teaches the offender how to become a caring member of the community."

The statement that whenever there is a direct victim, their pain needs to be addressed so the offender can see how his/her actions affected and damaged the lives of other people is a central tenet of restorative justice. Restorative justice is an approach to justice that focuses on repairing the harm caused by crime and restoring relationships between the offender, victim(s), and community.

In a restorative justice process, the offender is given an opportunity to take responsibility for their actions, acknowledge the harm they have caused, and make amends to the victim(s) and community. This process requires the offender to confront the impact of their actions on others, including the pain and suffering of the victim(s).

When the pain of the victim(s) is addressed, it can have a powerful impact on the offender. Seeing and understanding the direct impact of their actions on others can help the offender develop empathy and understanding, leading to a greater sense of remorse and accountability for their actions. This, in turn, can lead to a greater likelihood of the offender taking steps to make amends, and less likely to reoffend.

Addressing the pain of the victim(s) is also an important aspect of healing and recovery for the victim(s). By being given a voice and having their pain acknowledged, victims can feel empowered and validated. They may also be more likely to forgive the offender and move forward in their own healing process.

In conclusion, addressing the pain of the victim(s) is a crucial aspect of the restorative justice process. It allows the offender to confront the impact of their actions, develop empathy and understanding, and take responsibility for their behavior. It also empowers and validates the victim(s) and can contribute to their own healing and recovery.

11. Research shows that it is much easier to continue to offend an abstraction than it is to re-offend human beings.

The statement that research shows it is much easier to continue to offend an abstraction than it is to re-offend human beings highlights an important aspect of restorative justice. Restorative justice recognizes that crime is not just a violation of the law, but also a violation of human relationships and social bonds. Therefore, it seeks to address the harm caused by crime by restoring those relationships and bonds.

In traditional criminal justice systems, the focus is on punishing the offender and protecting society from further harm. This often involves treating the offender as an abstract criminal, rather than a human being who has caused harm to others. This approach can lead to a cycle of re-offending, as the offender does not fully understand the harm they have caused and may not be motivated to change their behavior.

Restorative justice, on the other hand, seeks to hold the offender accountable for their actions by making them confront the harm they have caused and take responsibility for it. By engaging with the victim(s) and the community, the offender is able to see the real impact of their actions and to develop empathy and understanding.

Research has shown that this approach is effective in reducing reoffending rates. When offenders are given the opportunity to make amends and to rebuild relationships with their victims and community, they are less likely to reoffend. This is because they have a greater understanding of the harm they have caused and are motivated to change their behavior to prevent future harm.

In conclusion, restorative justice recognizes that crime is not just a violation of the law, but also a violation of human relationships and social bonds. By focusing on repairing harm and restoring relationships, restorative justice is able to address the underlying causes of offending behavior and reduce reoffending rates. This is because it is much easier to continue to offend an abstraction than it is to reoffend human beings, and by making offenders confront the harm they have caused and take responsibility for it, restorative justice creates an environment in which offenders are motivated to change their behavior and make amends for the harm they have caused.

11. Describe a mentor's role with the offender.:

>   a) is to be a friend,
>
>   b) to advise,
>
>   c) to help
>
>   d) and to model the Christian life for the offender.

Proverbs 27:17 says, "Iron sharpeneth iron; so a man sharpeneth the countenance of his friend." Personal and spiritual growth is a communal affair, as Scripture reminds us in various ways. In the beginning, God did not make just one human being but two (Genesis 1:26–27).

David had Nathan the prophet, a faithful friend who brought him to repentance (2 Samuel 12:1–15). And Jesus appointed not just one overseer; rather, He has chosen for His church to be governed by a body of elders and deacons (Acts 6:1–7). Not just ex-offenders, but we ALL need others in our lives to sharpen us and encourage us in our daily walk.

Those of us who have at least one friend upon whom we can count for loving, constructive criticism are blessed. If we do not have any such people in our lives, we should be looking for them. We should also be asking the Lord to help develop us into people who can offer such criticism to others and to enable us to persist in love toward our friends and others.

In a restorative justice context, a mentor plays an important role in supporting and guiding the offender as they work to repair the harm caused by their actions and take steps to prevent future offending behavior.

The mentor's role is to act as a positive role model for the offender and to provide guidance, support, and encouragement throughout the restorative justice process. This can involve helping the offender to understand the impact of their actions on others, to take responsibility for their behavior, and to develop strategies for making amends and preventing future harm.

In addition, the mentor may provide practical support to the offender, such as helping them to access education or employment opportunities, or connecting them with other resources in the community. The mentor may also work with the offender's family and community to help create a supportive environment that encourages positive change.

The mentor's role is not to judge or punish the offender, but rather to support them in their harm caused by their actions and to become a responsible and productive member of the community. The mentor should be non-judgmental, empathetic, and respectful of the offender's feelings and experiences.

Accordingly, the mentor's role with the offender is to help them to develop the skills and attitudes necessary to make positive changes in their lives and to prevent future harm. By providing guidance, support, and encouragement, the mentor can help the offender to see the potential for positive change and to take concrete steps towards a more positive future.

12. Which aspect of criminal justice ministry could easily be listed with the victims of crime?

The offender's family and loved ones should always be listed with the victims of crime because they too suffer from the offender's criminal behavior. Even the sanctions levied against the offender, as a result of their crime, is felt by their family and loved ones.

One aspect of criminal justice ministry that could easily be listed with the victims of crime is the need for healing and restoration. Crime can cause significant harm to victims, including physical, emotional, and psychological trauma. Victims may experience feelings of fear, anxiety, anger, and hopelessness, and may struggle to trust others or feel safe in their communities.

Criminal justice ministry can play an important role in supporting victims in their journey towards healing and restoration. This can involve providing emotional support, counseling, and other resources to help victims cope with the aftermath of the crime. It can also involve advocating for victims' rights and needs within the criminal justice system, such as ensuring that victims are informed about court proceedings and have the opportunity to share their story in court.

In addition, criminal justice ministry can work to promote a restorative justice approach that emphasizes repairing the harm caused by crime and restoring relationships between victims, offenders, and the community. This approach recognizes that crime is not just a violation of the law, but also a violation of human relationships and social bonds, and seeks to address the underlying causes of offending behavior.

By focusing on healing and restoration, criminal justice ministry can help victims to feel heard, supported, and empowered in the aftermath of a crime. It can also help to prevent future harm by addressing the root causes of offending behavior and promoting a more just and peaceful society.

13. Incarceration produces what has been dubbed a prison widow or widower, and the prison orphan.

Incarceration can have significant negative impacts not only on the individual who is incarcerated, but also on their loved ones and family members. The term "prison widow" or "prison widower" is used to describe the partners of incarcerated individuals who may experience a sense of loneliness, isolation, and loss while their loved one is in prison. These individuals may struggle to maintain relationships, raise children, and manage the responsibilities of daily life while their partner is incarcerated.

Similarly, the term "prison orphan" is used to describe children who have one or both parents incarcerated. These children may experience emotional distress, academic challenges, and financial hardship as a result of their parent's incarceration. They may also face stigma and social exclusion due to their parent's status as an incarcerated individual.

The impact of incarceration on family members and loved ones can be profound and long-lasting, and may contribute to cycles of intergenerational poverty, trauma, and social exclusion. As a result, criminal justice systems and ministries should consider the needs and experiences of families and loved ones of incarcerated individuals as they work to address the harms caused by crime and promote a more just and equitable society.

Restorative justice approaches that prioritize healing, restoration, and community engagement may offer a more effective and humane response to crime that recognizes the interconnectedness of individuals and families within communities. By addressing the harms caused by crime in a way that involves and supports all members of the community, including families and loved ones of incarcerated individuals, we can work towards a more just and peaceful society for all.

14. As the offender's family waits on them, they need help spiritually, emotionally and financially.

When a family member is incarcerated, it can have significant emotional, financial, and spiritual impacts on their loved ones. The experience of having a family member in prison can be stressful, traumatic, and isolating, and can leave family members struggling to cope with a range of challenges.

Spiritually, family members may experience a sense of guilt or shame, as well as a sense of disconnection from their faith community. They may struggle to reconcile their love for their incarcerated family member with their own sense of moral values and beliefs.

Emotionally, family members may experience a range of negative emotions such as anxiety, depression, anger, and grief. They may feel a sense of loss, isolation, and shame, as well as a sense of responsibility for their loved one's actions.

Financially, incarceration can impose significant costs on families, including legal fees, travel expenses, and loss of income due to the incarceration of a family member. This can lead to economic hardship, debt, and financial insecurity for the family.

Given these challenges, criminal justice ministries and other support systems can play an important role in helping families of incarcerated individuals. This can include providing emotional and spiritual support, counseling services, and financial assistance. It can also involve working with families to help them stay connected to their incarcerated loved one, such as through visitation programs or letter writing campaigns.

By addressing the spiritual, emotional, and financial needs of families of incarcerated individuals, we can help to mitigate the negative impacts of incarceration and promote healing, restoration, and community engagement. This can also help to prevent future offending behavior and promote a more just and peaceful society for all.

15. There is a great need for marriage seminars that could save literally hundreds of offender marriages, and, as a result, break the generational cycle of crime and brokenness in these families.:

Approximately 90% of all marriages end in divorce when the incarceration period exceeds one year. If the offender can come home to a loving, waiting, Christian family, they have a greater chance of avoiding crime and staying out of prison in the future.

Marriage seminars can be a powerful tool for addressing the needs of families affected by incarceration and breaking the cycle of crime and brokenness that can be passed down from generation to generation. When a family member is incarcerated, it can have significant impacts on their relationships, including their marriage or intimate partner relationships. The stress, trauma, and financial strain associated with incarceration can strain these relationships and lead to divorce or separation.

By providing marriage seminars that address the unique needs of families affected by incarceration, criminal justice ministries and other support systems can help to strengthen relationships, promote healthy communication and conflict resolution skills, and provide a sense of hope and healing to families who may be struggling. These seminars can also help to address the specific challenges faced by families of incarcerated individuals, such as financial strain and emotional distress.

By promoting healthy relationships and strengthening families, marriage seminars can also help to break the cycle of crime and brokenness that can be passed down from generation to generation. Research has shown that children of incarcerated parents are at higher risk for involvement in criminal behavior themselves. By addressing the needs of families affected by incarceration, we can help to prevent future offending behavior and promote a more just and peaceful society for all.

In addition to marriage seminars, criminal justice ministries and other support systems can also provide a range of other services to support families affected by incarceration, such as counseling, financial assistance, and job training. By taking a holistic and restorative approach to criminal justice, we can work towards a more just and equitable society that values the needs and well-being of all members of our communities, including families affected by incarceration.

16. Which aspect of criminal justice ministry is the most difficult?

One thing we can do is to recognize and encourage criminal justice professionals who are positively impacting prisoners by their efforts, and inspiring them to become productive members of our community upon release. Theirs is not an easy job.

Criminal justice ministry can be a challenging and complex field, with many different aspects and challenges to consider. However, one of the most difficult aspects of criminal justice ministry is likely working with offenders who are resistant to change or who are struggling with addiction, mental health issues, or other challenges that make it difficult for them to fully engage in the restorative justice process.

When working with offenders, criminal justice ministries may encounter individuals who are deeply entrenched in their patterns of behavior and who may not be receptive to the idea of taking responsibility for their actions or making amends to their victims. This can be challenging, as it requires a great deal of patience, compassion, and persistence to work with these individuals over time and to help them see the value of the restorative justice process.

In addition, many offenders may be struggling with addiction or mental health issues, which can further complicate their ability to fully engage in the restorative justice process. These individuals may require additional support and resources to address these underlying issues and to fully participate in the restorative justice process.

Wherefore, working with offenders who are resistant to change or who are struggling with addiction or mental health issues requires a great deal of patience, compassion, and perseverance. It can be a difficult and emotionally taxing aspect of criminal justice ministry, but it is also an essential component of promoting healing, restoration, and community engagement. By working with these individuals over time and providing them with the support and resources they need to fully participate in the restorative justice process, we can help to break the cycle of crime and promote a more just and peaceful society for all.

17. The first step in ministering to a criminal justice professional is the building of a relationships.

The building of relationships is a crucial first step in ministering to criminal justice professionals for several reasons.

Firstly, criminal justice professionals often work in highly stressful and challenging environments that can take a toll on their mental and emotional well-being. By building relationships with these individuals, criminal justice ministries can provide them with a sense of support, connection, and community that can help to mitigate the effects of this stress and promote greater resilience.

Secondly, building relationships with criminal justice professionals can help to break down barriers and build trust between these individuals and the broader community. Many criminal justice professionals may feel isolated or misunderstood by the communities they serve, and building relationships with them can help to bridge this divide and promote greater understanding and collaboration.

Thirdly, building relationships with criminal justice professionals can help to promote the values of restorative justice and community engagement within the criminal justice system. By demonstrating the importance of building relationships and promoting healing and restoration, criminal justice ministries can help to shift the focus of the criminal justice system away from punitive measures and towards a more restorative and community-centered approach.

Therefore, building relationships with criminal justice professionals is a crucial first step in ministering to these individuals and promoting greater healing and restoration within the criminal justice system. By providing these individuals with a sense of support, connection, and community, criminal justice ministries can help to promote greater well-being and resilience among criminal justice professionals and help to shift the focus of the criminal justice system towards a more restorative and community-centered approach.

18. Establishing a relationship requires much patience, because the correctional staff in many ways is a closed community that shuns outsiders.

Establishing relationships with correctional staff can be a challenging and time-consuming process, as these individuals often work in a closed and insular community that can be resistant to outside influence or involvement.

Correctional staff work in a highly stressful and challenging environment, where their safety and the safety of those in their care is a constant concern. This can create a sense of isolation and distrust among correctional staff, who may view outsiders as a potential threat or interference to their work.

To build relationships with correctional staff, it is important to approach them with respect, sensitivity, and an understanding of the challenges they face on a daily basis. This may require a significant amount of patience and persistence, as trust and rapport are built slowly over time.

One way to build relationships with correctional staff is to seek out opportunities for collaboration and partnership. This might involve offering to provide training or support to staff members, or working with them to identify areas where restorative justice principles could be integrated into their work.

It is also important to be mindful of the boundaries and limitations of the correctional setting, and to work within the constraints of the system in order to build relationships with staff members. This may require flexibility and a willingness to adapt to the unique needs and culture of the correctional environment.

Thus, building relationships with correctional staff requires patience, persistence, and a deep commitment to promoting restorative justice principles within the criminal justice system. By approaching staff members with respect and sensitivity, and by seeking out opportunities for collaboration and partnership, criminal justice ministries can help to break down barriers and build trust with those working in the correctional system, ultimately promoting greater healing, restoration, and community engagement for all.

19. Because of varying work hours, a church should be willing to schedule special activities and develop programs to include ...: these unique individuals

Because of varying work hours, criminal justice professionals may have difficulty participating in traditional church activities and programs. To include these unique individuals, churches should be willing to schedule special activities and develop programs that are tailored to their specific needs and schedules.

One way to do this is to offer flexible scheduling for worship services and other church activities, such as Bible studies or prayer groups. This might involve offering multiple service times or scheduling events on different days of the week to accommodate the varying work schedules of criminal justice professionals.

In addition to flexible scheduling, churches can also develop specialized programs that are designed specifically for criminal justice professionals. This might include support groups for those who work in the correctional system or specialized training programs that address the unique challenges of this work.

It is also important for churches to be intentional about creating a welcoming and supportive environment for criminal justice professionals. This might involve developing specialized outreach efforts or partnering with organizations that work directly with criminal justice professionals.

Wherefore, churches can play an important role in supporting and ministering to criminal justice professionals by offering flexible scheduling, developing specialized programs, and creating a welcoming and supportive environment. By making an effort to include these unique individuals, churches can help to promote greater healing, restoration, and community engagement within the criminal justice system.

12. To the degree possible, offenders should attempt to reconcile the damages they have caused to those affected by their crime.

Restorative justice emphasizes the importance of offenders taking responsibility for their actions and attempting to make amends for the harm they have caused. One key aspect of this process is the concept of reconciliation, which involves making efforts to repair the harm that has been done to those affected by the crime.

Reconciliation can take many forms, depending on the circumstances of the crime and the needs of the victim(s) and their community. In some cases, it may involve a direct apology or a face-to-face meeting between the offender and the victim, where the offender can express remorse and take steps to make things right.

In other cases, reconciliation may involve the offender making restitution to the victim, such as paying for damages or providing financial support. This can be particularly important in cases where the victim has suffered financial or material losses as a result of the crime.

In addition to making amends to the victim(s), reconciliation can also involve efforts to address the root causes of the offender's behavior and to prevent future offenses. This might include participation in counseling or rehabilitation programs, or making efforts to address the social and environmental factors that contributed to the offender's criminal behavior.

While reconciliation can be a challenging and difficult process, it can be an important step towards healing and restoration for both the offender and the victim(s). By taking responsibility for their actions and making efforts to repair the harm they have caused, offenders can demonstrate their commitment to making things right and to contributing to the well-being of their communities.

13. Discover within James 5:16 two prerequisites to healing.:

a) Confess your faults one to another, and pray one for another

b) that ye may be healed

These two prerequisites to healing move both the victim and offender toward restoration. In many cases lasting friendships are also developed.

James 5:16 states: "Therefore, confess your sins to each other and pray for each other so that you may be healed. The prayer of a righteous person is powerful and effective."

From this verse, we can identify two prerequisites to healing:

1. Confession of sins: James emphasizes the importance of confessing our sins to each other as a prerequisite to healing.

Confession involves acknowledging and taking responsibility for our actions, as well as seeking forgiveness from those we have wronged. This act of humility and repentance can be a powerful step towards healing and reconciliation.

2. Prayer for each other: In addition to confession, James also emphasizes the importance of praying for each other as a means of healing. By lifting up one another in prayer, we demonstrate our care and concern for each other's well-being, and we invite God's healing power into our lives.

Taken together, these two prerequisites to healing suggest that the process of healing involves both personal responsibility and communal support. We must be willing to confess our sins and seek forgiveness, while also relying on the prayers and support of our fellow believers to help us in our journey towards healing and restoration.

14. An offender also needs to understand how his/her crime has affected the community.

Once the offender understands how their crime has affected the community, they will begin to see how they contribute to its stability. As a result, they will take measures to change.

When an offender commits a crime, the harm caused is not limited to just the victim(s). The wider community can also be affected by the crime, either directly or indirectly. For example, a violent crime may cause fear and anxiety in the community, leading to a sense of insecurity and distrust.

Understanding the impact of the crime on the community is an important aspect of restorative justice. It helps the offender to see the wider consequences of their actions beyond the immediate victim(s), and to take responsibility for their role in causing harm.

By understanding the impact of their crime on the community, the offender can begin to see the need for repairing the harm and making amends. This might involve participating in community service or restitution programs, or taking steps to address the root causes of their behavior, such as addiction or mental health issues.

In addition, by engaging with the community and taking steps towards making amends, the offender can also begin to rebuild trust and restore their relationships with others. This can be an important step towards reintegrating back into society and moving forward in a positive direction.

Finally, understanding the impact of their crime on the community is an important aspect of the offender's journey towards restoration and rehabilitation, and is an important component of the restorative justice process.

15. Every time an offense occurs in a community, the trust level between people decreases and the element of fear increases.

Fearing crime is a common and prevalent issue in modern society. The level or extent of the fear of crime depends on various factors like age, gender, and past experiences.

When an offense occurs in a community, it can have a significant impact on the level of trust between individuals. This is particularly true when the offense is violent or involves a breach of trust, such as theft or fraud. When people feel like they cannot trust those around them, it can lead to a breakdown in community cohesion and a sense of isolation.

In addition to the impact on trust, offenses can also increase the level of fear within a community. This is particularly true for violent crimes or crimes that are perceived as a threat to public safety, such as gang activity or drug trafficking. When people are afraid, they may avoid certain areas or activities, leading to a further breakdown in community cohesion and a sense of isolation.

Both the decrease in trust and the increase in fear can have negative consequences for a community. When people do not trust each other, it can be difficult to build strong relationships or work together to address community issues. When people are afraid, they may be less likely to engage with their community or to participate in activities that promote social cohesion and well-being.

Restorative justice can help to address these issues by promoting healing, reconciliation, and forgiveness. By bringing together victims, offenders, and community members to discuss the impact of the offense and to work towards repairing the harm caused, restorative justice can help to rebuild trust and promote a sense of community. By addressing the root causes of crime and taking steps towards preventing future offenses, restorative justice can also help to reduce fear and increase feelings of safety within the community.

Please note that offenses can have a significant impact on community trust and fear, but restorative justice offers a promising approach for addressing these issues and promoting healing and reconciliation.

16. What are some of the things that people may begin doing, as they become increasingly suspicious of other people? (Answers may vary.):

     a) they begin to secure their homes,

     b) with extra lights

     c) locks,

     d) sturdier fences,

     e) Others may even go to the extreme of purchasing a fire arm.

As people become increasingly suspicious of others, they may begin to do the following:

1. Avoiding interactions: They may avoid interacting with others, fearing that they may be harmed or betrayed.
2. Checking up on people: They may become obsessive about monitoring other people's actions and whereabouts.
3. Questioning others' motives: They may start to question the motives of others, even those close to them, and suspect that they are up to no good.
4. Secrecy: They may become more secretive themselves, guarding their own actions and thoughts, believing that others might use this information against them.
5. Isolation: They may choose to isolate themselves, withdrawing from social situations and avoiding interactions with others altogether.
6. Guarding their possessions: They may become overly protective of their belongings and property, thinking that someone might steal or damage them.
7. Increased vigilance: They may become more vigilant, always watching out for potential threats or suspicious behavior in others.
8. Paranoia: In severe cases, they may experience paranoia, believing that everyone is out to get them or harm them in some way.

Taken to the extreme, "scelerophobia" is the fear of burglars, bad men or crime in general. For those with this phobia, many normal things become difficult for the suffering individual. For example, a person might go to great lengths to prevent crime (such as locking one's home or constantly checking and rechecking locks to an extent that it becomes an obsession). Many refuse to step out of their home after dark or travel to lonely places for the fear of being attacked or robbed. Their phobia leads to constant fatigue as it causes them to believe that they need to be vigilant all the time.

A brief testimony, there was a young lady who wanted to be counseled by email. She had not left the house in 30 years. She was afraid of everything, and actually collects disability for her anxiety issues. She keeps roosters, hens, and dogs in the yard for protection. The roosters and hens are there to alert her to someone approaching, in case the dogs fall asleep.

Her first email to me was full of initials for all the diagnoses she had received from doctors over the years. I told her that may be the way the world sees her and what the doctors see in her, but this is NOT the way the Lord sees her. I began to write a series of devotionals for her to begin her day, highlighting what the Lord says she is. She made index cards with the verses, and left them all over the house.

However, the email therapy did NOT work. The day she got a letter of inquiry from Social Security about her disability payments, she went into the fetal position in bed for three days, paralyzed by fear. She went back on her meds, and decided to discontinue her email counseling. But at the end, she agreed to allow me to convert these personalized devotionals into a course. I deleted personal comments, and she even edited the final product for me. She did an AMAZING job of finding errors or better ways to say the same thing. She excelled because she was in her comfort zone – at home.

17. When offenders are encouraged to address the harm that results from their crime, they can begin to see that their actions are not isolated, and that their families, as well as friends and neighbors, suffer from their crime.

When offenders are encouraged to address the harm that results from their crime, they are given an opportunity to see the impact of their actions on others beyond just themselves. This can be a powerful experience that can help offenders to take responsibility for their behavior and work towards making amends.

One of the key ways in which offenders can begin to see the wider impact of their actions is through restorative justice programs. These programs aim to bring together the offender, the victim, and other affected parties to discuss the harm caused by the crime and work towards repairing it. By hearing from those directly affected by their actions, offenders can start to understand the full extent of the damage they have caused.

In particular, when offenders see how their crime has impacted their families, friends, and neighbors, they can begin to recognize that their actions do not just affect themselves, but have a ripple effect throughout the community. They may see that their loved ones have been hurt by their behavior, and that their relationships with others have been damaged as a result.

This realization can be a powerful motivator for offenders to make changes in their lives and work towards making amends for the harm they have caused. They may become more invested in repairing relationships with those they have hurt, and in taking steps to prevent future harm.

Thus, encouraging offenders to address the harm caused by their crime can be a valuable tool in helping them to take responsibility for their actions and work towards repairing the damage they have caused. By seeing the wider impact of their behavior, offenders can start to recognize the importance of making amends and working towards a better future for themselves and their communities.

18. What happens when the offender focuses on the ills of the prison system, rather than address the harm that resulted from his crime?

The offender is not held accountable for the damage they have caused through their offense.

When an offender focuses solely on the ills of the prison system and neglects to address the harm they caused, it can be a form of denial and avoidance of responsibility. This can be problematic for a few reasons:

1. Failure to take responsibility: By deflecting attention away from their own behavior and onto the prison system, offenders may fail to take responsibility for their actions and the harm they have caused. This can hinder the healing process for victims and the community.

2. Lack of accountability: If offenders do not address the harm they caused, they may not be held accountable for their actions. This can lead to a sense of injustice for victims and can undermine the legitimacy of the justice system.

3. Failure to address root causes: By focusing solely on the prison system, offenders may fail to address the root causes of their behavior. It is important for offenders to understand the underlying factors that contributed to their actions, so that they can take steps to address them and prevent future harm.

4. Lack of rehabilitation: If offenders do not take responsibility for their actions and work towards making amends, they may miss out on opportunities for rehabilitation and growth. This can make it more difficult for them to successfully reintegrate into society after their release.

Accordingly, while it is important to acknowledge and address issues within the prison system, it is also important for offenders to take responsibility for their own behavior and the harm they have caused. By doing so, they can begin the process of healing and growth, both for themselves and for the community.

They forget that what they have done harmed others, and also avoid feeling accountable for the harm they have caused through their actions.

19. A Christian offender needs to be willing to confront the pain he has caused, and discover a way to rebuild the trust that was destroyed by his actions.

As a Christian, an offender must take responsibility for their actions and be willing to confront the pain they have caused to others. This requires a willingness to face the consequences of their behavior and work towards making amends.

To rebuild trust, the offender must first acknowledge the harm they have caused and express genuine remorse for their actions. This involves taking responsibility for their behavior and recognizing the impact it has had on others. The offender must be willing to listen to the victim and other affected parties, and take their feelings and needs into account.

In addition, the offender must be committed to making things right. This may involve making restitution, participating in restorative justice programs, and taking steps to prevent future harm. The offender may also need to seek counseling or therapy to address any underlying issues that contributed to their behavior.

Ultimately, rebuilding trust is a process that requires patience, persistence, and a genuine desire to change. It may take time for the victim and others to forgive the offender, and it is important for the offender to be respectful of this process and continue to take responsibility for their behavior.

As a Christian, the offender may also seek guidance and support from their faith community. This can provide a source of strength and encouragement as they work towards rebuilding trust and making amends.

20. Ministry, using the restorative justice paradigm, ends in the restoration of both the victim and the offender back into the community.

Restorative justice is a paradigm that seeks to repair harm and restore relationships between those who have been affected by crime. This approach involves bringing together the victim, the offender, and the community to work towards a shared goal of healing and reconciliation.

In a ministry context, the use of the restorative justice paradigm can be particularly powerful. By focusing on restoration and reconciliation, this approach aligns with many Christian values, such as forgiveness, compassion, and love.

In a restorative justice ministry context, the goal is to restore both the victim and the offender back into the community. This involves providing support and resources to both parties as they work towards healing and reconciliation. The victim may receive counseling or other forms of support to help them cope with the trauma they have experienced. The offender may receive counseling or other forms of support to help them address the underlying issues that contributed to their behavior.

In addition, restorative justice ministry may involve community involvement, including support groups, mentoring programs, and other forms of community engagement. By involving the broader community in the restoration process, both the victim and the offender can feel supported and valued.

Ultimately, the goal of restorative justice ministry is to promote healing and reconciliation, and to create a sense of community that is based on forgiveness, compassion, and love. Through this approach, both the victim and the offender can be restored back into the community and can move forward in a positive and healthy way.

21. The Church, as an accepting community, can help with the issues of restoration, and facilitate reintegration for both the victim and the offender back into the community.

The Church can play a significant role in promoting restoration and facilitating reintegration for both the victim and the offender back into the community. As an accepting and supportive community, the Church can provide a safe and nurturing space for those affected by crime to heal and find support.

For victims of crime, the Church can offer pastoral care, counseling, and other forms of support to help them cope with the trauma they have experienced. The Church can also offer a supportive community where victims can connect with others who have had similar experiences and find comfort and healing.

For offenders, the Church can offer a space for confession, repentance, and redemption. Through pastoral counseling, mentoring, and other forms of support, the Church can help offenders address the underlying issues that contributed to their behavior and find a path towards rehabilitation and restoration.

In addition, the Church can play a role in facilitating reintegration for both the victim and the offender back into the community. Through community outreach programs, support groups, and other forms of community engagement, the Church can help to bridge the gap between those affected by crime and the broader community.

Ultimately, the Church can help to promote healing, reconciliation, and restoration for all those affected by crime. By creating a supportive and accepting community, the Church can provide a space for both the victim and the offender to heal, find redemption, and be welcomed back into the community.

22. What is required of a ministry, in order to be holistic?

a) It must consider both the offender and victim;

b) it attempts to meet the spiritual as well as the physical and emotional needs of those involved;

c) and it addresses the offender in prison, as well as after they are released back to the community.

Putting it in simple terms, you must cover all the bases in order to be holistic.

A holistic ministry is one that addresses the needs of the whole person - body, mind, and spirit. This approach recognizes that people have complex and interconnected needs, and that addressing one area of need can have a positive impact on other areas of their life.

To be holistic, a ministry must take into account the diverse needs of the people it serves. This may involve providing support and resources in a variety of areas, including:

1. Spiritual: A holistic ministry should provide opportunities for people to connect with God and deepen their faith. This may involve offering worship services, Bible studies, or prayer groups.
2. Emotional: A holistic ministry should provide support and resources to help people cope with emotional challenges such

as anxiety, depression, or trauma. This may involve offering counseling services, support groups, or other forms of emotional support.

3. Physical: A holistic ministry should provide resources and support to help people maintain physical health and well-being. This may involve offering health education, exercise classes, or access to medical care.

4. Social: A holistic ministry should provide opportunities for people to connect with others and build relationships. This may involve offering social events, community service projects, or other forms of social support.

5. Financial: A holistic ministry should provide resources and support to help people meet their basic needs and achieve financial stability. This may involve offering job training, financial counseling, or emergency assistance.

By addressing the diverse needs of the people, it serves, a holistic ministry can help to promote healing, growth, and transformation in the lives of those it serves. This approach recognizes the interconnectedness of our physical, emotional, and spiritual needs and provides a framework for supporting the whole person.

CHAPTER VII
HOW THE CHURCH CAN IMPACT
CORRECTIONS

1. How did Jesus define the Church's clear mandate to do criminal justice ministry in Matthew 25:35-36? **35** For I was an hungred, and ye gave me meat: I was thirsty, and ye gave me drink: I was a stranger, and ye took me in: **36** Naked, and ye clothed me: I was sick, and ye visited me: I was in prison, and ye came unto me.

a) vs. 35a: for I was hungry and you gave Me food;

b) vs. 35b: I was thirsty and ye gave me drink:

c) vs. 35c: I was a stranger, and ye took me in:

d) vs. 36a: naked and ye clothed me:

e) vs. 36b: I was in prison,

f) vs. 36c: and ye came unto me

The hungry, thirsty, stranger, naked and sick are obvious concerns for ministry; but Jesus went beyond these groups to point out the outcast prisoner's need for love and compassion.

In Matthew 25:35-36, Jesus defined the Church's clear mandate to do criminal justice ministry by saying:

"For I was hungry and you gave me something to eat, I was thirsty and you gave me something to drink, I was a stranger and you invited me in, I needed clothes and you clothed me, I was sick and you looked after me, I was in prison and you came to visit me."

These words of Jesus highlight the importance of caring for those who are in need, including those who are imprisoned. Jesus emphasizes that by ministering to those who are hungry, thirsty, or in prison, we are ministering to Him.

This passage provides a clear mandate for the Church to engage in criminal justice ministry by providing support and resources to those who are incarcerated or impacted by the criminal justice system. This may involve visiting those in prison, offering counseling or mentoring to offenders, or providing support to the families of those who are incarcerated.

In addition, this passage highlights the importance of viewing those impacted by the criminal justice system as individuals who are in need of care and support, rather than simply as criminals. By offering compassion and support to those who are impacted by crime and the criminal justice system, the Church can help to promote healing, restoration, and reconciliation.

2. The broad spectrum of criminal justice ministries that the Church can bring to corrections can be divided into four categories.:

    a) Victims

    b) Offenders

    c) Family

    d) And criminal justice professionals

The Church has a vital role to play in bringing a range of criminal justice ministries to the corrections system. These ministries can be broadly categorized into four categories: victims, offenders, family, and criminal justice professionals.

a) Victims: The Church can bring its resources to bear to support and minister to victims of crime. This could include offering counseling, pastoral care, and other forms of support to help them recover from the trauma of their experience. The Church can also work to advocate for the rights of victims and promote awareness of the impact of crime on individuals, families, and communities.

b) Offenders: The Church has a unique perspective on the issue of crime and punishment. It can offer pastoral care, counseling, and spiritual guidance to offenders, helping them to find a path towards repentance, restoration, and healing. The Church can also advocate for restorative justice approaches that seek to address the harm caused by the offender and work towards repairing the relationships that have been broken.

c) Family: The Church can provide support and care to the families of offenders and victims alike. It can help them to navigate the criminal justice system and provide a range of pastoral and practical services to help them cope with the challenges they face.

d) Criminal justice professionals: The Church can play an important role in supporting the work of criminal justice professionals, including police officers, prosecutors, judges, and corrections staff. This could include offering pastoral care, counseling, and spiritual support to help these professionals deal with the stresses and challenges of their work. The Church can also work to promote a greater understanding of the issues and challenges facing those who work in the criminal justice system.

In summary, the Church can bring a broad range of criminal justice ministries to the corrections system. By ministering to victims, offenders, families, and criminal justice professionals alike, the Church can help to promote healing, restoration, and reconciliation in our communities.

3. Criminal justice ministry is a mission to suffering people, clearly needing the love and compassion of Christ and His Church.

Criminal justice ministry is a mission to suffering people, who are often in need of the love and compassion of Christ and His Church, for several reasons:

1. Criminal justice involves harm and brokenness: Crime and the criminal justice system often involve harm and brokenness, including victims of crime, families affected by the actions of offenders, and offenders who have committed harm. These individuals are often in need of the love and compassion of Christ and His Church, which can offer healing, restoration, and hope.

2. Criminal justice ministry is a calling to serve: For many Christians, criminal justice ministry is a calling to serve those who are often overlooked or forgotten. It is an opportunity to live out the gospel message of love, mercy, and justice, and to share the hope of Christ with those who are in need.

3. The criminal justice system can be dehumanizing: The criminal justice system can be dehumanizing, both for offenders and for those who work within it. Criminal justice ministry offers an alternative perspective that values the dignity and worth of every person, regardless of their actions or circumstances.

4. The Church has a unique role to play: The Church has a unique role to play in criminal justice ministry, as it offers spiritual care, pastoral support, and a community of faith that can help to sustain individuals as they navigate the criminal justice system. Through its ministries, the Church can bring the hope and compassion of Christ to those who are suffering.

In conclusion, criminal justice ministry is a mission to suffering people who are in need of the love and compassion of Christ and His Church. Through its ministries, the Church can offer healing, hope, and a sense of purpose to those who are affected by crime and the criminal justice system.

4. One of the greatest ways the Church can impact the victims of crime is the ministry of presence.

Remember the popular cliche "actions speak louder than words" as you minister in silence to victims of crime.

The ministry of presence is a powerful way in which the Church can impact the victims of crime. It involves being present with those who have experienced harm, listening to their stories, and offering emotional and spiritual support.

When a person experiences the trauma of crime, they may feel isolated, alone, and overwhelmed. They may struggle with feelings of fear, anger, sadness, and confusion. The ministry of presence involves showing up in these moments, being willing to sit with the person, and offering comfort, care, and compassion.

The ministry of presence can take many forms, including:

1. Visiting victims in hospitals or homes: The Church can offer practical assistance by visiting victims in hospitals or their homes. This could involve offering prayer, bringing meals, providing transportation, or simply being present to listen and offer comfort.

2. Providing counseling and pastoral care: The Church can offer professional counseling and pastoral care to victims of crime, helping them to process their emotions, cope with trauma, and find hope and healing.

3. Offering support groups and peer counseling: The Church can offer support groups and peer counseling for victims of crime, providing a safe and supportive environment for people to share their experiences, connect with others who have gone through similar experiences, and find hope and healing.

4. Advocating for victims' rights: The Church can advocate for victims' rights by raising awareness of the impact of crime, promoting policies that prioritize victim support, and providing resources for victims to access legal and other support services.

In all these ways, the ministry of presence offers a powerful way for the Church to impact the victims of crime. By showing up, listening, and offering care and compassion, the Church can help victims to feel less alone, more supported, and more hopeful as they navigate the difficult aftermath of crime.

5. As Christians, we should be able to refrain from giving reasons, advice, or asking questions, and simply walk with the victims through their period of crisis.:

As Christians, one of the most important ways we can support victims of crime is by being present with them in their time of crisis.

This means being willing to walk alongside them, without judgment or the need to offer reasons, advice, or questions.

Here are some reasons why refraining from giving reasons, advice, or asking questions can be important:

1. It shows respect for the victim's experience: When we listen without judgment, we show respect for the victim's experience and validate their feelings. By not trying to explain away their pain or offer quick solutions, we demonstrate our willingness to be present with them in their suffering.

2. It creates a safe space for the victim to process their emotions: Victims of crime may experience a wide range of emotions, including fear, anger, and sadness. By creating a safe space where they can express themselves without fear of judgment or criticism, we allow them to process their emotions in a healthy way.

3. It allows the victim to take ownership of their healing: By refraining from giving advice or solutions, we allow the victim to take ownership of their own healing process. They can choose the pace and direction of their healing journey, and we can support them by simply being present.

4. It reflects the love and compassion of Christ: When we walk with victims without judgment or the need to offer advice or solutions, we reflect the love and compassion of Christ. We show them that they are not alone in their suffering and that God is present with them in their pain.

In conclusion, as Christians, our role in supporting victims of crime is to be present with them in their time of crisis. By refraining from giving reasons, advice, or asking questions, we can create a safe space for victims to process their emotions, take ownership of their healing, and experience the love and compassion of Christ.

6. Give two reasons why offenders seem to be the easiest group to which you can minister.:

a) because they are a captive audience with plenty of time on their hands

b) and usually, they understand their need for help

The ministry of presence could also be effectively used with the offender. This approach could be carried out through correspondence and visits to the prison.

Ministering to offenders can be a unique and fulfilling experience for several reasons. Two reasons why offenders seem to be the easiest group to which one can minister are:

a) They are a captive audience with plenty of time on their hands: Offenders are often incarcerated and have a lot of time on their hands. This means that they may be more open and receptive to spiritual and personal growth than those who are not incarcerated. They may also have a greater desire to connect with others and build community.

b) They usually understand their need for help: Offenders often have a deep understanding of their own struggles and shortcomings. This awareness can create a sense of humility and openness to receiving help and guidance from others. They may be more willing to seek out and engage with resources that can help them address their issues and grow as individuals.

These two factors can make offenders a receptive audience for ministry and personal growth. However, it is important to note that not all offenders will be open to or interested in spiritual growth, and there may be significant barriers to engaging with this population, such as security concerns and limited resources. Additionally, ministering to offenders can be complex and may require specialized training and support. Overall, while offenders may be a unique and potentially receptive group to minister to, it is important to approach this work with humility, sensitivity, and careful consideration of the needs and challenges involved.

7. Christianity is so powerful because it offers these individuals the opportunity for forgiveness and the ability to start their lives over.

Christianity is a faith that is centered around forgiveness and redemption. The core message of the Christian faith is that Jesus Christ died on the cross to forgive the sins of humanity, and through his resurrection, he offers the promise of eternal life. This message of forgiveness and redemption is particularly powerful for individuals who have been involved in the criminal justice system.

One of the most significant challenges that offenders face is the stigma and shame associated with their past actions. This can lead to feelings of hopelessness, isolation, and despair. However, the Christian message of forgiveness offers these individuals a way to move beyond their past mistakes and start over with a renewed sense of purpose and hope.

Through the teachings of Jesus Christ, offenders can find a path to forgiveness and healing. This can involve seeking forgiveness from God, as well as from those who have been impacted by their actions. By taking responsibility for their past mistakes and working towards making amends, offenders can begin the process of healing and transformation.

Christianity also offers a sense of community and support that can be vital for offenders who are trying to rebuild their lives. Through church communities and other Christian organizations, offenders can connect with others who share their faith and their struggles. This can provide a sense of belonging and accountability that can help them stay on track and avoid falling back into old patterns of behavior.

In conclusion, the Christian message of forgiveness and redemption can be a powerful tool for individuals who have been involved in the criminal justice system. By offering the opportunity for forgiveness and the ability to start over, Christianity can provide a path towards healing, transformation, and a renewed sense of purpose.

8. Establishing a relationship with an offender is imperative.

Many will shy away from establishing a relationship with an offender because of fear. Precautionary measures should be taken before making contact. For instance, if your method of establishing a relationship is through correspondence, use your church's address or a post office box instead of your home address.

Establishing a relationship with an offender is imperative for several reasons. Here are a few:

1. Building trust: Offenders may be wary of people in authority, including those who work in the criminal justice system. By establishing a relationship with an offender, you can build trust and create an environment in which they feel comfortable sharing their thoughts, feelings, and struggles.

2. Providing support: Offenders often feel isolated and alone, particularly if they have few friends or family members who are able or willing to support them. By establishing a relationship with an offender, you can provide them with emotional support and guidance. This can be particularly important during times of crisis or when the offender is feeling overwhelmed.

3. Encouraging personal growth: Offenders may have deep-seated issues that have contributed to their involvement in the criminal justice system. By establishing a relationship with an offender, you can encourage them to reflect on their past actions, take

responsibility for their mistakes, and work towards personal growth and development.

4. Offering hope: For many offenders, the future may seem bleak and hopeless. By establishing a relationship with an offender, you can offer them a sense of hope for the future. This can involve helping them set realistic goals, connecting them with resources and support, and encouraging them to believe in their ability to change and grow.

5. Reducing recidivism: Studies have shown that establishing a positive relationship with an offender can reduce the likelihood that they will reoffend. By building a relationship with an offender, you can help them feel valued and supported, which can decrease the likelihood that they will return to criminal behavior.

In conclusion, establishing a relationship with an offender is essential for providing support, encouraging personal growth, and reducing recidivism. By building trust, providing emotional support, offering hope, and encouraging personal growth, you can make a positive impact on the lives of offenders and help them to find a path towards healing and transformation.

9. Name one of the best things that prison ministers can do.:

"Arrive early to fellowship or sit with the offenders"

One of the best things that prison ministers can do is to provide ongoing support and follow-up care to offenders after they are released from prison. Many offenders face significant challenges when reintegrating into society, including finding employment, securing housing, and rebuilding relationships with family and friends. By providing ongoing support and follow-up care, prison ministers can help offenders navigate these challenges and stay on track towards a successful reintegration. This can involve connecting offenders with community resources, providing emotional support, and offering guidance and encouragement. Ultimately, by providing ongoing support, prison ministers can help to reduce recidivism and improve the overall well-being of offenders as they transition back into society.

In addition, the simple gesture of memorizing the offenders' names speaks volumes to these individuals. In prison they are known only by an identification number, so when you speak their name, you make them feel like real people.

10. An effective criminal justice ministry program will include a variety of outreach, nurturing, and educational activities using Church volunteers.:

An effective criminal justice ministry program is one that includes a variety of outreach, nurturing, and educational activities that engage both offenders and the broader community. Church volunteers play a crucial role in these efforts, as they can offer a range of skills, experiences, and perspectives that can help to make these programs more effective.

Here are a few examples of the types of activities that an effective criminal justice ministry program might include:

1. Outreach: One of the most important aspects of a criminal justice ministry program is outreach to offenders and their families. This might involve visiting prisons or jails, organizing letter-writing campaigns, or connecting with families of offenders. Church volunteers can play a key role in these efforts by providing emotional support, offering encouragement, and connecting offenders with resources and support.

2. Nurturing: Many offenders have experienced trauma, abuse, or neglect in their lives. A criminal justice ministry program can provide a nurturing environment that promotes healing and growth. This might involve offering counseling or therapy services, providing mentorship and role modeling, or creating opportunities for spiritual growth and reflection.

3. Education: Education is another critical component of a criminal justice ministry program. This might involve offering vocational training, educational classes, or life skills workshops. Church volunteers can help to facilitate these activities by providing instruction, mentorship, or support services.

4. Community engagement: A criminal justice ministry program should also engage the broader community in efforts to reduce recidivism and support offender reentry. This might involve organizing community events, partnering with local businesses and organizations, or creating opportunities for community members to volunteer or offer support.

In conclusion, an effective criminal justice ministry program will include a variety of outreach, nurturing, and educational activities that engage both offenders and the broader community. Church volunteers can play a critical role in these efforts by providing emotional support, mentorship, instruction, and other support services. By working together, we can create a more just and compassionate society that supports the needs of all its members, including those who have been involved in the criminal justice system.

11. Describe a mentor's role with the offender.:

a) is to be a friend,

b) to advise,

c) to help

d) and to model the Christian life for the offender.

A mentor's role with an offender is to provide guidance, support, and accountability as the offender works to reintegrate into society and lead a more positive and productive life. A mentor can be an invaluable resource for offenders, offering them a positive role model, someone to talk to, and someone to hold them accountable for their actions.

Here are some specific ways that a mentor can help an offender:

1. Providing emotional support: Mentors can offer offenders emotional support and encouragement as they work to overcome the challenges they face. This might involve listening to the offender's concerns, offering guidance and advice, and providing a sounding board for their ideas.

2. Setting goals: A mentor can help an offender set goals and work towards achieving them. This might involve developing a plan for finding a job, securing housing, or building healthy relationships.

3. Offering guidance: A mentor can offer guidance and advice on a range of issues, from managing finances to dealing with legal problems. They can also help offenders navigate the complexities of the criminal justice system and connect them with resources and support services.

4. Providing accountability: A mentor can hold an offender accountable for their actions, helping them stay on track towards their goals and avoid negative behaviors that might lead to recidivism.

Ultimately, a mentor's role is to be a positive influence in an offender's life, helping them to build the skills, relationships, and support networks they need to succeed. By providing guidance, support, and accountability, a mentor can help an offender navigate the challenges of reentry and build a brighter future for themselves and their families.

Proverbs 27:17 says, "Iron sharpeneth iron; so a man sharpeneth the countenance of his friend." Personal and spiritual growth is a communal affair, as Scripture reminds us in various ways. In the beginning, God did not make just one human being but two (Genesis 1:26–27).

David had Nathan the prophet, a faithful friend who brought him to repentance (2 Samuel 12:1–15). And Jesus appointed not just one overseer; rather, He has chosen for His church to be governed by a body of elders and deacons (Acts 6:1–7). Not just ex-offenders, but we ALL need others in our lives to sharpen us and encourage us in our daily walk.

Those of us who have at least one friend upon whom we can count for loving, constructive criticism are blessed. If we do not have any such people in our lives, we should be looking for them. We should also be asking the Lord to help develop us into people who can offer such criticism to others and to enable us to persist in love toward our friends and others.

12. Which aspect of criminal justice ministry could easily be listed with the victims of crime?

"Because they too suffer from the actions of the offender."

The offender's family and loved ones should always be listed with the victims of crime because they too suffer from the offender's criminal behavior. Even the sanctions levied against the offender, as a result of their crime, is felt by their family and loved ones.

The aspect of criminal justice ministry that could easily be listed with the victims of crime is the ministry of presence. This is because victims of crime often experience emotional trauma, pain, and isolation, and may feel that no one understands what they are going through. The ministry of presence involves simply being there for the victim, listening to their concerns, and offering emotional support and encouragement. This can be a powerful way to help victims feel seen, heard, and valued, and to remind them that they are not alone in their struggle.

Additionally, the ministry of presence can help victims to begin the process of healing and recovery, as they feel supported and encouraged to move forward with their lives. Therefore, the ministry of presence is a crucial aspect of criminal justice ministry that can be listed with the victims of crime.

13. Incarceration produces what has been dubbed a prison widow or widower, and the prison orphan.

Incarceration can have far-reaching effects on the families of those who are incarcerated. The term "prison widow or widower" is used to describe the partners of incarcerated individuals who must endure the hardships of separation and often struggle to maintain the relationship while their loved one is in prison. The term "prison orphan" is used to describe children who have a parent in prison and may face a range of emotional, social, and economic challenges as a result.

The impact of incarceration on families can be significant and long-lasting. Here are some of the ways that incarceration can produce a prison widow or widower and a prison orphan:

1. Emotional trauma: Families of incarcerated individuals often experience emotional trauma as a result of the separation. Partners may feel abandoned, betrayed, or hopeless, while children may feel confused, anxious, or depressed. These emotional challenges can be difficult to overcome and may have lasting effects on the family.

2. Economic challenges: Incarceration can also have significant economic impacts on families. Partners of incarcerated individuals may struggle to make ends meet without the support of their loved one, while children may experience financial hardship and be forced to rely on social services for support.

3. Social isolation: Families of incarcerated individuals may also experience social isolation, as they may feel stigmatized or ashamed of their loved one's incarceration. This can lead to a sense of isolation and loneliness, which can further exacerbate the emotional challenges they face.

4. Difficulty maintaining relationships: Maintaining relationships with incarcerated individuals can be challenging, as families must navigate the logistics of prison visits, phone calls, and correspondence. This can be especially difficult for children, who may struggle to understand why their parent is not with them and may feel disconnected from them as a result.

In conclusion, the impact of incarceration on families can be significant and long-lasting. Partners of incarcerated individuals can become prison widows or widowers, while children can become prison orphans. The emotional trauma, economic challenges, social isolation, and difficulty maintaining relationships that families of incarcerated individuals face can be difficult to overcome, but with support and resources, they can work towards healing and rebuilding their lives.

14. As the offender's family waits on them, they need help spirituality, emotionally and financially.

When an offender is incarcerated, it can be a challenging time for their family members who are left behind. They may experience a range of difficulties, including spiritual, emotional, and financial challenges.

Spiritual Support: The family of an incarcerated person may experience a crisis of faith or struggle to understand why this has happened to their loved one. They may also feel isolated from their church community, as they may be reluctant to share their situation with others. Therefore, they need spiritual support, such as prayer, scripture, and counseling, to help them find peace and comfort in their faith.

Emotional Support: The family members of incarcerated persons may feel a range of emotions, such as shame, guilt, anger, frustration, sadness, and anxiety. They may worry about the welfare of their loved one, and the uncertainty of their situation can cause stress and anxiety. Therefore, they need emotional support, such as counseling and therapy, to help them cope with the challenges they face.

Financial Support: Incarceration can also have significant financial impacts on families. They may struggle to make ends meet without the support of their loved one's income, and they may also have to pay for legal fees or other expenses related to the incarceration. Therefore, they need financial support, such as government assistance programs or support from community organizations, to help them maintain their financial stability.

In conclusion, the family of an incarcerated person may need help spiritually, emotionally, and financially as they wait for their loved one to be released. They need spiritual support to find comfort in their faith, emotional support to help them cope with their feelings, and financial support to help them maintain their financial stability. Therefore, it is important for criminal justice ministries to provide holistic support to the families of incarcerated persons, in addition to supporting the offenders themselves.

15. There is a great need for marriage seminars that could save literally hundreds of offender marriages, and, as a result, break the generational cycle of crime and brokenness in these families.:

Approximately 90% of all marriages end in divorce when the incarceration period exceeds one year. If the offender can come home to a loving, waiting, Christian family, they have a greater chance of avoiding crime and staying out of prison in the future.

Marriage seminars are an essential component of criminal justice ministry because they offer support and guidance to offenders and their families. Offender marriages often face unique challenges, such as separation, financial difficulties, and communication issues, which can put a significant strain on their relationship. Without proper support and guidance, these marriages are at risk of failing, which can lead to a cycle of brokenness and crime in the family.

Marriage seminars can provide essential resources and tools for offender couples to help them build strong and healthy relationships. These seminars can offer guidance on topics such as communication, conflict resolution, financial management, and parenting, which can help couples address the challenges they face and build stronger relationships. The seminars can also provide an opportunity for couples to connect with other couples facing similar challenges and to share experiences and support.

By helping to save offender marriages, these seminars can break the cycle of generational crime and brokenness in these families. When offender couples have strong and healthy relationships, they are better equipped to provide a stable and supportive home environment for their children, which can help to break the cycle of criminal behavior and incarceration.

Moreover, research has shown that strong family connections and support can reduce recidivism rates among offenders. Offenders who have positive relationships with their families and receive support and guidance are more likely to successfully reintegrate into society and avoid returning to a life of crime.

In conclusion, marriage seminars are an essential component of criminal justice ministry as they offer support and guidance to offender couples and help to break the cycle of generational crime and brokenness in families. By providing essential resources and tools, these seminars can help to save hundreds of offender marriages and reduce recidivism rates. Therefore, it is crucial to incorporate marriage seminars into criminal justice ministry programs.

16. Which aspect of criminal justice ministry is the most difficult?

The criminal justice professionals (officers and officials)

One thing we can do is to recognize and encourage criminal justice professionals who are positively impacting prisoners by their efforts, and inspiring them to become productive members of our community upon release. Theirs is not an easy job.

It is challenging to identify one specific aspect of criminal justice ministry as the most difficult since each component of the ministry presents unique challenges. However, working with offenders, especially those who have committed heinous crimes, can be one of the most challenging aspects of criminal justice ministry.

Ministering to offenders can be emotionally and mentally challenging for many reasons. Firstly, offenders may be hostile, manipulative, or resistant to change, which can make it challenging to establish a relationship of trust and empathy. Secondly, ministers may have to confront their own biases and preconceptions about offenders, which can interfere with their ability to minister effectively. Thirdly, offenders may have experienced trauma, abuse, or addiction, which can make it challenging to address their spiritual and emotional needs effectively.

Moreover, working with offenders can be challenging because ministers may face opposition from others who believe that offenders do not deserve compassion or forgiveness. There may be negative attitudes toward offenders from the public or even from within the Church, which can make it challenging to advocate for the needs of offenders and to promote restorative justice principles.

In conclusion, while each component of criminal justice ministry presents unique challenges, working with offenders can be one of the most challenging aspects of the ministry due to various factors such as resistance to change, the need for emotional and mental support, addressing spiritual and emotional needs, confronting one's own biases, and negative attitudes from others towards offenders.

17. The first step in ministering to a criminal justice professional is the building of a relationships.

The first step in ministering to a criminal justice professional is building a relationship because it allows the minister to understand the unique challenges and stressors faced by those working in the criminal justice system.

Criminal justice professionals, such as police officers, correctional officers, and judges, often face high levels of stress, trauma, and burnout due to the nature of their work. They are exposed to violence, crime scenes, and the suffering of victims and offenders on a daily basis. They may also face challenges in balancing their personal and professional lives and may feel isolated or unsupported in their work environment.

By building a relationship, the minister can demonstrate empathy and understanding of the challenges faced by criminal justice professionals. This can help to establish trust and rapport, which are essential for effective ministry. It can also provide an opportunity for the minister to listen and offer emotional and spiritual support, as well as practical resources and referrals to professional services if needed.

Furthermore, building a relationship with a criminal justice professional can help to break down barriers between the Church and the criminal justice system. Criminal justice professionals may have negative attitudes toward the Church or religion, or they may be skeptical of outside influences in their work environment. Building a relationship based on mutual respect and understanding can help to overcome these barriers and promote positive change in the criminal justice system.

In summary, building a relationship is the first step in ministering to a criminal justice professional because it allows the minister to understand the unique challenges faced by these individuals, demonstrate empathy and support, offer practical resources and referrals, and break down barriers between the Church and the criminal justice system.

18. *Establishing a relationship requires much patience, because the correctional staff in many ways is a closed community that shuns outsiders.*

Establishing a relationship with correctional staff can be a challenging task because they often work in a closed community that may be suspicious or unwelcoming of outsiders. This is particularly true in correctional facilities, where staff members are responsible for maintaining the safety and security of the institution and its inmates.

In order to establish a relationship with correctional staff, it is important to approach them with sensitivity, understanding, and patience. It is important to recognize that these individuals are under a great deal of stress and may be skeptical of outsiders, particularly those who are affiliated with a religious organization.

One effective approach is to start by simply being present in the correctional facility and offering to assist with any needs or concerns that staff members may have. This could include offering to lead a Bible study or prayer group, providing resources on topics such as stress management or conflict resolution, or simply being available to listen and offer support.

It is also important to be respectful of the boundaries and protocols established by the correctional facility. This may include obtaining the necessary approvals and clearances to enter the facility, adhering to the rules and regulations established by the institution, and respecting the privacy and confidentiality of staff members and inmates.

Additionally, it is important to recognize the unique challenges and stressors faced by correctional staff members, and to offer support and encouragement in a non-judgmental and compassionate manner. This may involve offering resources and referrals for mental health or addiction services, providing opportunities for staff members to participate in support groups or counseling sessions, or simply being a supportive and empathetic presence.

In summary, establishing a relationship with correctional staff requires patience, sensitivity, and understanding. By being present, offering support and resources, and respecting the boundaries and protocols established by the institution, ministers can build trust and rapport with correctional staff members and promote positive change in the correctional system.

19. Because of varying work hours, a church should be willing to schedule special activities and develop programs to include ...: these unique individuals

Correctional staff work in a unique and challenging environment that requires them to maintain a high level of alertness and vigilance at all times. As a result, their work schedules can be unpredictable and may involve long hours, irregular shifts, and weekend and holiday work.

In order to minister effectively to correctional staff, it is important for the Church to be flexible and accommodating in scheduling activities and developing programs. This may involve scheduling activities and events at times when correctional staff are more likely to be available, such as early morning, late evening, or weekends. It may also involve developing programs and activities that can be accessed remotely or on a flexible schedule, such as online Bible studies, devotional materials, or prayer groups.

In addition to scheduling activities and programs at convenient times, it is important to create an environment that is welcoming and supportive of correctional staff. This may involve providing resources and support for common challenges faced by correctional staff, such as stress management, self-care, and mental health resources. It may also involve providing opportunities for correctional staff to connect with one another and build community, such as support groups, social events, and networking opportunities.

Ultimately, the church must be willing to adapt and be creative in order to minister effectively to correctional staff. By recognizing the unique challenges and needs of this group, and by providing support and resources in a flexible and accommodating manner, the church can build meaningful relationships and promote positive change in the correctional system.

CHAPTER IX
ORGANIZATIONAL CHANGE

1. Convincing justice system officials to embrace a new justice paradigm is a difficult task.

Convincing justice system officials to embrace a new justice paradigm can be a difficult task for several reasons.

Firstly, justice system officials are often trained and experienced in a particular approach to justice that may be deeply ingrained in their thinking and decision-making processes. This can make it challenging to convince them to adopt a new approach, particularly if they perceive it as a significant departure from their current methods.

Secondly, justice system officials may be subject to political pressures or constraints that limit their ability to make significant changes to the justice system. For example, they may be subject to budgetary constraints, mandates from lawmakers or other government officials, or pressure from interest groups or the media.

Thirdly, justice system officials may be wary of adopting a new justice paradigm if they are not convinced of its effectiveness or if they perceive it as too risky. This may be particularly true if the new paradigm involves significant changes to existing practices or procedures.

Finally, justice system officials may be resistant to change due to a lack of awareness or understanding of alternative justice paradigms. They may not be familiar with the latest research or evidence-based practices, or they may not have had the opportunity to learn about alternative approaches to justice.

In order to overcome these challenges, advocates for a new justice paradigm must be persistent, strategic, and collaborative in their efforts to engage with justice system officials. They must be able to effectively communicate the benefits and potential risks of the new approach, and they must be able to demonstrate its effectiveness through research and evidence-based practices. They must also be able to build partnerships and coalitions with other stakeholders, such as community leaders, advocacy groups, and policymakers, in order to create a supportive environment for change.

b) However, it is important to know that no barrier is insurmountable.

Change is often met with resistance because of fear of the unknown. The current punitive system has been in place for years and some are convinced that it is the only way to carry out criminal justice.

That's true! While there may be challenges and barriers to implementing a new justice paradigm, it is important to remember that no barrier is insurmountable. With dedication, persistence, and creativity, advocates for change can find ways to overcome even the most difficult obstacles.

One way to do this is by building relationships and fostering collaboration among stakeholders. By working together and finding common ground, justice system officials, advocates, and community members can create a shared vision for a more just and equitable system, and develop strategies to bring that vision to life.

Another important approach is to be open to feedback and be willing to adapt and adjust as needed. If initial efforts to implement a new justice paradigm are met with resistance or challenges, it may be necessary to re-evaluate and make changes to the approach in order to achieve success.

Finally, it is important to remain focused on the ultimate goal: creating a justice system that is fair, effective, and compassionate. By keeping this goal in mind and working towards it with persistence and determination, advocates for change can overcome even the most daunting barriers and create a better future for all members of society.

2. In implementing any restorative justice programs and practices, it is necessary to determine what good will come from restorative justice principles, and to identify any possible challenges.

Implementing restorative justice programs and practices can be a complex and challenging process, as it involves a shift in the way the justice system approaches crime and justice. In order to successfully implement restorative justice principles, it is important to determine what benefits can be gained from this approach, as well as any possible challenges that may arise.

One of the key benefits of restorative justice is that it can help to repair harm caused by crime and promote healing for both victims and offenders. By involving all parties in the process and focusing on addressing the root causes of the crime, restorative justice can help to reduce recidivism and create a safer, more just society.

However, implementing restorative justice programs and practices can also present challenges. For example, there may be resistance from justice system officials or the public, who may be more familiar with traditional punitive approaches to justice. Additionally, it can be challenging to ensure that all parties involved in the process feel heard and respected, particularly if there are power imbalances or unresolved trauma.

To address these challenges, it is important to engage in ongoing education and dialogue with justice system officials, community members, and other stakeholders. By providing information and resources about the benefits of restorative justice and addressing any concerns or questions, advocates for this approach can help to build support and understanding for these programs and practices. Additionally, it is important to ensure that restorative justice processes are implemented in a way that is culturally responsive and trauma-informed, taking into account the unique needs and experiences of all participants.

In summary, implementing restorative justice programs and practices requires careful consideration of the benefits and challenges involved. By engaging in ongoing education, dialogue, and culturally responsive and trauma-informed approaches, advocates for restorative justice can help to create a more just and equitable justice system for all.

3. How might the results of a "benefit assessment" help in the implementation of restorative justice programs and practices?

a) Developing marketing messages for various constituencies, including community members, offenders and their advocates, victims and service providers, justice practitioners, elected officials, the news media, and allied professionals.

b) Comparing existing approaches to justice in the context of a more beneficial approach, i.e., cost effectiveness, victim involvement, offender competency development, community appreciation of justice practices, etc. . . .

c) Building programs on perceived strengths.

d) Evaluating programs, especially when benefits for these are tangible and can be measured in terms of performance outcomes.

Overall, Restorative justice offers many benefits compared to the traditional criminal justice:

- *It substantially reduces repeat offending for some offenders, although not all.*
- *It reduces repeat offending more than prison for adults and at least as well as prison for youth.*
- *It helps reduce the costs of criminal justice.*
- *It provides both victims and offenders with more satisfaction that justice had been done than did traditional criminal justice.*
- *It reduces crime victims' post-traumatic stress symptoms and the related costs.*
- *It reduces crime victims' desire for violent revenge against their offenders.*

- A "benefit assessment" is a process used to evaluate the potential benefits and drawbacks of implementing a particular policy or program. In the case of restorative justice programs and practices, a benefit assessment can help identify the specific ways in which these approaches can benefit victims, offenders, and the community as a whole.

- The results of a benefit assessment can be useful in several ways in the implementation of restorative justice programs and practices. First, it can help to build support and understanding for these approaches among justice system officials, community members, and other stakeholders. By highlighting the potential benefits of restorative justice, such as reduced recidivism and increased victim satisfaction, advocates can help to build momentum for the implementation of these programs and practices.

- Second, a benefit assessment can help to guide the development and implementation of restorative justice programs and practices. By identifying specific areas where restorative justice can have the greatest impact, such as reducing racial disparities in the justice system or addressing trauma and mental health issues among offenders, advocates can help to ensure that these programs are tailored to the unique needs and circumstances of the community.

- Finally, a benefit assessment can help to measure the effectiveness of restorative justice programs and practices over time. By regularly evaluating the outcomes and impacts of these programs, advocates can make adjustments and improvements to ensure that they are achieving their intended goals.

- In summary, a benefit assessment can provide valuable information and guidance for the implementation of restorative justice programs and practices, helping to build support, guide development, and measure effectiveness over time.

4. In what ways can the results of a "barrier assessment" assist in implementing any restorative justice programs and practices?

a): Early identification of potential opponent's arguments against restorative justice approaches.

b): Focusing planning and implementation on reducing

c): or eliminating possible barriers

d): Evaluating program effectiveness based upon success in overcoming any barriers.

A "barrier assessment" is a process used to identify and address potential obstacles or barriers to the successful implementation of a particular policy or program. In the case of restorative justice programs and practices, a barrier assessment can help identify specific challenges or obstacles that may need to be addressed in order to implement these approaches effectively.

The results of a barrier assessment can be useful in several ways in the implementation of restorative justice programs and practices. First, it can help to anticipate and address potential challenges before they become major obstacles. By identifying potential barriers, such as resistance from justice system officials or limited funding, advocates can develop strategies to overcome these challenges and ensure that the programs are implemented successfully.

Second, a barrier assessment can help to ensure that restorative justice programs and practices are tailored to the unique needs and circumstances of the community. By identifying specific challenges or barriers in the local context, advocates can develop programs that are more responsive and effective in meeting the needs of victims, offenders, and the community as a whole.

Finally, a barrier assessment can help to build support and buy-in for restorative justice programs and practices. By openly acknowledging and addressing potential challenges or obstacles, advocates can demonstrate a commitment to implementing these approaches in a thoughtful and effective way, which can help to build trust and support among justice system officials, community members, and other stakeholders.

In summary, a barrier assessment can help to identify potential challenges or obstacles to the successful implementation of restorative justice programs and practices, tailor these approaches to the unique needs and circumstances of the community, and build support and buy-in for these approaches.

5. Changing the criminal justice system requires a disciplined long-term commitment with creative leadership and vision.

All efforts to change the current criminal justice system should not include criticism but be informative and suggestive in nature.

Changing any established system, including the criminal justice system, is a complex and challenging task that requires a disciplined long-term commitment with creative leadership and vision. This is because the criminal justice system is deeply rooted in the political, social, and cultural fabric of society. It has a long history, and its practices and procedures are often deeply ingrained in the minds of those who work within it.

To bring about meaningful change, a sustained effort is required that involves multiple stakeholders, including policymakers, criminal justice professionals, community members, and those directly impacted by the system. It is important to engage in ongoing dialogue and collaboration with these stakeholders to ensure that their needs and perspectives are taken into account.

In addition, change often requires overcoming resistance to new ideas and practices. This can be especially challenging in a system that is highly bureaucratic and hierarchical, where individuals may be resistant to change or may feel threatened by new approaches. It is important to have leaders who can effectively communicate the benefits of restorative justice and build a coalition of support among stakeholders.

Finally, meaningful change requires resources, including funding, time, and expertise. It is important to develop a clear plan for implementing restorative justice programs and practices and to secure the necessary resources to ensure success. This requires both short-term and long-term planning and a commitment to ongoing evaluation and improvement.

6. What are some steps you can take to prepare yourself in becoming a restorative justice advocate?

a) Read and learn as much as you can about the principles and practices of restorative justice.

b) Understand the restorative justice paradigm well enough that you can introduce it properly and be able to explain it to those who want to hear about it.

c) Recognize that a comprehensive change process will take a long time and that many justice agencies are currently using some restorative practice.

Examining and participating in local restorative intervention programs can also help prepare you in becoming a restorative justice advocate. In other words, get some hands-on experience.

If you want to become a restorative justice advocate, here are some steps you can take to prepare yourself:

1. Educate yourself: Learn as much as you can about restorative justice principles, practices, and theories. Read books, articles, and research studies on the subject. Attend conferences, seminars, and workshops related to restorative justice.

2. Get trained: Take courses and training programs on restorative justice. Many organizations and universities offer training programs on restorative justice.

3. Volunteer: Find a local restorative justice organization and volunteer your time. You can help with community outreach, victim support, or facilitation of restorative justice meetings.

4. Build relationships: Connect with individuals and organizations involved in restorative justice work. Attend local meetings, join online groups, and engage with like-minded people.

5. Advocate: Speak out in support of restorative justice. Write letters to your local government officials, attend public hearings, and share information about restorative justice on social media.

6. Practice: Apply restorative justice principles in your daily life. Practice active listening, empathy, and forgiveness in your personal and professional relationships.

By taking these steps, you can become a knowledgeable and effective advocate for restorative justice.

7. Your objective is to make the criminal justice system more restorative over time by encouraging the public to examine existing beliefs about the purpose of crime intervention.

Encouraging the public to examine existing beliefs about the purpose of crime intervention is a crucial step in making the criminal justice system more restorative over time. Some steps that can be taken to achieve this objective are:

1. Education: Educate yourself about restorative justice principles and practices, and the ways in which they differ from traditional criminal justice interventions. Read books and articles on the subject, attend workshops and conferences, and connect with other advocates and practitioners.

2. Awareness: Raise awareness about the benefits of restorative justice, and the limitations of traditional punitive approaches. Use social media, public speaking, and other platforms to share stories and information about restorative justice, and its potential to create healing and transformation for all parties involved.

3. Advocacy: Advocate for restorative justice policies and programs at the local, state, and national levels. Join or support organizations that are working to promote restorative justice, and engage with elected officials and policymakers to express your support for restorative justice initiatives.

4. Collaboration: Collaborate with other individuals and organizations in your community to promote restorative justice principles and practices. Work with schools, faith-based organizations, and community groups to implement restorative justice programs, and build partnerships with law enforcement agencies and other criminal justice stakeholders to promote restorative justice initiatives.

5. Self-reflection: Engage in self-reflection and examine your own biases and assumptions about crime, punishment, and justice. Challenge yourself to see individuals who have committed harm as human beings with the capacity for change, and recognize the importance of healing and restoration for all parties involved in the criminal justice system.

8. What are some tips on action planning for the community?

a) Go to where the energy is (80/20).

b) Reclaim their moral authority.

c) Be guided by shared principles

d) Establish collaborative, diverse and multi-disciplinary teams

Here are some tips on action planning for the community:

1. Start with a clear goal: Determine the specific objective you want to achieve with your action plan.
2. Identify stakeholders: Determine who will be impacted by the plan and who can support the plan's implementation.
3. Develop a timeline: Break down the goal into smaller tasks and set deadlines for each step.
4. Assign responsibilities: Determine who will be responsible for each task and ensure that they have the necessary resources and support to complete it.
5. Develop a budget: Estimate the costs associated with implementing the plan and identify potential sources of funding.
6. Identify potential challenges: Anticipate potential obstacles and develop contingency plans to address them.
7. Measure progress: Determine how progress will be measured and establish benchmarks to evaluate success.
8. Communicate the plan: Share the plan with stakeholders and the community to build support and gain feedback.
9. Implement the plan: Take action on the plan and continually monitor progress to ensure that it is on track.
10. Evaluate the plan: Conduct a formal evaluation of the plan to determine its effectiveness and identify areas for improvement.

9. What are some tips on action planning for the government?

a) Delegate power to shape and decide.

b) Be patient and listen.

Developing a credible and diverse coalition for restorative justice requires advocates to draw in leaders in the victims' rights movement, offender-advocates, law enforcement officials, politicians (from both liberal and conservative ideologies), and other opinion makers.

It is necessary to promote the vision of restorative justice while responding patiently and respecting the position of systemic and political realities.

c) Give information.

d) Practice restraint.

e) Be clear on roles and expectations

Programs called "restorative" do not always reflect a restorative vision and values. Evaluation using the right criteria will help government programs become more restorative in their treatment of victims, offenders and community members.

Here are some tips on action planning for the government to promote restorative justice:

1. Build relationships with community stakeholders: The government can work to build relationships with community stakeholders to understand their perspectives on restorative justice and involve them in the decision-making process.

2. Conduct a needs assessment: The government can conduct a needs assessment to identify the gaps and opportunities in the current justice system and develop strategies to address them.

3. Develop policies and guidelines: The government can develop policies and guidelines that support restorative justice practices and integrate them into existing criminal justice policies and procedures.

4. Provide training and support: The government can provide training and support to justice professionals, such as judges, prosecutors, and defense attorneys, on restorative justice principles and practices.

5. Allocate resources: The government can allocate resources to support restorative justice initiatives, such as funding for victim services and community-based programs.

6. Evaluate and monitor progress: The government can evaluate and monitor the progress of restorative justice initiatives to ensure they are effective and make adjustments as necessary.

7. Engage in public education and outreach: The government can engage in public education and outreach to raise awareness of restorative justice and its benefits for both victims and offenders.

10. Which isolating system features should be addressed in action planning?

      a) Data privacy success.

      b) Sterilization of information.

      c) Removal of emotion from process.

      d) Intimidating and foreign structures

e) Professionalism

f) Public service convenience

Goals must be carefully delineated and implementation must be deliberate and monitored, re-evaluated and improved upon to establish the legitimacy of a restorative response to crime.

In action planning for restorative justice, the following isolating system features should be addressed:

1. Dehumanization: The system often views offenders as less than human, which can lead to further isolation and stigmatization. Addressing this feature involves promoting human dignity and respect for all individuals, including offenders.

2. Institutionalization: The prison system can become a self-contained world that is isolated from the outside community. Addressing this feature involves finding ways to connect offenders to the outside world, such as through education or vocational training programs.

3. Powerlessness: Offenders often feel powerless and disempowered within the criminal justice system. Addressing this feature involves giving offenders a sense of agency and empowerment, such as through restorative justice processes where they have a voice in the process.

4. Normlessness: The prison environment can be devoid of positive social norms, leading to the development of negative behaviors and attitudes. Addressing this feature involves creating a positive and supportive environment within the criminal justice system, including providing opportunities for personal growth and development.

5. Marginalization: Offenders can be marginalized from society and may have limited social support networks. Addressing this feature involves finding ways to reintegrate offenders into society and provide them with a sense of belonging, such as through community-based programs and support groups.

11. How does crime provoke community responsibility?

a) Calling attention to social problems and harmful social conditions.

b) Providing opportunity for the community to affirm its values and behavioral norms.

c) Causing a community obligation to provide a process through which this conflict can be resolved.

Crime can provoke a sense of responsibility in the community because it can be seen as a threat to the safety and well-being of everyone in the community, not just the direct victims of the crime. When a crime occurs, it can create a sense of fear and insecurity among community members, leading them to want to take action to prevent similar crimes from happening in the future. This can include working with law enforcement and other community organizations to address the root causes of crime and develop strategies for prevention, as well as providing support to victims and their families.

Additionally, communities may organize neighborhood watch programs, community patrols, or other initiatives aimed at deterring criminal activity and promoting a sense of safety and security. By taking action in response to crime, communities can demonstrate their commitment to creating a safe and healthy environment for all residents.

12. Give three solutions to sustain community involvement.:

a) Must win support of the public.

b) Train citizens and practitioners

c) Get organizations involved

Here are three solutions to sustain community involvement:

1. Provide ongoing education and training: It is important to provide the community with ongoing education and training about restorative justice principles and practices. This can be done through workshops, seminars, and community events that promote awareness and understanding of the issues.

2. Foster collaboration: Collaboration among community members and organizations is critical to sustaining involvement. This can be achieved through partnerships and alliances that share resources and expertise, and work together to address community issues.

3. Empower community members: Empowering community members to take ownership of restorative justice initiatives is key to sustaining involvement. This can be done by providing opportunities for community members to lead and participate in projects, and by recognizing and celebrating their contributions to the community.

13. What are some of the challenges to sustaining community involvement?

a): History of justice system.
b): Citizen cooperation
c): Lack of organizational involvement
d) Lack of understanding.
e) Previous victim experience.
f) Community diversity.

There are several challenges to sustaining community involvement in restorative justice efforts, including:

1. Lack of resources: Restorative justice programs often rely on volunteers, but it can be challenging to recruit and retain volunteers over time. This can be due to limited resources for training, supervision, and support.
2. Resistance to change: Some community members may be resistant to the idea of restorative justice or may prefer traditional punitive approaches to crime intervention.
3. Limited awareness and understanding: Many people may not be aware of restorative justice or may not fully understand how it works. This can make it difficult to generate community support and engagement.
4. Lack of political will: Restorative justice programs may require political support and funding to be sustainable, and there may be competing priorities for government resources.
5. Trauma and burnout: Restorative justice work can be emotionally taxing, and community members may experience burnout or vicarious trauma if they are not adequately supported.
6. Cultural barriers: Restorative justice programs may need to be adapted to meet the needs and cultural norms of diverse communities, which can present additional challenges.

Addressing these challenges requires ongoing effort and collaboration between community members, government officials, and other stakeholders.

14. Give four general principles about behavioral change.

a) Behavior is derived from thoughts

Proverbs 23:7 says, "For as he thinketh in his heart, so is he." People do the things they do, because they believe the things they believe. The battlefield really IS the mind.

b) Relationships count.

c) Community accountability counts.

d) Humans do not always follow principles.

1. Behavioral change takes time and requires persistence: Change rarely happens overnight, and it often requires consistent effort over a long period of time.
2. Behavioral change requires motivation: People are more likely to change their behavior if they are motivated to do so. Motivation can come from a variety of sources, including personal values, social pressure, and external rewards.
3. Behavioral change is most effective when it is tailored to the individual: Different people have different needs, motivations, and obstacles to change. Effective behavioral change programs take these individual differences into account and provide personalized support.
4. Behavioral change requires a supportive environment: People are more likely to change their behavior when they are surrounded by a supportive network of family, friends, and community members. A supportive environment can provide encouragement, accountability, and resources to help individuals achieve their goals.

CHAPTER X
CONCLUSION

---

1. Our country is becoming less free as Americans call for the passing of new laws, harsher punishment, and longer sentences.

Laws are created as a result of crime. In many instances they affect everyone. An example would be medicines that are sold over the counter but because of abuse a law is passed mandating that they be prescribed by a doctor. Some laws are designed to protect us but in doing so they rob us of certain freedoms and privileges.

There is a trend towards more punitive measures in the criminal justice system, which can be seen as a reflection of a broader cultural shift towards a desire for increased safety and security. While it is certainly understandable that people want to feel safe in their communities, there are some potential problems with this approach.

Firstly, the passing of new laws, harsher punishments, and longer sentences may not necessarily lead to a reduction in crime. In fact, research has shown that longer sentences may have little deterrent effect on crime rates and may even contribute to higher rates of recidivism.

Secondly, the increased use of punitive measures can lead to over-incarceration, particularly of people from marginalized communities who are disproportionately impacted by the criminal justice system. This can have long-term negative consequences for individuals, families, and communities, as well as a significant financial cost to taxpayers.

Thirdly, there are concerns about the erosion of civil liberties and the expansion of government power that can result from a focus on punitive measures. This can include issues such as the use of invasive surveillance, the erosion of privacy rights, and the militarization of law enforcement.

Ultimately, while it is important to prioritize public safety, there is a need for a balanced approach that takes into account the potential harms of punitive measures and recognizes the importance of rehabilitation, restorative justice, and addressing the root causes of crime.

2. Local governments feel "freed" when they send the offender away for years, but in reality they have only postponed and compounded the problem.

Many elected officials seem not to consider the long-term affects of sending the offender away for years or the need to resolve the problems created by criminal behavior. "Out of sight, out of mind" will never serve as an effective measure of intervention.

This statement highlights the issue of mass incarceration and the belief that simply sending offenders to prison does not solve the root causes of crime or address the needs of both victims and offenders. Instead, it perpetuates a cycle of incarceration that disproportionately affects communities of color and low-income individuals, creates a burden on the criminal justice system and tax payers, and often fails to address issues such as mental health, addiction, and poverty that may have contributed to the criminal behavior in the first place.

Furthermore, incarceration often strains families, leaving spouses without partners and children without parents, leading to negative long-term effects on their emotional and financial well-being. This can ultimately contribute to intergenerational poverty and perpetuate the cycle of crime. Therefore, simply relying on imprisonment as a solution to crime is not effective and requires a more holistic approach that addresses the underlying causes of criminal behavior, provides support for victims, and offers opportunities for rehabilitation and reintegration of offenders back into society.

3. The reality is that it is better to help successfully rehabilitate the offender than to deal with their continued criminal behavior.

Successful rehabilitation of offenders can have numerous benefits for society. Here are a few reasons why it is better to help rehabilitate offenders:

1. Reduced Recidivism: Successful rehabilitation helps offenders break the cycle of criminal behavior and reduces the likelihood of reoffending. This can reduce the burden on the criminal justice system and help keep communities safe.

2. Improved Public Safety: Rehabilitated offenders are more likely to become law-abiding citizens, leading to improved public safety.

3. Cost-Effective: It is often more cost-effective to rehabilitate offenders than to incarcerate them. Rehabilitation programs

can be tailored to meet the specific needs of each offender and can be less expensive than maintaining a prison population.

4. Humanitarian: Successful rehabilitation can help offenders turn their lives around and lead productive, fulfilling lives. This can have a positive impact on their families and communities.

5. Restorative Justice: Rehabilitation programs can incorporate restorative justice principles, which focus on repairing harm caused by crime and addressing the needs of both the victim and the offender. This can lead to healing and reconciliation, promoting a more just and peaceful society.

4. How does rehabilitation of the offender reap benefits to many people?

a) The offender benefits because they are able to live a different lifestyle.

b) Their families benefit because they are restored to their position in the family as a contributor to the household.

c) Other families, businesses and neighborhoods benefit because there is a reduction in crime,

d) and the community benefits because the offender no longer is a tax burden but rather a tax payer.

The rehabilitation of an offender can reap benefits to many people in several ways. First and foremost, it benefits the offender themselves by helping them address the underlying issues that led to their criminal behavior and providing them with the necessary tools and skills to lead a productive and law-abiding life. This, in turn, reduces the likelihood of them reoffending, which benefits their families, communities, and society as a whole.

Rehabilitation can also benefit the victims of crime by providing them with a sense of closure and healing. Through restorative justice practices, offenders can take responsibility for their actions and make amends to their victims, which can help the victims feel heard and validated.

Additionally, rehabilitation programs can provide job training, education, and other resources to offenders, which can increase their chances of finding employment and becoming self-sufficient. This, in turn, can reduce the burden on social welfare programs and benefit taxpayers.

Finally, a focus on rehabilitation can help shift the criminal justice system away from a punitive model and towards a more restorative and holistic approach. This can improve public trust in the justice system and reduce the negative impacts of mass incarceration on communities.

5. The shifting of responsibility from community to state is epidemic.

The shifting of responsibility from community to state is a phenomenon that has been observed in various aspects of society, including criminal justice. This shift is often due to the increasing complexity of issues and the perceived inability of individuals and local communities to effectively address these problems.

In the criminal justice system, this shift of responsibility is seen in the increased reliance on incarceration and the development of a punitive mindset. The belief is that punishment through incarceration will deter criminal behavior and provide justice for victims, while simultaneously removing the offender from society and shifting the responsibility for their rehabilitation to the state.

However, this approach has proven to be ineffective, as the high rates of recidivism and overcrowding in prisons demonstrate. Moreover, this approach has shifted the responsibility for addressing criminal behavior from the community to the state, leading to a loss of community involvement and empowerment.

Instead of shifting responsibility to the state, it is important to recognize that the community has a critical role to play in addressing criminal behavior. Communities can provide support and guidance for individuals who have been involved in criminal activity, helping them to turn their lives around and reintegrate into society. Communities can also provide opportunities for education and job training, which can help individuals to avoid criminal behavior in the first place.

Therefore, it is important to focus on rehabilitation and community involvement in addressing criminal behavior. This will require a shift in mindset from punishment and incarceration to support and guidance for offenders, and a renewed focus on empowering communities to take responsibility for the well-being of their members.

6. Building more prisons and merely locking people away is doomed to continued failure.

Consider this illustration. What would happen if we built more hospitals for the sick and merely gave them rooms without the medical care needed? Would the sick get well? Of course, they would not! Simply building hospital without providing medical care for the patients would be doomed to failure.

The strategy of building more prisons and relying solely on incarceration as a means of addressing crime has been widely criticized by many experts in the criminal justice field. While incarceration may be necessary in certain cases to protect public safety, it is not a sustainable solution for reducing crime rates in the long run. Here are some reasons why:

1. High Cost: The cost of building and maintaining prisons is extremely high, with taxpayers bearing the brunt of the expense. This puts a strain on government budgets and diverts resources away from other important social services, such as education, healthcare, and housing.

2. Overcrowding: The continued focus on incarceration has led to a significant increase in the number of people behind bars, resulting in overcrowded prisons that are often inhumane and unsafe. This not only puts prisoners at risk of harm but also creates a breeding ground for criminal activity and recidivism.

3. Lack of Rehabilitation: Prisons are often seen as a place of punishment rather than a place of rehabilitation, with limited opportunities for prisoners to receive education, job training, and mental health services. This makes it difficult for individuals to successfully reintegrate back into society upon release, leading to higher rates of recidivism.

4. Racial Disparities: The overreliance on incarceration has disproportionately affected communities of color, perpetuating systemic racism and social inequality. This is evidenced by the fact that Black Americans make up only 13% of the U.S. population but account for nearly 40% of the prison population.

5. Ignoring Root Causes: Incarceration alone does not address the root causes of crime, such as poverty, lack of education, and mental health issues. Focusing solely on punishment ignores the underlying factors that contribute to criminal behavior and fails to provide the necessary support for individuals to make positive changes in their lives.

In conclusion, building more prisons and relying solely on incarceration is not an effective long-term solution to reducing crime rates. Instead, a more comprehensive approach that focuses on prevention, rehabilitation, and addressing the root causes of crime is needed to create a safer and more just society.

7. Smart justice realizes that community-based, restorative justice is what works.

Smart justice recognizes that community-based, restorative justice is a more effective approach than simply locking people away in prisons. Restorative justice focuses on repairing harm caused by the offender and restoring relationships between the offender and the victim, as well as the community.

By involving the community in the process, restorative justice creates a sense of accountability and responsibility for the offender's actions. It allows for a more individualized approach to addressing the underlying issues that led to the criminal behavior, such as substance abuse, mental health issues, or a lack of education and employment opportunities.

Restorative justice also takes into account the needs and perspectives of the victim, providing them with a sense of closure and satisfaction. It allows them to have a voice in the process and to play an active role in the resolution of the situation.

In contrast, a punitive justice system that relies solely on incarceration and punishment often leads to further harm to the offender, the victim, and the community. It can result in a cycle of recidivism, as offenders are released from prison with little support or resources to reintegrate into society.

Therefore, smart justice recognizes that community-based, restorative justice is a more effective and sustainable approach to addressing crime and repairing harm caused by criminal behavior.

8. Criminal justice using the restorative justice paradigm ends in the restoration of both the victim and the offender back into the community.

Restorative justice is a paradigm shift from the traditional retributive justice approach, which focuses on punishing the offender for their crime. Restorative justice recognizes that the harm caused by the crime extends beyond the offender and affects the victim, the community, and even the offender themselves. Therefore, it seeks to repair the harm and restore relationships that have been damaged by the crime.

One of the core principles of restorative justice is the involvement of the victim in the process. Victims are given a voice and an opportunity to express their feelings, needs, and expectations. This allows them to participate in the decision-making process regarding the outcome of the case, which can lead to a sense of empowerment and healing.

Offenders are also encouraged to take responsibility for their actions and make amends for the harm they have caused. This could involve apologies, restitution, community service, or other forms of restorative action. The goal is to reintegrate the offender back into the community as a responsible and productive member, reducing the likelihood of future criminal behavior.

Restorative justice also recognizes the importance of the community in the process. Community members may be involved in supporting the victim, holding the offender accountable, or providing opportunities for the offender to make amends. By involving the community in the process, restorative justice promotes a sense of accountability and responsibility for the safety and well-being of the community as a whole.

In conclusion, the restorative justice approach recognizes the interconnectedness of individuals, communities, and the criminal justice system. By focusing on repairing harm, restoring relationships, and reintegrating offenders back into the community, restorative justice can lead to a more just and peaceful society.

9. A victim loses his/her sense of security and community stability, and desperately needs assistance to go on with their life.

When someone becomes a victim of a crime, their life can be severely impacted, both physically and emotionally. Victims often experience a loss of sense of security and stability in their community, as they may fear for their safety or the safety of their loved ones. This can lead to feelings of vulnerability and helplessness.

Victims also may suffer from a range of emotional and psychological trauma, such as anxiety, depression, and post-traumatic stress disorder (PTSD). These can have long-lasting effects on their mental health and well-being.

It is important that victims receive support and assistance in coping with the aftermath of the crime. This may include counseling and therapy, financial assistance, and other resources to help them rebuild their lives. Restorative justice programs can also provide opportunities for victims to have a voice in the criminal justice process and to receive restitution from the offender, which can help them feel a sense of justice and closure.

Community members and organizations can play a crucial role in supporting victims of crime. They can provide emotional support and practical assistance, such as transportation, child care, and help with household chores. They can also advocate for victims' rights and promote restorative justice practices in their communities.

Accordingly, it is important to recognize the needs of victims of crime and to provide them with the support and resources they need to recover and move forward with their lives.

10. *The offender needs to become a caring member of the community.*

The restorative justice paradigm recognizes that the offender is not just a lawbreaker but also a member of the community who has caused harm. Therefore, the process of restoration involves helping the offender recognize the harm they have caused and take responsibility for their actions. This process also involves helping the offender understand how their actions have impacted the victim and the community as a whole.

Restorative justice seeks to provide the offender with the opportunity to make amends and take actions to repair the harm they have caused. This could include financial compensation, community service, or other forms of restitution. In addition, the offender is encouraged to actively participate in their own rehabilitation and take steps to become a responsible member of society.

Restorative justice recognizes that the offender is not simply a passive recipient of punishment but an active agent in their own rehabilitation and restoration. By involving the offender in the process of repairing the harm they have caused, restorative justice seeks to promote personal growth, accountability, and social responsibility.

So, the goal of restorative justice is not just to punish the offender but also to help them become a caring member of the community. This approach recognizes that everyone in the community has a stake in preventing crime and promoting healing, and that the best way to achieve this is by working together towards the common goal of restoration.

11. *Restorative justice is smart justice.*

True. Restorative justice was born out of the belief that crime is something more than just breaking a law, and that the role of the criminal justice system should be about more than catching, convicting and punishing the guilty. The expanding and still evolving vision of restorative justice presents new perspectives and new tools that offer the future of an effective paradigm of justice - one focused on accountability, inclusion, problem-solving and healing.

Restorative justice is an approach to justice that emphasizes the restoration of harm caused by criminal behavior. This approach seeks to provide justice by repairing the harm caused by crime, addressing the needs of victims, and helping offenders take responsibility for their actions and make amends. Restorative justice is often contrasted with traditional retributive justice, which emphasizes punishment for wrongdoing rather than repairing harm.

Restorative justice is a smart justice approach for several reasons. First, it provides a more effective way to prevent future crime. By addressing the underlying causes of criminal behavior, restorative justice programs can help reduce recidivism rates and promote long-term rehabilitation. This is particularly important given the high rates of repeat offending in the criminal justice system.

Second, restorative justice can help improve public safety by promoting stronger, more connected communities. When offenders are held accountable for their actions and take responsibility for repairing the harm they have caused, they become more invested in the community and more likely to act in ways that promote public safety.

Third, restorative justice can help reduce the costs of the criminal justice system. Traditional retributive justice is often expensive and time-consuming, requiring extensive court proceedings, incarceration, and supervision. Restorative justice programs, on the other hand, can be less costly and more efficient, while also providing better outcomes for victims and communities.

Fourth, restorative justice can help address the harms caused by the criminal justice system itself. The traditional criminal justice system can be traumatizing and dehumanizing for both victims and offenders, perpetuating cycles of harm and dysfunction. Restorative justice offers a more humane and healing approach that prioritizes the needs of victims and focuses on repairing harm rather than punishing wrongdoing.

Hence, restorative justice is a smart justice approach that can help reduce crime, promote public safety, reduce costs, and address the harms caused by the criminal justice system itself. By prioritizing the needs of victims, promoting rehabilitation and reintegration of offenders, and strengthening communities, restorative justice offers a more effective, efficient, and compassionate approach to justice.

www.ingramcontent.com/pod-product-compliance
Lightning Source LLC
Chambersburg PA
CBHW061244120726
48001CB00001B/124